EATCS
Monographs on Theoretical Computer Science
Volume 12

EATCS Monographs on Theoretical Computer Science

Vol. 1: K. Mehlhorn: Data Structures and Algorithms 1: Sorting and Searching. XIV, 336 pages, 87 figs. 1984.

Vol. 2: K. Mehlhorn: Data Structures and Algorithms 2: Graph Algorithms and NP-Completeness. XII, 260 pages, 54 figs. 1984.

Vol. 3: K. Mehlhorn: Data Structures and Algorithms 3: Multidimensional Searching and Computational Geometry. XII, 284 pages, 134 figs. 1984.

Vol. 4: W. Reisig: Petri Nets. An Introduction. X, 161 pages, 111 figs. 1985.

Vol. 5: W. Kuich, A. Salomaa: Semirings, Automata, Languages. IX, 374 pages, 23 figs. 1986.

Vol. 6: H. Ehrig, B. Mahr: Fundamentals of Algebraic Specification 1. Equations and Initial Semantics. XI, 321 pages. 1985.

Vol. 7: F. Gécseg: Products of Automata. VIII, 107 pages, 18 figs. 1986.

Vol. 8: F. Kröger: Temporal Logic of Programs. VIII, 148 pages. 1987.

Vol. 9: K. Weihrauch: Computability. X, 517 pages. 1987.

Vol. 10: H. Edelsbrunner: Algorithms in Combinatorial Geometry. XV, 423 pages, 93 figs. 1987.

Vol. 11: J. L. Balcázar, J. Díaz, J. Gabarró: Structural Complexity I. IX, 191 pages, 57 figs. 1988.

Vol. 12: J. Berstel, C. Reutenauer: Rational Series and Their Languages. VIII, 151 pages. 1988.

Vol. 13: E. Best, C. Fernández C.: Nonsequential Processes. IX, 112 pages, 44 figs. 1988.

Vol. 14: M. Jantzen: Confluent String Rewriting. Approx. 136 pages. 1988.

Vol. 15: S. Sippu, E. Soisalon-Soininen: Parsing Theory, Vol. I: Languages and Parsing. VIII, 228 pages, 55 figs. 1988.

Vol. 16: P. Padawitz: Computing in Horn Clause Theories. XI, 322 pages, 7 figs. 1988.

Jean Berstel
Christophe Reutenauer

Rational Series and Their Languages

Springer-Verlag Berlin Heidelberg New York
London Paris Tokyo

Authors
Prof. Jean Berstel
Dr. Christophe Reutenauer
LITP, Université Pierre et Marie Curie
Tour 45–55
4, place Jussieu, F-75252 Paris Cedex 05

Editors
Prof. Dr. Wilfried Brauer
Institut für Informatik, Technische Universität München
Arcisstr. 21, D-8000 München 2, Germany

Prof. Dr. Grzegorz Rozenberg
Institute of Applied Mathematics and Computer Science
University of Leiden, Niels-Bohr-Weg 1, P.O. Box 9512
NL-2300 RA Leiden, The Netherlands

Prof. Dr. Arto Salomaa
Department of Mathematics, University of Turku
SF-20500 Turku 50, Finland

Exclusively authorized English version of the original French edition
Berstel, J., Reutenauer, Chr.: Les séries rationnelles et leurs langages

ISBN 3-540-18626-3 Springer-Verlag Berlin Heidelberg New York
ISBN 0-387-18626-3 Springer-Verlag New York Berlin Heidelberg

Library of Congress Cataloging-in-Publication Data.
Berstel, Jean, 1941– [Séries rationnelles et leurs langages. English]
Rational series and their languages/Jean Berstel, Christophe Reutenauer. p. cm.
(EATCS monographs on theoretical computer science; v. 12).
Translation of: Les séries rationnelles et leurs langages. Bibliography: p. Includes index.
ISBN 0-387-18626-3 (U.S.)
1. Sequential machine theory. 2. Formal languages. 3. Power series.
I. Reutenauer, Christophe. II. Title. III. Series.
QA267.5.S4B4713 1988 511.3–dc 19 88-12286 CIP

Dataconversion: Brühlsche Universitätsdruckerei, Giessen
Offsetprinting: Color-Druck, Berlin. Bookbinding: Lüderitz & Bauer, Berlin.
2145/3020-543210 – Printed on aced-free paper

Preface

This book is an introduction to rational formal power series in several noncommutative variables and their relations to formal languages and to the theory of codes.

Formal power series have long been in use in all branches of mathematics. They are invaluable in enumeration and combinatorics. For this reason, they are useful in various branches of computer science. As an example, let us mention the study of ambiguity in formal grammars.

It has appeared, for the past twenty years, that rational series in noncommutative variables have many remarkable properties which provide them with a rich structure. Knowledge of these properties makes them much easier to manipulate than, for instance, algebraic series. The depth and number of results for rational series are similar to those for rational languages. The aim of this text is to present the basic results concerning rational series.

The point of view adopted here seems to us to be a natural one. Frequently one observes that a set of results becomes a theory when the initial combinatorial techniques are progressively replaced by more algebraic ones. We have tried wherever possible to substitute an algebraic approach for a combinatorial description. This has made it possible for us to give a unified and more complete presentation that is hopefully also easier to understand. We feel that, in this manner, the fundamental mechanisms and their interactions are easier to grasp.

The first part of the book, comprising the first two chapters, illustrates very well how the introduction of an algebraic concept, namely syntactic algebra, can give a unified presentation. These two chapters contain the most important general results and discuss in particular the equality between rational and recognizable series and the construction of the reduced linear representation.

The following two chapters are devoted to the two applications which seemed most important to us. First, we describe the relationship with the families of formal languages studied in theoretical computer science. Next, we establish the correspondence with the rational functions in one variable as studied in number theory.

Chapter V presents arithmetic properties of rational series and their relations to the nature of their coefficients. These results are fairly profound, and there is a constant interaction with number theory. Let us mention the analytic characterization of N-rational series, which is the first result of this kind.

The next chapter presents several results on decidability. We describe only some positice results which are of increasing importance. Those given here are directly related to the Burnside problem.

The last two chapters are devoted to the study of polynomials in noncommutative variables, and to their application to coding theory. Because of noncommutativity, the structure of polynomials is much more complex than it would be in the case of commutativity, and the results are rather delicate to prove. We present here basic properties concerning factorization, without trying to be complete. The main purpose of Chapter VII is to prepare the ground for the final chapter, which contains the generalization of a result of M. P. Schützenberger concerning the factorization of a polynomial associated with a finite code.

Exercises are provided for most chapters and also short bibliographical notes.

The algebraic and arithmetic approach adopted in this book implies a choice in the set of possible applications. We do not describe several important applications, such as the use of polynomials in control theory, where formal series in noncommutative variables are employed to represent the behavior of systems and replace the Volterra series (Fliess 1981, Isidori 1985). Another area of application is combinatorial graph theory. Enumeration of graphs by well-chosen encodings leads to systems of equations in noncommutative formal series whose solutions give the desired enumeration. Cori (1975) gives an introduction to this topic. The analysis of algorithms also leads to the study of formal series in a somewhat larger context (see Steyaert and Flajolet 1983; Berstel and Reutenauer 1982).

This book issued from an advanced course held several times by the authors, at the University Pierre et Marie Curie, Paris and at the University of Saarbrücken. Parts of the book were also taught at several different levels, at other places. Any concept from algebra that might not be familiar to the reader can be found in S. Lang's Algebra (1965). Finally, thanks are due Rosa de Marchi who carefully typed the manuscript.

Paris – Montréal
August 1988

Jean Berstel
Christophe Reutenauer

Note to the Reader

Following usual notation, items such as sections, theorems, corollaries, etc. are numbered within a chapter. When cross-referenced the chapter number is omitted if the item is within the current chapter. Thus, "Theorem 1.1" means the first theorem in the first section of the current chapter, and "Theorem II.1.3" refers to the equivalent theorem in Chap. II. Exercises are numbered accordingly and the section number should help the reader to find the section relevant to that exercise.

Contents

Chapter I
Rational Series

This chapter contains the definitions of the basic concepts, namely, rational and recognizable series in several noncommutative variables. It also gives a short account of some preliminary notions that will appear frequently throughout the book.

We start with the definition of a semiring, followed by the notation for the usual objects in free monoids and formal series. The topology on formal series is only treated to the extent required for later reference.

Section 4 contains the definition of rational series, together with some elementary properties and the fact that certain morphisms preserve the rationality of series.

Recognizable series are introduced in Sect. 5. An interesting algebraic characterization is given. We also prove (Theorem 5.1) that the Hadamard product preserves recognizability.

The fundamental theorem of Schützenberger (equivalence between rational and recognizable series, Theorem 6.1) is the concern of the last section. This theorem is the starting point for the developments given in the subsequent chapters.

1 Semirings

Recall that a *monoid* is a set equipped with an associative, binary operation and having a neutral element for this law.

A *semiring* is, roughly speaking, a ring without subtraction. More precisely, it is a set K equipped with two operations $+$ and $\cdot$ (sum and product) such that the following properties hold:

(i) $(K,+)$ is a commutative monoid with neutral element denoted by 0.
(ii) $(K,\cdot)$ is a monoid with neutral element denoted by 1.
(iii) The product is distributive with respect to the sum.
(iv) For all a in K, $0a=a0=0$.

The last property is not a consequence of the others, as is the case for rings. Sometimes, semirings without a neutral element for the product are considered, but we will not use them here.

A semiring K is *commutative* if its product is commutative. A *subsemiring* of K is a subset of K containing 0 and 1, which is stable for the operations of K.

A *semiring morphism* is a function

$$f: K \to K'$$

of a semiring K into a semiring K' that maps the 0 and 1 of K into the corresponding elements of K' and that respects sum and product.

Let us give some examples of semirings. Among them are, of course, fields and rings. Next, the set $\mathbf{N}$ of natural numbers, the sets $\mathbf{Q}_+$ of nonnegative rational numbers and $\mathbf{R}_+$ of nonnegative real numbers are semirings. The *Boolean semiring* $\mathbf{B}=\{0,1\}$ is completely described by the relation $1+1=1$ (see Exercise 1.1). If M is a monoid, the set of subsets of a monoid is naturally equipped with the structure of a semiring: the sum of two subsets A and B of M is simply $A\cup B$ and their product is

$$\{ab \mid a\in A,\ b\in B\}$$

Let K be a semiring and let P, Q be two finite sets. We denote by $K^{P\times Q}$ the set of $P\times Q$-matrices with coefficients in K. The sum of such matrices is defined in the usual way, and if R is a third finite set, a product

$$K^{P\times Q}\times K^{Q\times R}\to K^{P\times R}$$

is defined in the usual manner. In particular, $K^{Q\times Q}$ thus becomes a semiring. If $P=\{1,\ldots,m\}$ and $Q=\{1,\ldots,n\}$, we will write $K^{m\times n}$ for $K^{P\times Q}$; moreover, $K^{1\times 1}$ will be identified with K.

For the rest of this chapter, we fix a semiring K.

2 Formal Series

Let X be a finite, nonempty set called *alphabet*. The *free monoid* X^* generated by X is the set of finite sequences

$$x_1\ldots x_n$$

of elements of X, including also the empty sequence denoted by 1. This set is a monoid, the product being the concatenation defined by

$$(x_1\ldots x_n)\cdot(y_1\ldots y_p)=x_1\ldots x_n y_1\ldots y_p$$

and with neutral element 1. An element of the alphabet is called a *letter*, an element of X^* is a *word* and 1 is the *empty word.* The *length* of a word

$$w=x_1\ldots x_n$$

is n; it is denoted by $|w|$. The length $|w|_x$ relative to a letter x is defined to be the number of occurrences of the letter x in w. We denote by X^+ the set $X^*\backslash 1$. A *language* is a subset of X^*.

A *formal series* (or formal power series) S is a function

$$X^*\to K$$

The image by S of a word w is denoted by (S, w) and is called the *coefficient* of w in S. The *image* of S is denoted by $Im(S)$. The *support* of S is the language

$$supp(S) = \{w \in X^* \mid (S, w) \neq 0\}$$

The set of formal series over X with coefficients in K is denoted by $K\langle\langle X\rangle\rangle$. A structure of a semiring is defined on $K\langle\langle X\rangle\rangle$ as follows. If S and T are two formal series, their *sum* is given by

$$(S+T, w) = (S, w) + (T, w)$$

and their *product* by

$$(ST, w) = \sum_{uv=w} (S, u)(T, v)$$

Observe that this sum is finite.

Furthermore, two external operations of K on $K\langle\langle X\rangle\rangle$, one acting on the left, the other on the right, are defined, for $a \in K$, by

$$(aS, w) = a(S, w), \qquad (Sa, w) = (S, w)a$$

There is a natural injection of the free monoid into $K\langle\langle X\rangle\rangle$ as a multiplicative submonoid; the image of a word w is still denoted by w. Thus the neutral element of $K\langle\langle X\rangle\rangle$ for the product is 1. Similarly, there is an injection of K into $K\langle\langle X\rangle\rangle$ as a subsemiring: to each $a \in K$ is associated $a \cdot 1 = 1 \cdot a$, simply denoted by a. Thus we identify X^* and K with their images in $K\langle\langle X\rangle\rangle$.

A *polynomial* is a formal series with finite support. The set of polynomials is denoted by $K\langle X\rangle$. It is a subsemiring of $K\langle\langle X\rangle\rangle$. The *degree* of a polynomial is the maximal length of the words in its support (and is $-\infty$ if the polynomial is zero).

When $X = \{x\}$ has just one element, one gets the usual sets of formal power series $K\langle\langle x\rangle\rangle = K[[x]]$ and of polynomials $K[x]$.

For the rest of this chapter, we fix an alphabet X.

3 The Topology of $K\langle\langle X\rangle\rangle$

We have seen that $K\langle\langle X\rangle\rangle$ is the set of functions $X^* \to K$. In other words,

$$K\langle\langle X\rangle\rangle = K^{X^*}$$

Thus, if K is equipped with the *discrete topology*, the set $K\langle\langle X\rangle\rangle$ can be equipped with the product topology.

This topology can be defined by an *ultrametric distance*. Indeed, let

$$\omega: K\langle\langle X\rangle\rangle \times K\langle\langle X\rangle\rangle \to \mathbf{N} \cup \infty$$

be the function defined by

$$\omega(S, T) = \inf\{n \in \mathbf{N} \mid \exists w \in X^*, |w| = n \text{ and } (S, w) \neq (T, w)\}$$

For any real number σ with $0 < \sigma < 1$, the function

$$d: K\langle\langle X\rangle\rangle \times K\langle\langle X\rangle\rangle \rightarrow \mathbf{R}$$

$$d(S, T) = \sigma^{\omega(S, T)}$$

is an ultrametric distance which defines the topology given above (Exercise 3.1). Furthermore, $K\langle\langle X\rangle\rangle$ is *complete* for this topology, and it is a *topological semiring* (i.e. sum and product are continuous functions).

Let $(S_i)_{i \in I}$ be a familie of series. It is called *summable* if there exists a formal series S such that, for all $\varepsilon > 0$, there exists a finite subset I' of I such that every finite subset J of I containing I' satisfies the inequality

$$d\left(\sum_{j \in J} S_j, S\right) \leqq \varepsilon$$

The series S is then called the *sum* of the family (S_i) and is unique.

A family $(S_i)_{i \in I}$ is called *locally finite* if for every word w there exists only a finite number of indices $i \in I$ such that $(S_i, w) \neq 0$. It is easily seen that every locally finite family is summable. The sum of such a family can also be defined simply for $w \in X^*$ by

$$(S, w) = \sum_{i \in I} (S_i, w)$$

observing that the support of this sum is finite because the family (S_i) is locally finite. However, it is not true that a summable family is always locally finite (see Exercise 3.2), but we shall need mainly the second concept.

Let S be a formal series. Then the family of series $((S, w)w)_{w \in X^*}$ clearly is locally finite, since each of these series has a support formed of at most one single word, and supports are pairwise disjoint. Thus the family is summable, and its sum is just S. This gives the usual notation

$$S = \sum_{w \in X^*} (S, w)w$$

It follows in particular that $K\langle X\rangle$ is *dense* in $K\langle\langle X\rangle\rangle$ which thus is the completion of $K\langle X\rangle$ for the distance d.

4 Rational Series

A formal series $S \in K\langle\langle X\rangle\rangle$ is *proper* if the coefficient of the empty word (i.e. the *constant term* of S) vanishes, thus if $(S, 1) = 0$. In this case, the family $(S^n)_{n \geqq 0}$ is locally finite. Indeed, for any word w, the condition $n > |w|$ implies that $(S^n, w) = 0$. Thus the family is summable. The sum of this family is denoted by S^*

$$S^* = \sum_{n \geqq 0} S^n$$

and is called the *star* of S. Similarly, S^+ denotes the series

$$S^+ = \sum_{n \geqq 1} S^n$$

The fact that $K\langle\langle X\rangle\rangle$ is a topological semiring and the usual properties of summable families imply that

$$S^* = 1 + S^+ \quad \text{and} \quad S^+ = SS^* = S^*S$$

From these, it follows that if K is a ring, then S^* is just the inverse of $1 - S$, since $S^*(1-S) = S^* - S^*S = S^* - S^+ = 1$. This also gives the following classical result: a series is invertible if, and only if, its constant term is invertible in K (still assuming K to be a ring); see Exercise 4.5.

Let us return to the general case of a semiring.

Lemma 4.1. *Let T and U be two formal series, with T proper. Then the unique solution S of the equation $S = U + TS$ (of $S = U + ST$) is the series $S = T^*U$ (the series $S = UT^*$, respectively).*

Proof. One has $T^* = 1 + TT^*$, whence $T^*U = U + TT^*U$. Conversely, since T is proper

$$\lim_n T^n = 0 \quad \text{and} \quad \lim_n \sum_{0 \leqq i \leqq n} T^i = T^*$$

From $S = U + TS$, it follows that

$$S = U + T(U + TS) = U + TU + T^2S$$

and inductively

$$S = (1 + T + \dots + T^n)U + T^{n+1}S$$

Thus, going to the limit, and using the fact that $K\langle\langle X\rangle\rangle$ is a topological semiring, one gets $S = T^*U$. □

Definition. The *rational operations* in $K\langle\langle X\rangle\rangle$ are the sum, the product, the two external products of K on $K\langle\langle X\rangle\rangle$ and the star operation. A subset of $K\langle\langle X\rangle\rangle$ is *rationally closed* if it is closed for the rational operations. The smallest subset containing a subset E of $K\langle\langle X\rangle\rangle$ and which is rationally closed is called the *rational closure* of E.

Definition. A formal series is *rational* if it is an element of the rational closure of $K\langle X\rangle$.

Observe that if K is a ring, then the rational closure of $K\langle X\rangle$ is the smallest subring of $K\langle\langle X\rangle\rangle$ containing $K\langle X\rangle$ and closed under inversion (in other words, the star operation and inversion play equivalent roles).

Example 4.1. Denote by $\underline{X}$ the series $\sum_{x\in X} x$. This series is proper, and

$$\underline{X}^* = \sum_{n\geq 0} \underline{X}^n$$

Since $\underline{X}^n$ is simply the sum of all words of length n, it follows that

$$\underline{X}^* = \sum_{w\in X^*} w$$

is the sum of all words in X^*.

Thus, this series is rational. Consider now a letter x. The series $\underline{X}^*x\underline{X}^*$, as a product of $\underline{X}^*$, x and $\underline{X}^*$, is also rational. By the definition of product,

$$(\underline{X}^*x\underline{X}^*, w) = \sum_{uvt=w} (\underline{X}^*, u)\,(x, v)\,(\underline{X}^*, t)$$

Since $(x, v) = 0$ unless $v = x$ (and then $(x, v) = 1$), and since $(\underline{X}^*, u) = (\underline{X}^*, t) = 1$, one has $(\underline{X}^*x\underline{X}^*, w) = \sum_{uxt=w} 1$ which is just the number of factorizations $w = uxt$, i.e. the number $|w|_x$ of occurrences of the letter x in w. Thus

$$\underline{X}^*x\underline{X}^* = \sum_{w} |w|_x w$$

is a rational series.

Let Y be an alphabet, and let ϱ be a function

$$\varrho: X \to K\langle\langle Y\rangle\rangle$$

Then ϱ extends to a morphism of monoids

$$\varrho: X^* \to K\langle\langle Y\rangle\rangle$$

If K is commutative, then ϱ can be extended in a unique manner into a morphism of semirings

$$\varrho: K\langle X\rangle \to K\langle\langle Y\rangle\rangle$$

with $\varrho|_K = id$. Indeed, it suffices, for any polynomial $P = \sum_{w \in X^*} (P, w)\, w$ in $K\langle X\rangle$, to set

$$\varrho(P) = \sum_{w \in X^*} (P, w)\varrho(w)$$

which is a finite sum since P is a polynomial.

Assume now that for each letter $x \in X$, the series $\varrho(x)$ is proper. Then $\varrho: K\langle X\rangle \to K\langle\langle Y\rangle\rangle$ is uniformly continuous. Indeed, let P and Q be two polynomials with

$$\omega(P, Q) = n$$

Then, for any word u in Y^* of length $< n$,

$$(\varrho(P), u) = \sum_{w \in X^*} (P, w)(\varrho(w), u) = \sum_{|w| < n} (P, w)(\varrho(w), u)$$

since $(\varrho(w), u) = 0$ whenever $|w| \geqq n$ by the hypothesis on ϱ. Thus

$$(\varrho(P), u) = \sum_{|w| < n} (Q, w)(\varrho(w), u) = (\varrho(Q), u)$$

showing that

$$\omega(\varrho(P), \varrho(Q)) \geqq n$$

Since $K\langle\langle X\rangle\rangle$ is the completion of $K\langle X\rangle$ (see Sect. 3), the function ϱ extends uniquely to a morphism of semirings

$$K\langle\langle X\rangle\rangle \to K\langle\langle Y\rangle\rangle$$

which induces the identity mapping on K and which is continuous.

Proposition 4.2. *Suppose K is commutative. Let $\varrho: X \to K\langle\langle Y\rangle\rangle$ be a function such that, for all $x \in X$, the series $\varrho(x)$ is a proper rational series. Then ϱ extends uniquely to a morphism of semirings $K\langle\langle X\rangle\rangle \to K\langle\langle Y\rangle\rangle$ which induces the identity on K and which is continuous. Moreover, the image of any rational series is again rational.*

Proof. It suffices to show the last claim. If P is a polynomial, then $\varrho(P) = \Sigma(P, w)\varrho(w)$ is a rational series since $\varrho(x)$ is a rational series for each letter x in X. Next, if $\varrho(S)$ and $\varrho(T)$ are rational series, then so are $\varrho(S+T)$ and $\varrho(ST)$. Finally, if S is a proper series and $\varrho(S)$ is rational, then $\varrho(S)$ is proper and

$$\varrho(S^*) = \varrho\left(\sum_{n \geqq 0} S^n\right) = \sum_{n \geqq 0} \varrho(S^n) = \varrho(S)^*$$

by the continuity of ϱ, showing that $\varrho(S^*)$ is rational. This proves that ϱ preserves rationality. □

5 Recognizable Series

Definition. A formal series $S \in K\langle\langle X \rangle\rangle$ is called *recognizable* if there exists an integer $n \geq 1$ and a morphism of monoids

$$\mu: X^* \to K^{n \times n}$$

($K^{n \times n}$ with its multiplicative structure) and two matrices $\lambda \in K^{n \times 1}$ and $\gamma \in K^{n \times 1}$ such that, for all words w,

$$(S, w) = \lambda \mu w \gamma$$

In this case, the triple (λ, μ, γ) is called a *linear representation* of S, and n is its *dimension*.

We shall need the notion of module over a semiring.

A *left K-module* is a commutative monoid M with law denoted by $+$ and neutral element 0, equipped with an external law $K \times M \to M$ denoted by $(a, m) \mapsto am$ such that, for all a, b in K and m, n in M, the following relations hold:

$$a(m+n) = am + an$$

$$(a+b)m = am + bm$$

$$(ab)m = a(bm)$$

$$1m = m$$

$$0m = 0$$

A *submodule* of M is a subset of M containing 0 and closed for the operations of M.

The semiring $K\langle\langle X \rangle\rangle$ of formal power series is a left K-module, where the external law $K \times K\langle\langle X \rangle\rangle \to K\langle\langle X \rangle\rangle$ is the law already considered in Sect. 2:

$$(a, S) \mapsto aS$$

A left K-module M *is finitely generated* if there exist finitely many elements $m_1, \ldots, m_n \in M$ such that any element in M can be written as a linear combination

$$a_1 m_1 + \ldots + a_n m_n \quad (a_i \in K)$$

We now define an operation of X^* on $K\langle\langle X \rangle\rangle$. To each word u, and to each formal series S, we associate the series $u^{-1}S$ define by

$$u^{-1}S = \sum_{w \in X^*} (S, uw) w$$

In other words, for all words u and w, the coefficient of w in the series $u^{-1}S$ is (S, uw), thus

$$(u^{-1}S, w) = (S, uw)$$

A more combinatorial view of this fact is given in the case where $S=v$ is a single word. Then $u^{-1}v$ vanishes, unless v starts with u, i.e. $v=uv'$. In this case, $u^{-1}v=v'$.

Observe that this defines completely the operation

$$S \to u^{-1}S$$

since this operation is additive, i.e.

$$u^{-1}(S+T)=u^{-1}S+u^{-1}T$$

since it commutes with the external operations of K on $K\langle\langle X\rangle\rangle$, i.e.

$$u^{-1}(aS)=a(u^{-1}S),\ u^{-1}(Sa)=(u^{-1}S)a$$

for all a in K, and since, finally, this operation is continuous.

Example 5.1.

$$(xy)^{-1}(x^2+xyx^2+xyxy+xy^2+y)=x^2+xy+y$$

The same remark shows that if P is a polynomial, then $u^{-1}P$ is still a polynomial, with degree less than or equal to the degree of P.

Furthermore, this operation of X^* on $K\langle\langle X\rangle\rangle$ is associative in the following sense:

$$(uv)^{-1}S=v^{-1}(u^{-1}S)$$

as is easily verified. Another property is the following formula which holds for any series S:

$$S=(S,1)+\sum_{x\in X} x(x^{-1}S) \tag{5.1}$$

A subset M of $K\langle\langle X\rangle\rangle$ is called *stable* if, for all S in M and u in X^*, the series $u^{-1}S$ is in M.

Proposition 5.1. *A formal series $S\in K\langle\langle X\rangle\rangle$ is recognizable if, and only if, there exists a stable finitely generated left submodule of $K\langle\langle X\rangle\rangle$ which contains S.*

Proof. Assume that S is recognizable, and let (λ, μ, γ) be a linear representation of S of dimension n. Consider the formal series $S_1, \ldots, S_n$ defined by

$$(S_i, w)=(\mu w\gamma)_i$$

for all words w. Let M be the left K-module generated by the series S_i. Thus M is finitely generated. It contains S, since

$$(S, w)=\lambda\mu w\gamma=\sum_i \lambda_i(\mu w)_i=\sum_i \lambda_i(S_i, w)$$

showing that $S=\sum_i \lambda_i S_i$. Next, M is stable. Indeed, let u be a word. Then

$$(u^{-1}S_i, w) = (S_i, uw) = (\mu u \mu w \gamma)_i$$

$$= \sum_j (\mu u)_{i,j} (\mu w \gamma)_j = \sum_j (\mu u)_{i,j} (S_j, w)$$

Thus $u^{-1}S_i = \sum_j (\mu u)_{i,j} S_j \in M$.

Conversely, let M be a stable left submodule of $K\langle\langle X\rangle\rangle$, generated by $S_1, \ldots, S_n$, and containing S. Then

$$S = \sum_i \lambda_i S_i$$

for some λ_i in K. Moreover, for any letter x, there exists a matrix $\mu x \in K^{n\times n}$ such that, for all i,

$$x^{-1}S_i = \sum_j (\mu x)_{i,j} S_j$$

Let μ: $X^* \to K^{n\times n}$ be the morphism of monoids which extends this mapping. Then for any word w,

$$w^{-1}S_i = \sum_j (\mu w)_{i,j} S_j$$

Indeed, if this relation holds for some word w, then

$$(wx)^{-1}S_i = x^{-1}(w^{-1}S_i) = x^{-1}\left(\sum_k (\mu w)_{i,k} S_k\right)$$

$$= \sum_k (\mu w)_{i,k} (x^{-1}S_k) = \sum_k (\mu w)_{i,k} \sum_j (\mu x)_{k,j} S_j$$

$$= \sum_j \left(\sum_k (\mu w)_{i,k} (\mu x)_{k,j}\right) S_j = \sum_j (\mu w x)_{i,j} S_j$$

and consequently, the relation holds for all words.

Set $\gamma_j = (S_j, 1)$ and let $\gamma \in K^{n\times 1}$ be the matrix defined in this way. Then

$$(S_i, w) = (w^{-1}S_i, 1) = \left(\sum_j (\mu w)_{i,j} S_j, 1\right)$$

$$= \sum_j (\mu w)_{i,j} (S_j, 1) = \sum_j (\mu w)_{i,j} \gamma_j$$

$$= (\mu w \gamma)_i$$

Consequently,

$$\lambda\mu w\gamma = \sum_i \lambda_i (S_i, w) = (S, w)$$

showing that S is recognizable. □

Example 5.2. We use Proposition 5.1 to give an example of a recognizable series.

Let $X = \{x_0, x_1\}$ and let $K = \mathbf{N}$. For each word w, let $\langle w \rangle$ be the integer for which w is an expansion in base 2. More precisely, if

$$w = x_{i_k} \ldots x_{i_0}$$

then

$$\langle w \rangle = i_k 2^k + \ldots + i_1 2 + i_0$$

For $w = 1$, we set $\langle w \rangle = 0$. Let

$$S = \sum_{w \in X^*} \langle w \rangle w$$

Thus S starts as follows.

$$S = x_1 + x_0 x_1 + 2x_1 x_0 + 3x_1^2 + x_0^2 x_1 + 2x_0 x_1 x_0 + 3x_0 x_1^2 + 4x_1 x_0^2 + 5x_1 x_0 x_1 + 6x_1^2 x_0 + 7x_1^3 + \ldots$$

Given a word w, one has the relations

$$(S, x_0 w) = (S, w) \quad \text{and} \quad (S, x_1 w) = 2^{|w|} + (S, w)$$

where $|w|$ denotes the length of w. In other words,

$$x_0^{-1} S = S \quad \text{and} \quad x_1^{-1} S = T + S$$

where T is the series

$$T = \sum_w 2^{|w|} w$$

From the relations

$$(T, x_0 w) = 2(T, w), \qquad (T, x_1 w) = 2(T, w)$$

it follows that

$$x_0^{-1} T = x_1^{-1} T = 2T$$

This shows that the submodule M of $\mathbf{N}\langle\langle X\rangle\rangle$ generated by S and T is stable under the operations

$$U \to x^{-1}U \, (x \in X)$$

The associativity of the operation $U \to w^{-1}U$ implies that the submodule M is stable. Proposition 5.1 shows that S is recognizable.

Proposition 5.1 admits the following consequence.

Corollary 5.2. *Any linear combination of recognizable series is a recognizable series.* □

Definition. The *Hadamard product* of two formal series S and T is the series $S \odot T$ defined by

$$(S \odot T, w) = (S, w)(T, w)$$

Theorem 5.3 (Schützenberger 1962a). *Let K_1 and K_2 be two subsemirings of K such that each element of K_1 commutes with each element of K_2. If S_1 is a K_1-recognizable series and S_2 is a K_2-recognizable series, then $S_1 \odot S_2$ is K-recognizable.*

Proof. We apply Proposition 5.1. Let M_1 (M_2) be a left submodule of $K_1\langle\langle X\rangle\rangle$ (of $K_2\langle\langle X\rangle\rangle$) which contains S_1 (S_2), is stable, and is generated by the series $T_1^1, \ldots, T_1^n \in K_1\langle\langle X\rangle\rangle$ (the series $T_2^1, \ldots, T_2^m \in K_2\langle\langle X\rangle\rangle$, respectively).

Let M be the left submodule of $K\langle\langle X\rangle\rangle$ generated by $M_1 \odot M_2 = \{T_1 \odot T_2 \mid T_1 \in M_1, T_2 \in M_2\}$. Clearly $S_1 \odot S_2$ is in M. Morover, M is finitely generated. Indeed, if $T_1 = \sum_{1 \leq i \leq n} a_i T_1^i \in M_1$ with $a_i \in K_1$ and $T_2 = \sum_{1 \leq j \leq m} b_j T_2^j \in M_2$ with $b_j \in K_2$, then for any word w,

$$(T_1 \odot T_2, w) = (T_1, w)(T_2, w) = \sum_{i,j} a_i (T_1^i, w) b_j (T_2^j, w)$$

$$= \sum_{i,j} a_i b_j (T_1^i, w)(T_2^j, w)$$

since (T_1^i, w) and b_j commute. Thus

$$T_1 \odot T_2 = \sum_{i,j} a_i b_j T_1^i \odot T_2^j$$

showing that M is generated, as a K-module, by the series $T_1^i \odot T_2^j$.

Finally, M is stable, since for any word u, and for series $T_1 \in M_1$, $T_2 \in M_2$,

$$u^{-1}(T_1 \odot T_2) = (u^{-1}T_1) \odot (u^{-1}T_2) \in M$$ □

Example 5.3. For $n \in \mathbf{N}$, we denote by n the element $1 + \ldots + 1$ (n times) of K. Let x be a letter. Then the series $\sum_w |w|_x w$ is recognizable (it is also rational, as seen in Example

4.1). Indeed the series admits the linear representation (λ, μ, γ) defined by $\lambda = (1, 0)$, $\mu x = \begin{pmatrix} 1 & 1 \\ 0 & 1 \end{pmatrix}$, $\mu y = \begin{pmatrix} 1 & 0 \\ 0 & 1 \end{pmatrix}$ for $y \in X \backslash x$, and $\gamma = \begin{pmatrix} 0 \\ 1 \end{pmatrix}$. It is indeed easily seen that for any word w,

$$\mu w = \begin{pmatrix} 1 & |w|_x \\ 0 & 1 \end{pmatrix}$$

As an application, let $P(t_1, \dots, t_n)$ be a *commutative* polynomial with coefficients in K. Then the formal series (over the alphabet $X = \{x_1, \dots, x_n\}$)

$$S = \sum_{w \in X^*} P(|w|_{x_1}, \dots, |w|_{x_n})\, w$$

is recognizable. This follows from Theorem 5.3, Corollary 5.2 and from the recognizability of $\sum |w|_x w$.

6 The Fundamental Theorem

Theorem 6.1 (Schützenberger 1961a). *A formal series is recognizable if and only if it is rational.*

We start with several lemmas which will be needed for the proof.

Lemma 6.2. *Let S and T be two formal series and let x be a letter. Then*

$$x^{-1}(ST) = (x^{-1}S)T + (S, 1)(x^{-1}T)$$

If S is proper, then

$$x^{-1}(S^*) = (x^{-1}S)S^*$$

Proof. For any word w,

$$(x^{-1}(ST), w) = (ST, xw) = \sum_{uv = xw} (S, u)(T, v)$$

$$= (S, 1)(T, xw) + \sum_{uv = w} (S, xu)(T, v)$$

$$= (S, 1)(T, xw) + \sum_{uv = w} (x^{-1}S, u)(T, v)$$

$$= (S, 1)(x^{-1}T, w) + ((x^{-1}S)T, w)$$

This proves the first relation

For the second claim, observe that $S^* = 1 + SS^*$, whence $x^{-1}(S^*) = (x^{-1}S)S^*$, since $(S, 1) = 0$. □

Let m be an $n \times n$-matrix with coefficients in $K\langle\langle X\rangle\rangle$:

$$m \in K\langle\langle X\rangle\rangle^{n \times n}$$

The matrix m is *proper* if, for all indices i and j, the series $m_{i,j}$ is proper. In this case, the *star* of m can be defined as

$$m^* = \sum_{n \geq 0} m^n$$

The existence of m^* can be verified by considering the product topology induced by $K\langle\langle X\rangle\rangle$ on $K\langle\langle X\rangle\rangle^{n \times n}$ (the details are left to the reader). It is easily seen that

$$m^* = 1 + mm^* \tag{6.1}$$

where 1 is the identity matrix.

Lemma 6.3. *If m is a proper matrix with elements in $K\langle\langle X\rangle\rangle$, then all coefficients of m^* are in the rational closure of the coefficients of m.*

Proof. Let m be an $n \times n$-matrix. If $n=1$, the result is clear. Arguing by induction, assume $n>1$ and consider a decomposition into blocks

$$m = \begin{pmatrix} a & b \\ c & d \end{pmatrix}$$

where a and d are square matrices, and set

$$m^* = \begin{pmatrix} \alpha & \beta \\ \gamma & \delta \end{pmatrix}$$

where the blocks have the same dimensions as the corresponding blocks $\in m$.
By Eq. (6.1), we get

$$\alpha = 1 + a\alpha + b\gamma$$

$$\beta = a\beta + b\delta$$

$$\gamma = c\alpha + d\gamma$$

$$\delta = 1 + c\beta + d\gamma$$

Using Lemma 4.1 (or more precisely, its extension to matrix equations), we have

$$\beta = a^* b\delta, \ \gamma = d^* c\alpha$$

whence

$$\alpha = 1 + a\alpha + bd^{*}c\alpha$$

$$\delta = 1 + ca^{*}b\delta + d\delta$$

Again, Lemma 4.1 gives

$$\alpha = (a + bd^{*}c)^{*}$$

$$\delta = (ca^{*}b + d)^{*}$$

Finally,

$$\beta = a^{*}b(ca^{*}b + d)^{*}$$

$$\gamma = d^{*}c(a + bd^{*}c)^{*}$$

By the induction hypothesis, all coefficients of a^{*}, d^{*} are in the rational closure of the coefficients of m. The same holds for the coefficients of $a + bd^{*}c$ and $ca^{*}b + d$, and using again the induction hypothesis, the coefficients of α, δ, and also those of β and γ, are in this rational closure. □

Proof of Theorem 6.1. In order to show that any rational series is recognizable, we use Proposition 5.1. If P is a polynomial, then $w^{-1}P = 0$ for any word w of length greater than $\deg(P)$. Consequently, the set $\{w^{-1}P \mid w \in X^{*}\}$ is finite. Since it is stable, it generates a stable submodule which, moreover, is finitely generated, and also contains P (because $1^{-1}P = P$). Thus P is recognizable.

If S and T are recognizable, then there exist stable finitely generated left submodules M and N of $K\langle\langle X\rangle\rangle$ with $S \in M$ and $T \in N$. Then $M + N$ contains $S + T$, is finitely generated and is stable, showing that $S + T$ is recognizable.

Next let P be the submodule $P = MT + N$. Clearly P contains ST, and according to Lemma 6.2, P is stable. It is finitely generated because M and N are finitely generated.

Assume now that S is proper. Let Q be the submodule $Q = K + MS^{*}$. Then Q contains $S = 1 + SS^{*}$, and Q is stable, since by Lemma 6.2,

$$x^{-1}(S'S^{*}) = (x^{-1}S')S^{*} + (S', 1)(x^{-1}S)S^{*}$$

is in Q for all S' in M. Finally, Q is finitely generated.

Conversely, let S be a recognizable series and let (λ, μ, γ) be a linear representation of S of dimension n. Consider the proper matrix

$$m = \sum_{x \in X} \mu x x \in K^{n \times n}\langle\langle X\rangle\rangle = K\langle\langle X\rangle\rangle^{n \times n}$$

Then

$$m^{*} = \sum_{n \geq 0} m^{n} = \sum_{n \geq 0} \left(\sum_{x \in X} \mu x x \right)^{n} = \sum_{n \geq 0} \sum_{w \in X^{n}} \mu w w = \sum_{w \in X^{*}} \mu w w$$

Thus

$$m^*_{i,j} = \sum_w (\mu w)_{i,j}\, w$$

and since

$$S = \sum_{i,j} \lambda_i m^*_{i,j} \gamma_j$$

the series S is rational in view of Lemma 6.3. □

Exercises for Chapter I

1.1. Let $K = \{0, 1\}$ be a semiring composed of two elements. Show that, according to the value of $1+1$, K is either the field with two elements or the Boolean semiring.

1.2. Let K be a semiring; a *congruence* in K is an equivalence relation $\equiv$ which is compatible with the laws of K, i.e. for all $a, b, c, d \in K$,

$$a \equiv b,\ c \equiv d \quad \Rightarrow \quad a+c \equiv b+d,\ ac \equiv bd$$

a) Show that $K/\equiv$ has a natural structure of a semiring. Such a semiring is called a *quotient* of K.
b) Show that if K is a ring then there is a bijection between congruences and two-sided ideals in K.
c) Show that any quotient semiring of $\mathbf{N}$ which is not isomorphic to $\mathbf{N}$ is finite.

The *prime* subsemiring of a semiring K is the semiring L generated by 1. Show that every element in L commutes with every element in K and that L either is isomorphic to $\mathbf{N}$, or is finite.

1.3. Let K be a commutative semiring.

a) Define two operations on $K \times K$ by

$$(a, b) + (a', b') = (a+a', b+b')$$

$$(a, b)(a', b') = (aa'+bb', ab'+ba')$$

Show that these operations make $K \times K$ a semiring with zero $(0, 0)$ and unity $(1, 0)$. Show that

$$i : a \mapsto (a, 0)$$

is an injection of K in $K \times K$. Show that the relation $\equiv$ defined by

$$(a, b) \equiv (a', b') \Leftrightarrow \exists c : a+b'+c = '+b+c$$

is a congruence on $K \times K$. Show that $L = K \times K/\equiv$ is a ring.

b) Denote by p the canonical surjection

$$p: K \times K \to L$$

Show that $p \circ i: K \to L$ is injective if and only if for all $a, b, c \in K$

$$a+b=a+c \quad \Rightarrow \quad b=c$$

A semiring having this property is called *regular*. Show that K can be embedded into a ring if and only if it is regular.

c) Show that the ring L is entire if and only if for all $a, b, c, d \in K$

$$ac+bd=ad+bc \quad \Rightarrow \quad a=b \quad \text{or} \quad c=d$$

Show that K can be embedded into a field if and only if K is regular and this condition is satisfied.

d) K is *simplifiable* if for all $a, b, c \in K$

$$ab=ac \quad \Rightarrow \quad b=c \quad \text{or} \quad a=0$$

Show that if K can be embedded into a field, then it is regular and simplifiable.

e) Let a, b, c, d be commutative indeterminates and let I be the ideal of $\mathbf{Z}[a, b, c, d]$ generated by $(a-b)(c-d)$. Show that the image K of $\mathbf{N}[a, b, c, d]$ in $\mathbf{Z}[a, b, c, d]/I$ is a regular and simplifiable semiring, but that K cannot be embedded into any field.

3.1. Give complete proofs for the claims in Sect. 3.

3.2. Let $\mathbf{B}$ be the Boolean semiring and for all $n \in \mathbf{N}$, let $S_n = 1$. Show that the family $(S_n)_{n \in \mathbf{N}}$ is summable, but not locally finite.

3.3. Let K, L be two semirings and let X, Y be two alphabets. A function

$$\varrho: K\langle\langle X \rangle\rangle \to L\langle\langle Y \rangle\rangle$$

is a *morphism of formal series* if ϱ is a morphism of semirings and moreover is uniformly continuous.

a) Show that the mapping

$$L\langle\langle Y \rangle\rangle \to L$$

$$S \to (S, 1)$$

is a continuous morphism of semirings. Show that if

$$\varrho: K\langle\langle X \rangle\rangle \to L\langle\langle Y \rangle\rangle$$

is a morphism of semirings which is continuous at 0, then
(i) for all $a \in K$ and $x \in X$, the elements $\varrho(a)$ and $\varrho(x)$ commute,
(ii) the multiplicative subsemigroup of L generated by

$$\{(\varrho(x), 1) \mid x \in X\}$$

is nilpotent.
b) Let ϱ: $X \cup K \rightarrow L\langle\langle Y\rangle\rangle$ be a function satisfying conditions (i) and (ii) of (a). Show that ϱ extends in a unique manner to a morphism of formal series

$$K\langle\langle X\rangle\rangle \rightarrow L\langle\langle Y\rangle\rangle$$

3.4. Let M be a commutative monoid, with law denoted additively, having an ultrametric distance d which is subinvariant with respect to translation (i.e. such that $d(a+c, b+c) \leqq d(a, b)$ for $a, b, c \in M$). Show that every series that converges in M converges commutatively.

3.5. Assume that K is a commutative field. Recall that for any K-vector space E, for any subspace F and any vector v in $E \backslash F$, there exists a linear form ϱ on E such that $\varrho(E)=0$ and $\varrho(v) \neq 0$. We use here the identification of $K\langle\langle X\rangle\rangle$ and the dual of $K\langle X\rangle$ (see the beginning of Chap. II).

a) For each subspace V of $K\langle X\rangle$ (subspace W of $K\langle\langle X\rangle\rangle$), define its *orthogonal* in $K\langle\langle X\rangle\rangle$ (in $K\langle X\rangle$) to be given by

$$V^{\perp}=\{S \in K\langle\langle X\rangle\rangle \mid \forall P \in V,\ (S, P)=0\}$$

$$(W^{\perp}=\{P \in K\langle X\rangle \mid \forall S \in W,\ (S, P)=0\}, \text{ respectively})$$

Show that if V is a subspace of $K\langle X\rangle$, then $V^{\perp\perp}=V$.
b) Show that a linear form ϱ on $K\langle\langle X\rangle\rangle$ is continuous (for the discrete topology on K and the product topology on K^{X^*}) iff Ker ϱ contains all but a finite number of elements of X^*. Show that the topological dual space of $K\langle\langle X\rangle\rangle$ can be identified with $K\langle X\rangle$. Show that for any *closed* subspace W of $K\langle\langle X\rangle\rangle$, and for any formal series S not in W, there exists a *continuous* linear form ϱ on $K\langle\langle X\rangle\rangle$ such that $\varrho(S) \neq 0$ and $\varrho(W)=0$. Show from this that for any subspace W of $K\langle\langle X\rangle\rangle$, $W^{\perp\perp}$ is the adherence of W.

4.1. Let $S \in K\langle\langle X\rangle\rangle$, let a be its constant term and let T be the proper series with $S=a+T$.

a) Show that if $\sum S^n$ converges in $K\langle\langle X\rangle\rangle$, then $\sum a^n$ also converges in K (for the discrete topology).
b) Show that if $\sum a^n$ converges in K, then $\sum S^n$ converges in $K\langle\langle X\rangle\rangle$, and then

$$\sum_{n \geqq 0} S^n=\left(\left(\sum_{n \geqq 0} a^n\right) T\right)^*\left(\sum_{n \geqq 0} a^n\right)$$

c) Show that if S is rational and if $\sum S^n$ converges, then $\sum S^n$ is rational.
d) Show that if $\varrho: K\langle\langle X\rangle\rangle \rightarrow L\langle\langle Y\rangle\rangle$ is a morphism of formal series (see Exercise 3.3) such that $\varrho(S)$ is rational for all $S \in K \cup X$, then ϱ preserves rationality.

4.2. Let (S_n) be a sequence of proper series. Show that if $\lim S_n = S$ then S is proper and $\lim S_n^* = S^*$.

4.3. Recall that an element a of a ring K is called *quasiregular* (in the sense of Jacobson) if there exists some $b \in K$ such that $a+b+ab=0$. Recall also that the radical R of K is the greatest two-sided ideal of K having only quasiregular elements (it exists!).

a) Show that $S \in K\langle\langle X\rangle\rangle$ is quasiregular in $K\langle\langle X\rangle\rangle$ if and only if its constant term is quasiregular in K.
b) Show that the radical of $K\langle\langle X\rangle\rangle$ is

$$\{S \in K\langle\langle X\rangle\rangle \mid (S, 1) \in R\}$$

4.4. Let $k \geqq 2$ be an integer and let $X = \{x_0, \ldots, x_{k-1}\}$. For a word w over X, we denote by $\langle w\rangle$ the integer having w as an expansion in base k. For example,

$$\langle x_0 x_1 x_1 x_1\rangle = k^2 + k + 1$$

Let S, T be the series defined by

$$S = \sum_w \langle w\rangle w, \quad T = \sum_w k^{|w|} w$$

Show that

$$T = 1 + \sum_i k x_i T$$

$$(S, x_i w) = (S, w) + i(T, w)$$

Using the formula $S = (S, 1) + \sum x_i (x_i^{-1} S)$ show that

$$S = (x_1 + 2x_2 + \ldots + (k-1) x_{k-1}) T + (x_0 + \ldots + x_{k-1}) S$$

and show that

$$S = \left(\sum_i x_i\right)^* \left(\sum_i i x_i\right) \left(\sum_i k x_i\right)^*$$

(by applying Lemma 4.1), also showing that S is rational.

4.5. Assume that K is a ring. Show that a series is invertible in $K\langle\langle X\rangle\rangle$ iff its constant term is invertible in K.

5.1. a) Suppose that K is a field with an absolute value $|\ |$. Show that if $S \in K\langle\langle X\rangle\rangle$ is recognizable, then there exists a constant $C \in \mathbf{R}$ such that for all w in X^*

$$|(S, w)| \leqq C^{|w|+1}$$

b) Suppose that K is a (commutative) integral domain with quotient field F. Show that if $S \in F\langle\langle X\rangle\rangle$ is recognizable, there exists $C \in K \backslash 0$ such that the series

$$\sum C^{|w|+1} (S, w) w$$

has its coefficients in K and is K-recognizable ("Eisenstein's Criterion").

5.2. Let $w=x_1 \dots x_n$ be a word $(x_i \in X)$. For any subset $I=\{i_1<\dots<i_k\}$ of $\{1,\dots,n\}$, define $w|I$ to be the word $x_{i_1} \dots x_{i_k}$. Given two words u and v of length n and p respectively, define their *shuffle* product $u \sqcup\!\sqcup v$ to be the polynomial

$$u \sqcup\!\sqcup v = \sum w(I, J)$$

where the sum is over all partitions $\{1,2,\dots,n+p\}=I \cup J$, with $|I|=n$, $|J|=p$, and where $w(I, J)$ is defined by $w(I, J)|I=u$, $w(I, J)|J=v$. Moreover, $1 \sqcup\!\sqcup v = v \sqcup\!\sqcup 1 = 1$. For example,

$$xy \sqcup\!\sqcup xz = xyxz + 2x^2yz + 2x^2zy + xzxy$$

Let K be a commutative semiring. Extend the shuffle product to $K\langle\langle X \rangle\rangle$ by linearity and continuity, i.e.

$$S \sqcup\!\sqcup T = \sum_{u,v \in X^*} (S, u)(T, v) u \sqcup\!\sqcup v$$

Show that the shuffle product is commutative and associative. Show that the operator

$$S \mapsto x^{-1}S \quad (x \in X)$$

is a derivation for the shuffle, i.e.

$$x^{-1}(S \sqcup\!\sqcup T) = (x^{-1}S) \sqcup\!\sqcup T + S \sqcup\!\sqcup (x^{-1}T) \tag{*}$$

Show that the shuffle product of two recognizable series is still recognizable. (*Hint*: Proceed as in the proof of Theorem 5.3, and use Eq. (*).)

Notes to Chapter I

The theorem showing the equivalence between rationality and recognizability was first proved by Kleene (1956) for languages (which are the series with coefficients in the Boolean semiring) and later extended by Schützenberger (1961a, 1962a and b) to arbitrary semirings. Here we shall derive Kleene's theorem from Schützenberger's (see Chap. III). The condition "recognizable" ⇒ "rational", which is essentially Lemma 6.3, is proved by using an argument of Conway (1971). Other proofs are also given in Eilenberg (1974) and Salomaa and Soittola (1978). The characterization of recognizable series (Proposition 5.1) is taken from Jacob (1975) who extends to semiring a Hankel-like property given by Fliess (1974a) for fields. Closure under shuffle product (Exercise 5.2) is due to Fliess (1974b). We do not consider algebraic formal series in this book; the reader may consult Salomaa, Soittola (1978) and Kuich, Salomaa (1986).

Chapter II

Minimization

This chapter gives a new presentation of well-known results concerning the reduction of linear representations of recognizable series. The central concept of this study is the notion of syntactic algebra, which is introduced in Sect. 1. Rational series are characterized by the fact that their syntactic algebras are finite dimensional (Theorem 1.1). The syntactic right ideal, which is the analogue for series of the minimal automaton for languages, leads to the notions of rank and of Hankel matrix.

Sect. 2 is devoted to a detailed study of reduced linear representations. The relations between representations and syntactic algebra are given. Two reduced representations are shown to be similar (Theorem 2.4), and an explicit form of the reduced representation is given (Corollary 2.3).

The reduction algorithm for representations is presented in Sect. 3. We start with a study of prefix sets. The main application is a description of bases of right ideals of noncommutative polynomials (Theorem 3.2).

Several important consequences are given. Among them are the Schreier formula for right ideals and linear recurrence relations for the coefficients of a rational series. A detailed description of the reduction algorithm completes the chapter.

In this chapter, K denotes a commutative ring.

1 Syntactic Ideals

The algebra of polynomials $K\langle X\rangle$ is a free K-module having as a basis the free monoid X^*. Consequently, the set $K\langle\langle X\rangle\rangle$ of formal series can be identified with the dual of $K\langle X\rangle$. Each formal series S defines a linear form

$$K\langle X\rangle \to K$$

$$P \mapsto (S, P) = \sum_{w \in X^*} (S, w)(P, w)$$

the sum having a finite support because P is a polynomial. Thus, one may consider the kernel of S, denoted by $Ker\, S$:

$$Ker\, S = \{P \in K\langle X\rangle \mid (S, P) = 0\}$$

Next, any multiplicative morphism μ: $X^* \to M$, where M is a K-algebra, can be extended uniquely to a morphism of algebra

$$K\langle X\rangle \to M$$

This extension will also be denoted by μ. We shall use this convention tacitly in the following. Clearly

$$\mu(P) = \sum_{w \in X^*} (P, w)\mu(w)$$

Definition. The *syntactic ideal* of a formal series $S \in K\langle X \rangle$ is the greatest two-sided ideal of $K\langle X \rangle$ contained in the kernel of S. It is denoted by I_S.

Observe that this ideal always exists, since it is the sum of all ideals contained in *Ker S*,

$$I_S = \sum_{I \subset Ker\, S} I$$

Definition. The *syntactic algebra* of a formal series $S \in K\langle\langle X \rangle\rangle$, denoted by M_S, is the quotient algebra of $K\langle X \rangle$ by the syntactic ideal of S,

$$M_S = K\langle X \rangle / I_S$$

The canonical morphism $K\langle X \rangle \to M_S$ is denoted by μ_S. Since $Ker\, \mu_S = I_S \subset Ker\, S$, the series S induces on M_S a linear form denoted by φ_S. Consequently

$$S = \varphi_S \circ \mu_S$$

A K-algebra M is said to have *finite rank* (over K) if it is a finitely generated K-module.

Theorem 1.1 (Reutenauer 1978a, 1980a). *A formal series is rational iff its syntactic algebra has finite rank.*

Proof. If S is rational, S is recognizable and has a linear representation (λ, μ, γ), with $\mu: X^* \to K^{n \times n}$ a morphism. Since X is finite, the subring L of K generated by the coefficients of λ, $\mu(x)$ $(x \in X)$ and γ is a finitely generated ring. Therefore L is Noetherian. This in turn implies that the L-subalgebra $\mu(L\langle X \rangle)$ of $L^{n \times n}$ has finite rank over L. Consequently, the K-algebra $\mu(K\langle X \rangle)$ has finite rank over K. Now $Ker\, \mu$ is an ideal contained in $Ker\, S$. Thus by definition $Ker\, \mu \subset I_S$, and M_S, as a quotient of $\mu(K\langle X \rangle)$, has finite rank.

Conversely, suppose that the syntactic algebra of S has finite rank. Consider, for each word w in X^*, the K-endomorphism νw of M_S defined by

$$m \mapsto \mu_S(w) m$$

The function

$$\nu: X^* \to End(M_S)$$

is a morphism, and moreover

$$(S, w) = \varphi_S \circ \mu_S(w) = \varphi_S(\nu w(1))$$

In order to conclude, it suffices to apply the following lemma and Theorem I.6.1.

□

Lemma 1.2. (This lemma requires no hypothesis on K.) *Let M be a finitely generated right K-module, let φ be a K-linear form on M, let m_0 be an element of M and let v be a morphism $X^* \to End(M)$. Then the formal series*

$$S = \sum_{w \in X^*} \varphi(vw(m_0))$$

is recognizable. More precisely, if M has a generating system of n elements, then S admits a linear representation of dimension n.

Proof. Let $m_1, \ldots, m_n$ be generators of M. Then for each letter x in X, and each j in $\{1, \ldots, n\}$, there exist coefficients $\alpha^x_{i,j}$ such that

$$vx(m_j) = \sum_i m_i \alpha^x_{i,j}$$

The matrices $(\alpha^x_{i,j})_{i,j} \in K^{n \times n}$ define a function $\mu: X \to K^{n \times n}$ which extends to a morphism $\mu: X^* \to K^{n \times n}$. An induction shows that for any word w,

$$vw(m_j) = \sum_i m_i (\mu w)_{i,j}$$

Let $\lambda \in K^{1 \times n}$ and $\gamma \in K^{n \times 1}$ be given by $\lambda_i = \varphi(m_i)$ and $m_0 = \sum_j m_j \gamma_j$. Then

$$vw(m_0) = vw\left(\sum_j m_j \gamma_j\right)$$

thus

$$\varphi(vw(m_0)) = \sum_{i,j} \lambda_i (\mu w)_{i,j} \gamma_j = \lambda \mu w \gamma$$

which completes the proof. □

Definition. The *syntactic right ideal* of a formal series $S \in K\langle\langle X \rangle\rangle$ is the greatest right ideal of $K\langle X \rangle$ contained in $Ker\, S$. It is denoted by I^d_S.

The existence of I^d_S is shown in the same manner as that of I_S.

We now introduce an operation of $K\langle X \rangle$ on $K\langle\langle X \rangle\rangle$ on the right. Recall that, since $K\langle\langle X \rangle\rangle$ is the dual of $K\langle X \rangle$, each endomorphism f of the K-module $K\langle X \rangle$ defines an endomorphism, called the *transposed* morphism, of the K-module $K\langle\langle X \rangle\rangle$ by the relation

$$(S, f(P)) = ({}^t f(S), P)$$

for every series S and polynomial P. The function $f \mapsto {}^t f$ is an antimorphism:

$$^t(g \circ f) = {}^t f \circ {}^t g \qquad (1.1)$$

Given a polynomial P, we consider the endomorphism $Q \mapsto PQ$ of $K\langle X\rangle$ and its transposed morphism, denoted by $S \mapsto S \circ P$. Thus

$$(S, PQ) = (S \circ P, Q)$$

In particular, for all words u and v

$$(S, uv) = (S \circ u, v) \tag{1.2}$$

Consequently,

$$S \circ u = u^{-1} S$$

with the notation of Sect. I.5. Observe that the operation $\circ$ is already defined by Eq. (1.2); it suffices to extend it by linearity. In view of Eq. (1.1), one obtains

$$(S \circ P) \circ Q = S \circ PQ$$

Thus $K\langle\langle X\rangle\rangle$ is a right $K\langle X\rangle$-module.

Proposition 1.3. *The syntactic right ideal of a series S is*

$$I_S^d = \{P \in K\langle X\rangle \mid S \circ P = 0\}$$

Proof. Since the operation $\circ$ defines on $K\langle\langle X\rangle\rangle$ a structure of right $K\langle X\rangle$-module, it is clear that the right-hand side of the equation is a right ideal of $K\langle X\rangle$. It is contained in $Ker\, S$ because $S \circ P = 0$ implies $(S, P) = (S \circ P, 1) = 0$. It is the greatest right ideal with this property , since, given any polynomial P, the relation $PK\langle X\rangle \subset Ker\, S$ implies $(S \circ P, Q) = (S, PQ) = 0$ for all polynomials Q, whence $S \circ P = 0$. □

Corollary 1.4. *$K\langle X\rangle / I_S^d$ is isomorphic to $S \circ K\langle K\rangle$ as a right $K\langle X\rangle$-module.* □

This module is the analogue for series of the *minimal* automaton of a formal language.

We suppose from now on that K is a field.

Definition. The *rank* of a formal series S is the dimension of the space $S \circ K\langle X\rangle$.

Definition. The *Hankel matrix* of a formal series S is the matrix H indexed by $X^* \times X^*$ defined by

$$H(u, v) = (S, uv)$$

for all words u, v.

Theorem 1.5 (Carlyle and Paz 1971, Fliess 1974a). *The rank of a formal series S is equal to the codimension of its syntactic right ideal, and is equal to the rank of its Hankel matrix. The series S is rational if and only if this rank is finite and in this case, its rank is equal to the minimum of the dimensions of the linear representations of S.*

This theorem shows that the rank of a formal series could have been defined by an operation of $K\langle X\rangle$ on $K\langle\langle X\rangle\rangle$ on the left (analogous to $\circ$), or also by means of the syntactic left ideal (whose definition is clear). Indeed, the Hankel matrix is an object which is essentially unoriented.

Recall that the *rank* of a matrix (even an infinite one) can be defined to be the greatest dimension of a nonvanishing subdeterminant, and that it is equal to the rank of the rows (and to the rank of the columns).

Proof. The first equality, namely $rk(S)=codim(I_S^d)$ is a direct consequence of Corollary 1.4. Next, the space $S\circ K\langle X\rangle$ has as a set of generators $\{S\circ u | u\in X^*\}$. Thus $rk(S)$ is equal to the rank of this set. Since each $S\circ u$ can be identified with the row of index u in the Hankel matrix of S, the rank of S is equal to the rank of this matrix.

If S is rational, it has a linear representation (λ, μ, γ) of dimension n. The right ideal

$$J=\{P\in K\langle X\rangle \mid \lambda\mu(P)=0\}$$

is contained in $Ker\, S$, and its codimension is $\leqq n$. Consequently, J is contained in I_S^d, showing that $rk(S)=codim(I_S^d)\leqq codim(J)\leqq n$.

Conversely, let $r=rk(S)=dim(S\circ K\langle X\rangle)$. Let φ be the linear form

$$S\circ K\langle X\rangle\rightarrow K$$

$$T\mapsto(T, 1)$$

Then for any word w,

$$(S, w)=(S\circ w, 1)=\varphi(S\circ w) \tag{1.3}$$

Let μw be the matrix of the endomorphism of $S\circ K\langle X\rangle$ which maps a series T on $T\circ w$, in some base of $S\circ K\langle X\rangle$. (Each element of $S\circ K\langle X\rangle$ is represented by a vector in $K^{1\times n}$, and each endomorphism of $S\circ K\langle X\rangle$ is represented by a matrix in $K^{n\times n}$; thus $K^{n\times n}$ acts *on the right* on $K^{1\times n}$). In view of Eq. (1.2), one has $(\mu u)(\mu v)=\mu(uv)$ for any words u and v. Let λ be the row vector representing S in the chosen base, and let γ be the column representing φ. Then Eq. (1.3) can be expressed as

$$(S, w)=\lambda\mu w\gamma$$

showing that S is recognizable, with a linear representation of dimension r. □

This theorem justifies the following definition.

Definition. A *reduced linear representation* of a rational series S is a linear representation of S with minimal dimension among all its representations.

Example 1.1. The only series of rank 0 is the null series.

Example 1.2. Let S be a series of rank 1. It admits a representation (λ, μ, γ), with $\mu\colon K\langle X\rangle\rightarrow K$ a morphism of algebras and $\lambda, \mu\in K$. Set $\alpha_x=\mu(x)$ for each letter x, For

$w = x_1 \ldots x_n (x_i \in X)$, this gives

$$\mu w = \alpha_{x_1} \ldots \alpha_{x_n} = \prod_{x \in X} \alpha_x^{|w|_x}$$

Consequently

$$(S, w) = \lambda \gamma \prod_{x \in X} \alpha_x^{|w|_x}$$

Such a series is called *geometric*. It follows that

$$S = \lambda \gamma \left(\sum_{x \in X} \alpha_x x \right)^* = \lambda \gamma \left(1 - \sum_{x \in X} \alpha_x x \right)^{-1}$$

An example of a geometric series is the characteristic series of X^*:

$$S = \sum_{w \in X^*} w = \left(\sum_{x \in X} x \right)^* = \left(1 - \sum_{x \in X} x \right)^{-1}$$

Example 1.3. The series $S = \sum_{w \in X^*} |w|_x w$ has rank 2. Indeed, it has a linear representation of dimension 2 (see Example I.5.1) Next, the subdeterminant of its Hankel matrix corresponding to the coordinates 1, x is

$$\begin{vmatrix} 0 & 1 \\ 1 & 2 \end{vmatrix} = -1$$

Thus, S has rank $\geqq 2$. In view of Theorem 1.5, the rank of S is 2.

2 Reduced Linear Representations

K denotes a (commutative) field.

Proposition 2.1. *A linear representation (λ, μ, γ) of dimension n of a series S is reduced if and only if, setting $M = \mu(K\langle X \rangle)$,*

$$\lambda M = K^{1 \times n} \quad \text{and} \quad M\gamma = K^{n \times 1}$$

In this case,

$$I_S^d = \{P | \lambda \mu P = 0\}$$

Proof. Suppose that (λ, μ, γ) is reduced, and let $J = \{P | \lambda \mu P = 0\}$. Then J is a right ideal of $K\langle X \rangle$ and $codim(J) = dim(\lambda M) \leqq n$. Since $J \subset Ker\, S$, one has $J \subset I_S^d$ and $codim(J) \geqq codim(I_S^d) = n$ (Theorem 1.5). Consequently $codim(J) = n$, $J = I_S^d$ and $\lambda M = K^{1 \times n}$. The equality $M\gamma = K^{n \times 1}$ is derived symmetrically.

Conversely, assume $\lambda M = K^{1\times n}$ and $M\gamma = K^{n\times 1}$. Then there exist words $u_1, \ldots, u_n$ $(v_1, \ldots, v_n)$ such that $\{\lambda\mu u_1, \ldots, \lambda\mu u_n\}$ $(\{\mu v_1\gamma, \ldots, \mu v_n\gamma\})$ is a base of $K^{1\times n}$ (of $K^{n\times 1}$). Consequently

$$det(\lambda\mu u_i v_j\gamma)_{1\leqq i,\ j\leqq n} \neq 0$$

Since $\lambda\mu u_i v_j\gamma = (S, u_i v_j)$, the Hankel matrix of S has rank $\geqq n$. In view of Theorem 1.5, the representation (λ, μ, γ) is reduced. □

Corollary 2.2. *If the linear representation (λ, μ, γ) of the formal series S is reduced, then the kernel of μ is exactly the syntactic ideal of S, and consequently $\mu(K\langle X\rangle)$ is isomorphic to the syntactic algebra of S.*

Proof. Since $Ker\ \mu$ is contained in $Ker\ S$, it is contained in I_S. Conversely let $P \in I_S$. Then QPR is in I_S for all polynomials Q, R, and consequently $(S, QPR) = 0$. It follows that $\lambda\mu QPR\gamma = 0$ and in fact $\lambda\mu(K\langle X\rangle)\mu P\mu(K\langle X\rangle)\gamma = 0$. In view of Proposition 2.1. this implies $\mu P = 0$, whence $P \in Ker\ \mu$. □

Corollary 2.3 (Schützenberger 1961a). *If (λ, μ, γ) is a reduced linear representation of dimension n of a formal series S then there exist polynomials $P_1, \ldots, P_n, Q_1, \ldots, Q_n$ such that, for every word w*

$$\mu w = ((S, P_i w Q_j))_{1\leqq i,\ j\leqq n}$$

Proof. In view of Proposition 2.1, there are polynomials $P_1, \ldots, P_n, Q_1, \ldots, Q_n$ such that $(\lambda\mu P_i)_{1\leqq i\leqq n}$ gives the canonical base of $K^{1\times n}$ and similarly $(\mu Q_j\gamma)_{1\leqq j\leqq n}$ gives that of $K^{n\times 1}$. Thus

$$(\mu w)_{ij} = \lambda\mu P_i \mu w \mu Q_j \gamma = (S, P_i w Q_j)$$ □

Two linear representations (λ, μ, γ) and $(\lambda', \mu', \gamma')$ are called *similar* if there exists an invertible matrix m such that $\lambda' = \lambda m$, $\mu' w = m^{-1}\mu w m$ (for all words w), $\gamma' = m^{-1}\gamma$. Clearly, they recognize the same series.

Theorem 2.4 (Schützenberger 1961a, Fliess 1974a). *Two reduced linear representations of the same series are similar.*

Proof. Let (λ, μ, γ) be a reduced linear representation of a series S. Since, by Propositions 1.3 and 2.1,

$$I_S^d = \{P \in K\langle X\rangle | \lambda\mu P = 0\} = \{P \in K\langle X\rangle | S \circ P = 0\}$$

the two right $K\langle X\rangle$-modules $S \circ K\langle X\rangle$ and $K^{1\times n} = \lambda\mu(K\langle X\rangle)$ (with the action on $K^{1\times n}$ defined by $(v, P) = v\mu(P)$) are isomorphic. Consequently there exists a K-isomorphism

$$f: K^{1\times n} \to S \circ K\langle X\rangle$$

such that, for any polynomial P, and any $v \in K^{1\times n}$,

$$f(v\mu P) = f(v)\circ P$$

and moreover

$$f(\lambda) = S$$

Next, consider the linear form φ on $S\circ K\langle X\rangle$ defined by $\varphi(T) = (T, 1)$. Then for $v = \lambda\mu P$, one gets $\varphi(f(v)) = \varphi(f(\lambda\mu P)) = \varphi(f(\lambda)\circ P) = \varphi(S\circ P) = (S\circ P, 1) = (S, P) = \lambda\mu P\gamma = v\gamma$, which shows that

$$\varphi\circ f = \gamma$$

if γ is set to be the linear form $v \mapsto v\gamma$.

If $(\lambda', \mu', \gamma')$ is another reduced linear representation, there exists an analoguous isomorphism f'. Thus there exists an isomorphism

$$\psi = f^{-1}\circ f' : K^{1\times n} \to K^{1\times n}$$

such that

$$\psi(v\mu' P) = \psi(v)\mu P, \quad \psi(\lambda') = \lambda, \quad \gamma\circ\psi = \gamma'$$

It suffices to write these relations in matrix form to obtain the announced result. □

Corollary 2.5 (Schützenberger 1961a). *Let (λ, μ, γ) and $(\lambda', \mu', \gamma')$ be two linear representations of some series S, and assume the second representation is reduced. Then there exists a representation $(\bar{\lambda}, \bar{\mu}, \bar{\gamma})$ similar to (λ, μ, γ) and having a block decomposition of the form*

$$\bar{\lambda} = (\times, \lambda', 0), \qquad \bar{\mu} = \begin{bmatrix} \mu_1 & 0 & 0 \\ \times & \mu' & 0 \\ \times & \times & \mu_2 \end{bmatrix}, \qquad \bar{\gamma} = \begin{bmatrix} 0 \\ \gamma' \\ \times \end{bmatrix}.$$

Proof. Let n be the dimension of (λ, μ, γ). Let V_1 be the subspace of $K^{1\times n}$ given by

$$V_1 = \lambda\mu(K\langle X\rangle) \cap \{v \mid v\mu(K\langle X\rangle)\gamma = 0\}$$

Let V_2 be a subspace of $K^{1\times n}$ such that

$$V_1 \oplus V_2 = \lambda\mu(K\langle X\rangle)$$

and let V_3 be a subspace with

$$V_1 \oplus V_2 \oplus V_3 = K^{1\times n}$$

The subspaces V_1 and $V_1 \oplus V_2$ are both stable under the action of the matrices in $\mu(K\langle X\rangle)$. This shows that there exists a decomposition into blocks, relatively to the direct sum above, having the form

$$\lambda = (\lambda_1, \lambda_2, 0), \qquad \mu = \begin{bmatrix} \mu_1 & 0 & 0 \\ \times & \mu_2 & 0 \\ \times & \times & \mu_3 \end{bmatrix}, \qquad \gamma = \begin{bmatrix} 0 \\ \gamma_2 \\ \gamma_3 \end{bmatrix}.$$

Then $\lambda\mu w\gamma = \lambda_2\mu_2 w\gamma_2$, which shows that $(\lambda_2, \mu_2, \gamma_2)$ is a linear representation of S. From $V_1 \oplus V_2 = \lambda\mu(K\langle X\rangle)$, it follows that $V_2 = \lambda_2\mu_2(K\langle X\rangle)$. Similarly, since

$$0 = \{v \in V_2 | v\mu(K\langle X\rangle)\gamma = 0\} = \{v \in V_2 | v\mu_2(K\langle X\rangle)\gamma_2 = 0\}$$

one gets

$$V_2' = \mu_2(K\langle X\rangle)\gamma_2$$

where V_2' is the dual of V_2. Consequently, $(\lambda_2, \mu_2, \gamma_2)$ is reduced (Proposition 2.1). Thus it is similar to $(\lambda', \mu', \gamma')$, and this proves the corollary. □

3 The Reduction Algorithm

We now give an effective procedure for computing a reduced linear representation of a recognizable series.

Definition. A *prefix set* is a subset C of X^* such that $u, uv \in C$ implies $v = 1$ for all words u and v. It is *right complete* if CX^* meets every right ideal of X^*.

Definition. A subset P of X^* is *prefix-closed* if $uv \in P$ implies $u \in P$ for all words u and v.

In other words, a prefix-closed set contains all the left factors of its elements, while a prefix set contains none of them.

Proposition 3.1. *There exists a bijection between prefix sets and prefix-closed sets. To a prefix set C is associated the prefix-closed set $P = X^* \setminus CX^*$, and the reciprocal bijection is defined by $C = PX \setminus P$. In this case, $X^* = C^*P$. This bijection defines, by restriction, a bijection between finite right complete prefix sets and finite nonempty prefix-closed sets.*

Proof. (i) Let C be a prefix set. Since CX^* is a right ideal, its complement $P = X^* \setminus CX^*$ is prefix-closed. Let $C' = PX \setminus P$. If $w \in C$, and $w = ux$ for some $x \in X$, then u cannot be in CX^* because C is a prefix set. Thus $u \in P$, and $C \subset PX$. Since $C \cap P = \varnothing$, one has $C \subset C'$. Conversely, if $w \in C'$, then $w \notin P$, whence $w \in CX^*$ and $w = cu$ for some $c \in C$. Moreover, $w = px$ for some $p \in P$, $x \in X$, and thus $px = cu$. Since $p \notin CX^*$, one has $|p| < |c|$, whence $c = px$ and $u = 1$, which shows that w is in C. This proves that $C = C'$.

If C is assumed to be right complete and finite, let $n = \max\{|c|, c \in C\}$. Any word w of length at least n is in CX^*, since by hypothesis $wX^* \cap CX^* \neq \varnothing$. This proves that $P = X^* \setminus CX^*$ is finite.

(ii) Now let P be prefix-closed and let $C = PX \backslash P$. A word w not in P has a longest left factor in P, say p. Thus $w = pxu$ for some $x \in X$, showing that $px = c \in C$ and $w = cu$. Arguing by induction, this shows that

$$X^* = C^* P$$

Moreover, if $w \in C$, then $w = px$, and each proper left factor of w is a left factor of p and therefore is in P, showing that C is a prefix set.

Let $P' = X^* \backslash CX^*$. Since $P \cap C = \emptyset$ and P is prefix-closed, one has $P \cap CX^* = \emptyset$, showing that $P \subset P'$.

Conversely, let $w \notin P$. Then $w = pxu$ for some letter x and with p the longest left factor of w which is in P. Then $w \in CX^*$ and consequently $w \notin P'$. Thus $P' = P$.

If P is finite, then any word $w \notin P$ is, as before, in CX^*, which shows that $wX^* \cap CX^* \neq \emptyset$. If $w \in P$, then since P is finite, wX^* meets $X^* \backslash P = CX^*$. Thus $wX^* \cap CX^* \neq \emptyset$ for all $w \in X^*$, and C is right complete. Since $C \subset PX$, C is finite. □

Remark. In order to illustrate Proposition 3.1, let us consider the *tree representation* of the free monoid X^*. Let, for instance, $X = \{x, y\}$. Then X^* is represented by

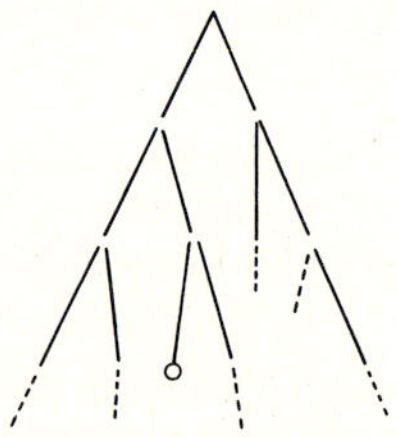

For instance, the circled node corresponds to xyx. A finite right complete prefix set C then is represented by a finite tree of the shape

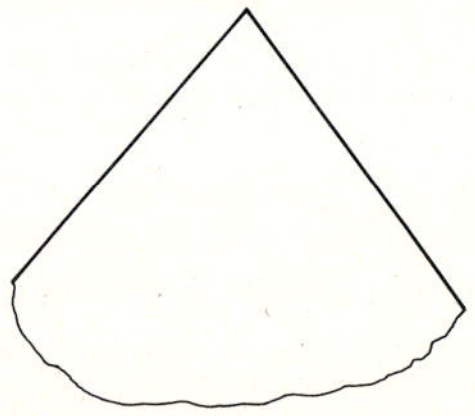

with the elements of the set being the tree's leaves, and the prefix-closed set associated with C being represented by its interior nodes.

Example 3.1. The tree

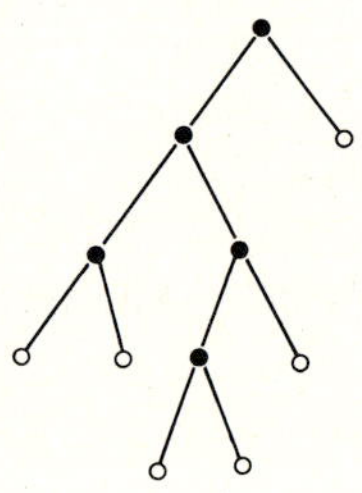

represents the prefix set

$$C = x^3 + x^2y + xyx^2 + xyxy + xy^2 + y$$

with

$$P = 1 + x + x^2 + xy + xyx$$

The white circles ○ represent the elements of the set, and the black circles ● the elements of P. This representation helps in understanding the heavy formalism of the proof.

In the following statement, K is assumed to be a commutative field.

Theorem 3.2. *Let I be a right ideal of $K\langle X\rangle$. There exists a prefix set C with associated prefix-closed set P, and coefficients $\alpha_{c,p}$ $(c \in C,\ p \in P)$, such that the polynomials $P_c = c - \sum_{p \in P} \alpha_{c,p}\, p\ (c \in C)$ generate freely I (as a right $K\langle X\rangle$-module) and such that P defines a K-base in $K\langle X\rangle/I$.*

Proof. Let

$$\varphi : K\langle X\rangle \to M = K\langle X\rangle/I$$

be the canonical morphism. Let P be a prefix-closed subset of X^* such that the elements $\varphi(p)$, for $p \in P$, are K-linearly independent in M, and maximal among the subsets of X^* having these properties.

Let $C = PX\backslash P$. Then C is a prefix set (Proposition 3.1). For each $c \in C$, the set $P \cup c$ is prefix-closed, and by the maximality of P, $\varphi(c)$ is in the subspace of M spanned by $\varphi(P)$. Thus there exist coefficients $\alpha_{c,p} \in K$ such that

$$P_c = c - \sum_{p \in P} \alpha_{c,p}\, p \in I \tag{3.1}$$

We now show that any polynomial R can be written as

$$R = \sum_{c \in C} P_c Q_c + \sum_{p \in P} \beta_p p \tag{3.2}$$

for some polynomials $Q_c\ (c \in C)$ and coefficients $\beta_p\ (p \in P)$. It suffices to prove this for the case where $R = w$ is a word, and even in the case where $w \notin P$. But then $w = cu\ (c \in C)$ since $X^*\backslash P = CX^*$ by Proposition 3.1. We argue by induction on the length of the word u. First, observe that by Eq. (3.1),

$$w = P_c u + \sum_{p} \alpha_{c,p}\, pu$$

Since each of the words pu is either in P or of the form $c'u'$ with $|p| < |c'|$, whence $|u'| < |u|$, the induction hypothesis completes the proof.

If the polynomial R of Eq. (3.2) is in I, then

$$0=\varphi(R)=\sum_p \beta_p \varphi(p)$$

Consequently $\beta_p=0$ for all p and

$$R=\sum_{c\in C} P_c Q_c$$

which shows that the right ideal I is generated by the P_c.

Let $\sum P_c Q_c=0$ be a relation of $K\langle X\rangle$-dependency between the P_c, and assume that not all the Q_c vanish. Then

$$\sum_c cQ_c=\sum_{p,c} \alpha_{c,p} pQ_c \tag{3.3}$$

Consider a word w for which there is a $c_0\in C$ with $(Q_{c_0}, w)\neq 0$, and which is a word of maximal length. For this word w, the coefficient of $c_0 w$ on the left-hand side of Eq. (3.3) is $(Q_{c_0}, w)\neq 0$ because C is a prefix set. Thus

$$(Q_{c_0}, w)=\sum_{p,c} \alpha_{c,p}(pQ_c, c_0 w)\neq 0$$

However, $pu=c_0 w$ implies that p is a proper left factor of c_0, thus $c_0=pv$ for some $v\neq 1$ and $u=vw$. Consequently

$$(Q_{c_0}, w)=\sum_{v\neq 1,\ c_0=pv} \alpha_{c,p}(Q_c, vw)=0$$

in view of the maximality of w, a contradiction. □

Corollary 3.3 (Cohn 1969). *Each right ideal of $K\langle X\rangle$ is a free right $K\langle X\rangle$-module.* □

Corollary 3.4 (Lewin 1969). *Let I be a right ideal of $K\langle X\rangle$ of codimension n and rank d (as a right $K\langle X\rangle$-module). Let r be the cardinality of X. Then*

$$d=n(r-1)+1$$

Proof. Indeed, if P is a finite prefix-closed set, with an associated prefix set C, then $X^*=C^*P$ by Proposition 3.1. This equality is easily seen to hold in $\mathbf{Z}\langle\langle X\rangle\rangle$, whence by inversion

$$C-1=P(X-1)$$

and $|C|=|P|(|X|-1)+1$. □

We also obtain *linear recurrence relations* for rational series which generalize those for one-variable series (see Chap. IV).

Corollary 3.5. *For any rational series S of rank n, there exist a prefix-closed set P of n elements, with an associated prefix set C, and coefficients $\alpha_{c,p}$ $(c \in C, p \in P)$ such that, for all words w and all c in C,*

$$(S, cw) = \sum_{p \in P} \alpha_{c,p} (S, pw) \tag{3.4}$$

Proof. It suffices to apply Theorem 3.2 to the syntactic right ideal of S which has codimension n. □

Corollary 3.6. *Let S be a rational series of rank $\leqq n$, such that $(S, w) = 0$ for all words w of length $\leqq n-1$. Then $S = 0$.*

Proof. This is a consequence of Corollary 3.5. Indeed, $|p| \leqq n-1$ and therefore $(S, p) = 0$ for all $p \in P$. Assume $S \neq 0$, and let w be a word with $(S, w) \neq 0$. Then $w = cu$ for some $c \in C$. We choose w in such a way that the corresponding word u has minimal length. By Eq. (3.4),

$$(S, cu) = \sum_{p \in P} \alpha_{c,p} (S, pu)$$

and by the choice of u, one has $(S, pu) = 0$ for all $p \in P$. Thus $(S, cu) = 0$, a contradiction. □

A subset T of X^* is *suffix-closed* if $uv \in T$ implies $v \in T$ for all words u and v.

Corollary 3.7. *Let S be a rational series of rank n. There exist a prefix-closed set P and a suffix-closed set T, both with n elements, such that*

$$\det((S, pt))_{p \in P, t \in T} \neq 0$$

Proof. Let (λ, μ, γ) be a reduced linear representation of S. It has dimension n. In view of Theorem 3.2, there exists a prefix-closed subset P such that $\lambda\mu(P)$ is a base of $K^{1 \times n}$, and symmetrically, there is a suffix-closed set T such that $\mu(T)\gamma$ is a base of $K^{n \times 1}$. Thus, the determinant of the matrix

$$(\lambda\mu p \mu t \gamma)_{p,t}$$

does not vanish. This proves the corollary. □

A careful analysis of the preceding proofs shows how to compute effectively a reduced linear representation of a rational series S given by any of its linear representations.

Indeed, let (λ, μ, γ) be such a representation, of dimension n. The first step consists in reducing the representation to satisfy $K^{1 \times n} = \lambda\mu(K\langle X \rangle)$. To do this, consider a prefix-closed subset P of X^* such that the vectors $\lambda\mu p$, for $p \in P$, are linearly independent, and which is maximal for this property. Then for each c in the prefix set $C=PX\backslash P$, there are coefficients $\alpha_{c,p}$ such that

$$\lambda\mu c=\sum_{p}\alpha_{c,p}\,\mu p$$

Consider, for each letter x, the matrix $\mu' x\in K^{P\times P}$ defined by

$$(\mu' x)_{p,q}=\begin{cases}1 & \text{if } px=q\\ \alpha_{c,q} & \text{if } px=c\in C\\ 0 & \text{otherwise}\end{cases}$$

In other words, $\mu' x$ is the matrix, in the base $\lambda\mu P$ of $\lambda\mu(K\langle X\rangle)$, of the endomorphism $v\mapsto v\mu x$. In this base the matrix for λ is λ' defined by $\lambda'_1=1$, and $\lambda'_p=0$ for $p\neq 1$; the matrix for γ is γ' defined by $\gamma'_p=\lambda\mu p\gamma=(S,p)$. Then (λ',μ',γ') is a linear representation of S, since for any word w, one has $\lambda\mu w\in\lambda\mu(K\langle X\rangle)$, whence $\lambda\mu w\gamma=\lambda'\mu' w\gamma'$. Moreover, the representation (λ',μ',γ') satisfies $K^{1\times P}=\lambda'\mu'(K\langle X\rangle)$. Indeed, since $\lambda'\mu' p$ represents the vector $\lambda\mu p$ in the base $\lambda\mu(P)$, one has $\lambda'\mu' p=(\delta_{p,q})_{q\in P}$, which shows that $\lambda'\mu'(K\langle X\rangle)$ contains the canonical base of $K^{1\times P}$.

If in the preceding construction, we assume moreover that $\mu(K\langle X\rangle)\gamma=K^{n\times 1}$, then also $\mu'(K\langle x\rangle)\gamma'=K^{P\times 1}$. Indeed, the first equality implies that every linear form on the space $\lambda\mu(K\langle X\rangle)$ is represented by a matrix of the form $\mu(R)\gamma$ for some $R\in K\langle X\rangle$. In the new base $\lambda'\mu'(P)$ of $\lambda'\mu'(K\langle X\rangle)$, this matrix becomes $\mu'(R)\gamma'$. Thus any linear form on $K^{1\times P}=\lambda'\mu'(P)$ is represented as some $\mu'(R)\gamma'$, which proves the claim.

Now the work is almost done. In a first step, one reduces the representation to satisfy the condition $\mu(K\langle X\rangle)=K^{n\times 1}$, using a construction which is symmetric to the preceding one, based on suffix sets and suffix-closed sets. In a second step, the representation is transformed to satisfy in addition $\lambda\mu(K\langle X\rangle)=K^{1\times n}$, and (λ,μ,γ) is reduced by Proposition 2.1.

Exercises for Chapter II

1.1. The *reversal* of a word w, denoted by ${}^t w$, is defined as follows. If $w=1$, then ${}^t w=1$; if $w=x_1\ldots x_n$ $(x_i\in X)$, then ${}^t w=x_n\ldots x_1$. A word is a *palindrome* if it is equal to its reversal. Let L be the set of palindrome words.

a) Assume $|X|\geqq 2$. Show that if $u, u_1,\ldots,u_n$ are words with $|u|\leqq|u_1|,\ldots,|u_n|$ and $u\neq u_1,\ldots,u_n$, then there exists v such that $uv\in L$, $u_1v,\ldots,u_nv\notin L$. (*Hint*: Take $v=x^p yyx^p({}^t u)$, where x and y are distinct letters and $p=\sup\{|u_i|-|u|\}$).
b) Let $S\in K\langle\langle X\rangle\rangle$ be such that $(S,w)=1$ if $w\in L$, and $(S,w)=0$ for $w\notin L$. Show that all syntactic ideals of S are null (see Reutenauer 1980a).
c) (K is a commutative semiring.) Let $S\in K\langle\langle X\rangle\rangle$ be a recognizable series. Show that $S'=\sum_{w}(S,{}^t w)w$ is recognizable.

1.2. A K-algebra M is *syntactic* if there exists a formal series S whose syntactic algebra is isomorphic to M.

a) Show that an algebra $M \neq 0$ is syntactic if and only if it contains a hyperplane which contains no nonnull two-sided ideal. (One may use infinite alphabets.)
b) Let $M = K \cdot 1 \oplus K \cdot \alpha \oplus K \cdot \beta$, with the multiplication defined by

$$\alpha^2 = \alpha\beta = \beta\alpha = \beta^2 = 0$$

Show that M is not syntactic.
c) Show that $K\langle X \rangle$ is syntactic (use Exercise 1.1).

Notes to Chapter II

The notions of syntactic ideal and algebra are introduced in Reutenauer (1978a, 1980a), which also contains Theorem 1.1. The notions of Hankel matrix and rank of a formal series, which are classical in the case of one variable, were introduced by Carlyle and Paz (1971) and Fliess (1974a). The reduced linear representation of a rational series was first studied by Schützenberger (1961a and b), mainly in connection with the linear recurrence relations (Corollary 3.4). His methods are used here to prove Theorem 3.2 and the reduction algorithm. Observe that this construction is closely related to Schreier's construction of a base of a subgroup of a free group (see Lyndon and Schupp 1977, Proposition I.3.7).

Chapter III
Series and Languages

This chapter describes the relations between rational series and languages. It contains a criterion for the support of a rational series to be a rational language, and also an iteration theorem for these supports.

We start by proving Kleene's theorem as a consequence of Schützenberger's theorem. Then we describe the cases where the support of a rational series is a rational language. The most important result states that if a series has finite image, then its support is a rational language (Theorem 2.7).

The family of languages which are supports of rational series have closure properties given in Sect. 3. The iteration theorem for rational series is proved in Sect. 4. The last section is concerned with an extremal property of supports which forces their rationality.

1 The Theorem of Kleene

Definitions. A *language* is a subset of X^*. A *congruence* in a monoid is an equivalence relation which is compatible with the operation in the monoid. A language L is *recognizable* if there exists a congruence with finite index in X^* that saturates L (i.e. L is union of equivalence classes).

It is equivalent to say that L is recognizable if there exists a finite monoid M, a morphism of monoids $\varphi: X^* \to M$ and a subset P of M such that $L = \varphi^{-1}(P)$.

The *product* of two languages L_1 and L_2 is the language $L_1 L_2 = \{uv \mid u \in L_1, v \in L_2\}$.

If L is a language, the submonoid generated by L is $\bigcup_{n \geq 0} L^n$. For this reason, it is denoted by L^*.

Definition. The set of *rational languages* (over X) is the smallest set of subsets of X^* containing the finite subsets and closed under union, product, and submonoid generation.

Theorem 1.1 (Kleene 1956). *A language is rational if and only if it is recognizable.*

We shall obtain this theorem as a consequence of Schützenberger's Theorem I.6.1.

Lemma 1.2. *Let K, L be two semirings and let $\varphi: K \to L$ be a morphism of semirings. If $S \in K\langle\langle X \rangle\rangle$ is recognizable, then $\varphi(S) = \sum \varphi((S, w))w \in L\langle\langle X \rangle\rangle$ is recognizable.*

Proof. If indeed S has a linear representation (λ, μ, γ) then $\varphi(S)$ admits the linear representation $(\varphi(\lambda), \varphi(\mu), \varphi(\gamma))$. □

Lemma 1.3. *A language L is recognizable if and only if it is the support of some recognizable series $S \in \mathbf{N}\langle\langle X \rangle\rangle$.*

Proof. If L is recognizable, there exist a finite monoid M, a morphism of monoids $\varphi: X \to M$ and a subset P of M such that $L = \varphi^{-1}(P)$. Consider the *right regular representation* of M

$$\psi: M \to \mathbf{N}^{M \times M}$$

defined by

$$\psi(m)_{m_1, m_2} = \begin{cases} 1 & \text{if} \quad m_1 m = m_2 \\ 0 & \text{otherwise}. \end{cases}$$

It is easy to verify that ψ is a morphism of monoids. Define $\lambda \in \mathbf{N}^{1 \times M}$ and $\gamma \in \mathbf{N}^{M \times 1}$ by

$$\lambda_m = \delta_{m,1}$$

$$\gamma_m = \begin{cases} 1 & \text{if} \quad m \in P \\ 0 & \text{otherwise}. \end{cases}$$

Then $\psi(m)_{1,m} = 1$ if and only if $m = m'$, and consequently $\lambda \psi(m) \gamma = 1$ if $m \in P$, and $= 0$ otherwise. Now let

$$\mu = \psi \circ \varphi : X^* \to \mathbf{N}^{M \times M}$$

and let S be the recognizable series with representation (λ, μ, γ). Then $S = \sum_{w \in L} w$, whence $L = supp(S)$.

Conversely, assume that $S \in \mathbf{N}\langle\langle X \rangle\rangle$ is recognizable and let $L = supp(S)$. Consider the Boolean semiring $\mathbf{B} = \{0,1\}$ with $1 + 1 = 1$. Then the function

$$\varphi: \mathbf{N} \to \mathbf{B}$$

defined by $\varphi(0) = 0$ and $\varphi(a) = 1$ for $a \geqq 1$ is a morphism of semirings. By Lemma 1.2, the series $\varphi(S) = \sum \varphi((S, w)) w \in \mathbf{B}\langle\langle X \rangle\rangle$ is $\mathbf{B}$-recognizable.

Thus there exists a linear representation (λ, μ, γ) of $\varphi(S)$ with

$$\mu: X^* \to \mathbf{B}^{n \times n}$$

Let $M = \mathbf{B}^{n \times n}$, and $P = \{m \in M \mid \lambda m \gamma = 1\}$. Since M is finite, the language

$$\{w \mid \mu(w) \in P\}$$

is recognizable; but this language is exactly $supp(\varphi(S)) = supp(S) = L$. □

Lemma 1.4. *A language L over X is rational if and only if it is the support of some rational series* $S \in \mathbf{N}\langle\langle X \rangle\rangle$.

Proof. The following relations hold for series S and T in $\mathbf{N}\langle\langle X \rangle\rangle$:

$$supp(S+T) = supp(S) \cup supp(T)$$

$$supp(ST) = supp(S)\, supp(T)$$

$$supp(S^*) = (supp(S))^*, \text{ if } S \text{ is proper}$$

It follows easily that the support of a rational series in $\mathbf{N}\langle\langle X \rangle\rangle$ is a rational language.

For the converse, one can use the same relations, provided one has proved that any rational language can be obtained from finite sets by union, product, and submonoid generation restricted to *proper* languages (i.e. languages not containing the empty word). We shall prove a stronger result, namely that for any rational language L, the language $L \backslash 1$ can be obtained from the finite subsets of $X^+ = X \backslash 1$ by union, product and generation of subsemigroup (i.e. $A \mapsto A^+ = \bigcup_{n \geq 1} A^n = AA^*$).

Indeed, if L_1 and L_2 have this property, then clearly so does $L_1 \cup L_2$ also, since $(L_1 \cup L_2) \backslash 1 = L_1 \backslash 1 \cup L_2 \backslash 1$, and $L_1 L_2$, since $L_1 L_2 \backslash 1 = (L_1 \backslash 1)(L_2 \backslash 1) \cup K$, where $K = L_1 \backslash 1$, $= L_2 \backslash 1$, $= L_1 \backslash 1 \cup L_2 \backslash 1$ according to whether L_2, L_1, or both contain the empty word. Finally, if L has the announced property, then so does L^*, since $L^* \backslash 1 = (L \backslash 1)^* \backslash 1 = (L \backslash 1)^+$. □

Kleene's Theorem 1.1 now is an immediate consequence of Lemmas 1.3, 1.4, and of Theorem I.6.1.

Corollary 1.5. *The complement of a rational language is rational.*

Proof. If L is saturated by a congruence with finite index, then $X^* \backslash L$ is saturated by the same congruence. □

Corollary 1.6. *A language L over X is rational if and only if the set of languages* $\{w^{-1}L \mid w \in X^*\}$ *is finite (with* $w^{-1}L = \{u \in X^* \mid wu \in L\}$*).*

Proof. This is a consequence of Lemma 1.3 and Proposition I.5.1. □

2 Series and Rational Languages

Definition. If L is a language, its *characteristic series* is the formal series

$$\underline{L} = \sum_{w \in L} w$$

In other words, $(\underline{L}, w) = 1$ for $w \in L$, and $(\underline{L}, w) = 0$ if $w \notin L$.

Proposition 2.1. *The characteristic series of a rational language is a rational series.*

Proof. This is the first part of the proof of Lemma 1.3, with "recognizable" replaced by "rational", which can be done in view of Theorem 1.1 and Theorem I.6.1. □

Corollary 2.2. *If S is a rational series and L is a rational language, then* $S \odot \underline{L} = \sum_{w \in L} (S, w) w$ *is rational.*

Proof. Let K_1 be the prime semiring of K, i.e. the semiring generated by 1. Then by Proposition 2.1, the series $\underline{L}$ is K_1-rational. Since the elements of K_1 and K commute, it suffices to apply Theorem I.5.3. □

Let S be a formal series, and let A be a subset of K. We denote by $S^{-1}(A)$ the language

$$S^{-1}(A) = \{w \in X^* \mid (S, w) \in A\}$$

Proposition 2.3. *If K is finite and if $S \in K\langle\langle X \rangle\rangle$ is rational, then $S^{-1}(A)$ is rational for any subset A of K. In particular, $supp(S)$ is rational.*

Proof. Since S is recognizable, it admits a linear representation (λ, μ, γ). Since K is finite, $K^{n \times n}$ is finite, and $S^{-1}(A)$ is saturated by a congruence with finite index. Thus $S^{-1}(A)$ is recognizable, hence rational. □

Corollary 2.4. *If $S \in \mathbf{Z}\langle\langle X \rangle\rangle$ is a rational series and $a, b \in \mathbf{Z}$, $b \neq 0$, then $S^{-1}(a + b\mathbf{Z})$ is a rational language.*

Proof. Let $\varphi: \mathbf{Z} \to \mathbf{Z}/b\mathbf{Z}$ be the canonical morphism. Then $\varphi(S)$ is rational by Lemma 1.1. Since $S^{-1}(a + b\mathbf{Z}) = \varphi(S)^{-1}(\varphi(a))$, the result follows from Proposition 2.3. □

Corollary 2.5. *If $S \in \mathbf{N}\langle\langle X \rangle\rangle$ is rational and if $a \in \mathbf{N}$, then the languages $S^{-1}(a)$, $S^{-1}(\{n \mid n \geqq a\})$, $S^{-1}(\{n \mid n \leqq a\})$ are rational.*

Proof. Let $\sim$ be the congruence of the semiring $\mathbf{N}$ generated by the relation $a+1 \sim a+2$; in this congruence, all integers $n \geqq a+1$ are in a single class, and each $n \geqq a$ is alone in its class. Let K be the quotient semiring and let $\varphi: \mathbf{N} \to K$ be the canonical morphism. Then $\varphi(S)$ is rational by Lemma 1.2, and it suffices to apply Proposition 2.3, K being finite. □

Corollary 2.6. *Let $S \in \mathbf{Z}\langle\langle X \rangle\rangle$ be a rational series. If there is an integer $d \in \mathbf{N}$ which divides none of the nonzero coefficients of S, then the support of S is a rational language.*

Proof. If this is true, then $supp(S) = X^* \setminus S^{-1}(d\mathbf{Z})$ and it suffices to apply Corollaries 2.4 and 1.5. □

We denote by $Im(S)$ the set of coefficients of S. It is called the *image* of S.

Theorem 2.7 (Schützenberger 1961a; Sontag 1975). *Assume that K is a commutative ring. If $S \in K\langle\langle X\rangle\rangle$ is a rational series with finite image, then $S^{-1}(A)$ is rational for any $A \subset K$. Thus in particular the support of S is rational.*

Proof. (i) We first show that S satisfies a linear recurrence rational close to that of Eq. (II.3.4). The result will be less precise because K is not assumed to be a field. Let (λ, μ, γ) be a linear representation of S. Consider the ring generated by the coefficients of the matrices λ, $\mu x (x \in X)$, and γ. It shows that we may assume K to be finitely generated, and thus to be Noetherian. Let n be the dimension of μ and consider a maximal submodule among the submodules of $K^{1\times n}$ generated by a set of the form $\{\lambda\mu p | p \in P\}$ with P a finite prefix-closed subset of X^* (see Sect. II.3.). Such a maximal submodule exists because K is Noetherian. Let C be the complete finite prefix set $C = PX \backslash P$ (ibid.). Then $P \cup c$ being prefix-closed for all $c \in C$, the maximality of the submodule shows that $\lambda\mu c = \sum_{p \in P} \alpha_{c,p} \lambda\mu p$ for some $\alpha_{c,p}$ in K. Multiplying on the right by $\mu w \gamma$ gives

$$(S, cw) = \sum_{p \in P} \alpha_{c,p} (S, pw) \tag{2.1}$$

(ii) We now consider the set E of sequences of words of the form $(pw)_{p \in P}$. For each word u, define a function f_u from E into E by

$$f_u((pw)_p) = (puw)_p$$

Then $f_v \circ f_u = f_{vu}$, since indeed $f_v \circ f_u((pw)_p) = f_v((puw)_p) = (pvuw)_p = f_{vu}((pw)_p)$.

Consider now the image of E by S, i.e. the set F of sequences $((S, pw))_{p \in P}$. The left action of X^* on E defined above defines an action of X^* on F, since if $((S, pw))_{p \in P} = ((S, pw'))_{p \in P}$ then also $((S, puw))_{p \in P} = ((S, puw'))_{p \in P}$. It suffices to prove this claim for $u = x \in X$. In this case, either $px \in P$ and then $(S, pxw) = (S, pxw')$, or $px = c \in S$, and then $(S, pxw) = (S, pxw')$ by Eq. (2.1).

(iii) We have defined a morphism of monoids of X^* into the monoid M of functions from F into F by

$$u \mapsto f_u$$

We now apply the hypothesis. Since $Im(S)$ is finite, the set F is finite, and consequently M is finite. Let P be the subset of M composed of those functions that map the sequence $((S, p))_{p \in P}$ onto an element F of the form $(\beta_p)_p$ with $\beta_1 \in A$. Thus

$$f_u \in P \Leftrightarrow (S, u) \in A \Leftrightarrow u \in S^{-1}(A)$$

The shows that $S^{-1}(A)$ is recognizable, whence rational. □

3 Supports

In this and the next section, we study the properties of languages which are supports of rational series. These languages strongly depend on the underlying semiring. Thus we have seen in Sects. 1 and 2 that the rational languages are exactly the supports of rational series when the semiring is **N** or is finite. This is not generally true.

Example 3.1. Let $K=\mathbf{Z}$, $X=\{x, y\}$, and let S be the series

$$S=\sum_w (|w|_x-|w|_y)\, w$$

This series is rational (Example I.5.3). Its support is the language

$$supp(S)=\{w\in X^* \mid |w|_x \neq |w|_y\}$$

and its complement is

$$L=\{w\in X^* \mid |w|_x=|w|_y\}$$

We shall prove that L is not a support of a rational series. This shows that L is not a rational language, by Proposition 2.1, and shows also that $supp(S)$ is not rational, by Corollary 1.5.

Arguing by contradiction, we assume that $L=supp(T)$ for some rational series T having a linear representation (λ, μ, γ) of dimension n. Then the matrix μx^n is a linear combination of the matrices $\mu 1, \mu x, \ldots, \mu x^{n-1}$, and

$$\mu x^n=\alpha_1 \mu 1+\ldots+\alpha_n \mu x^{n-1}$$

Multiplying on the left by λ and on the right by $\mu y^n \gamma$, one gets

$$(T, x^n y^n)=\alpha_1(T, y^n)+\ldots+\alpha_n(T, x^{n-1} y^n)$$

Since $x^i y^n \in L$ for $i \neq n$, the right-hand side of this equation vanishes, and the left-hand side is not zero, a contradiction.

Example 3.2. Recall that a *palindrome* word is a word w which is equal to its reversal, i.e. $w={}^t w$ (see Exercise II.1.1). We show that the language $L=\{w\in X^* \mid w \neq {}^t w\}$ of words which are not palindromes is the support of a rational series over **Z**.

Assume for simplicity that $X=\{x_0, x_1\}$, and consider the series

$$\sum_w \langle w\rangle w$$

where $\langle w\rangle$ is the integer represented by w in base 2. This series is rational (see Example I.5.2). Consequently, the series

$$\sum_w \langle {}^t w\rangle w$$

also is rational (see Exercise II.1.1). Thus the series

$$\sum_{w} (\langle w\rangle - \langle {}^t w\rangle) w$$

is rational, and its support is L. By a technique analogous to that of Example 3.1, one can show that $X^*\backslash L$ is not a support of a rational series.

For the rest of this section, we fix a subsemiring K of the field $\mathbf{R}$ of real numbers. We denote by $\mathbf{K}$ the family of languages which are supports of rational series, i.e. $L \subset X^*$ is in $\mathbf{K}$ if and only if $L = supp(S)$ for some rational series $S \in K\langle\langle X\rangle\rangle$. We shall see that $\mathbf{K}$ has all the closure properties usually considered in formal language theory, excepting complementation, as follows from Example 3.1.

The morphisms considered in the next statement are morphisms from one free monoid into another.

Theorem 3.1. (Schützenberger 1961a, Fliess 1971). *The family* $\mathbf{K}$ *contains the rational languages. Moreover,* $\mathbf{K}$ *is closed under finite union, intersection, product, submonoid generation, direct and inverse morphism.*

Proof. The first claim is a consequence of Proposition 2.1. Consider now a language $L \subset X^*$ in $\mathbf{K}$, and let $S \in K\langle\langle X\rangle\rangle$ be a rational series with $L = supp(S)$. If $\varphi: Y^* \to X^*$ is a morphism, then

$$\varphi^{-1}(S) = \sum_{w \in Y^*} (S, \varphi(w)) w$$

is rational. Indeed, if (λ, μ, γ) is a linear representation of S, then clearly $(\lambda, \mu \circ \varphi, \gamma)$ is a linear representation of $\varphi^{-1}(S)$. Consequently, $\varphi^{-1}(L) = supp(\varphi^{-1}(S))$ is in $\mathbf{K}$.

Next, let $L' \subset X^*$ be another language in $\mathbf{K}$, with $L' = supp(S')$ and S' rational. Then $L \cap L' = supp(S \odot S')$ is also in $\mathbf{K}$, by Theorem I.5.3.

In order to show that the submonoid L^* generated by L is also in $\mathbf{K}$, observe first that $L^* = (L\backslash 1)^*$ and that $L\backslash 1 = L \cap X^+$ is in $\mathbf{K}$. Thus we may assume that $1 \notin L$, i.e. $(S, 1) = 0$. Next we may suppose that S has only nonnegative coefficients, by considering $S \odot S$ instead of S, which is possible in view of Theorem I.5.3. Under these conditions,

$$L^* = supp(S^*)$$

showing that L^* is in $\mathbf{K}$.

It is easily seen that $\mathbf{K}$ is closed by union and product, using the formulas

$$supp(S + S') = supp(S) \cup supp(S')$$

$$supp(SS') = supp(S)\, supp(S')$$

which hold if S and S' have nonnegative coefficients.

Finally, consider a morphism $\varphi: X^* \to Y^*$.

(i) First we assume that $\varphi(X) \subset Y^+$. In this case, the family of series $((S, w)\varphi(w))_{w \in X^*}$, with each of these series reduced to a monomial, is locally finite, and its sum, the series

$$\varphi(S) = \sum_{w \in X^*} (S, w)\varphi(w)$$

is rational by Proposition I.4.2. If, moreover, S has nonnegative coefficients, then

$$supp(\varphi(S)) = \varphi(L)$$

showing that $\varphi(L)$ is in **K**.

(ii) Next, we assume that $X = Y \cup \{x\}$, with $x \notin Y$, and that φ is the projection $X^* \to Y^*$, i.e. $\varphi|_Y = id$, $\varphi(x) = 1$. Let n be the dimension of a linear representation (λ, μ, γ) of S, and set

$$P = X^* \backslash X^* x^n X^*$$

We claim that

$$\varphi(L) = \varphi(L \cap P) \tag{3.1}$$

Let indeed $w \in L$. If $w \notin P$, then $w = ax^n b$ for some words a and b. But the characteristic polynomial of μx shows that $(S, ax^n b)$ is a linear combination of the $(S, ax^i b)$ with $0 \leqq i \leqq n-1$. Consequently, there is such an i with $(S, ax^i b) \neq 0$, whence $ax^i b \in L$. Since $\varphi(w) = \varphi(ax^i b)$, induction on the length completes the proof.

Let ψ: $Y^* \to K\langle X \rangle$ be the morphism of monoids defined by

$$\psi(y) = (1 + \ldots + x^{n-1})y(1 + \ldots + x^{n-1})$$

Further, recall that we may assume that S has nonnegative coefficients. Let $T \in K\langle\langle Y \rangle\rangle$ be the rational series with linear representation $(\lambda, \mu \circ \psi, \gamma)$, with μ extended to $K\langle X \rangle$ by linearity.

Let $w = y_1 \ldots y_m \in Y^*$. The coefficient of w in T is $\lambda(\mu \circ \psi w)\gamma$. Since ψw is an **N**-linear combination of words of the form

$$x^{i_0} y_1 x^{i_1} \ldots y_m x^{i_m} \tag{3.2}$$

and since *any* word of the form given in Eq. (3.2) with $i_0, \ldots, i_m \in \{0, \ldots, n-1\}$ appears in this combination, by the definition of ψ, it follows that (T, w) is an **N**-linear combination of coefficients of the form

$$(S, x^{i_0} y_1 x^{i_1} \ldots y_m x^{i_m})$$

In view of Eq. (3.1), and by the fact that all coefficients are nonnegative, this implies that

$$\varphi(supp(S)) = supp(T)$$

(iii) Consider finally an arbitrary morphism $\varphi: X^* \to Y^*$ and L in **K**. We may assume that X and Y are disjoint. Then $\varphi = \varphi_2 \circ \varphi_1$, where $\varphi_1: X^* \to (X \cup Y)^*$ is defined by $\varphi(x) = x\varphi(x)$ for each letter x, and with $\varphi_2: (X \cup Y)^* \to Y^*$ defined by $\varphi_2(x) = 1$ for $x \in X$, and $\varphi_2(y) = y$ for $y \in Y$. In view of (i), $\varphi_1(L) \in \mathbf{K}$. Moreover, φ_2 can be factorized into a sequence of morphisms of the type considered in (ii). Thus $\varphi_2(\varphi_1(L)) \in \mathbf{K}$, and $\varphi(L) \in \mathbf{K}$. □

4 Iteration

In this section, we assume that K is a *commutative field.* We prove the following.

Theorem 4.1 (Jacob 1980). *Let L be a language which is support of a rational series. There exists an integer N such that for any word w in L, and for any factorization $w = aub$ satisfying $|u| \geqq N$, there exists a factorization $u = fgh$ such that the language*

$$L \cap afg^*hb$$

is infinite.

We need a definition and a lemma.

Definition. A *quasipower of order* 0 is any nonempty word. A *quasipower of order* $n+1$ is a word of the form uvu, where u is a quasipower of order n.

Example 4.1. If $u \neq 1$, then $uvuwuvu$ is a quasipower of order 2.

Lemma 4.2 (Schützenberger 1961b). *Let X be a (finite) alphabet. There exists a sequence of integers (c_n) such that any word on X of length at least c_n has a factor which is a quasipower of order n.*

Proof. Let $d = |X|$, $c_0 = 1$ and inductively

$$c_{n+1} = c_n(1 + d^{c_n})$$

Suppose that any word of length c_n contains a factor which is a quasipower of order n. Let w be a word of length at least $c_{n+1} = c_n(1 + d^{c_n})$. Then w has a factor of the form $u_1 u_2 \ldots u_r$ with each u_i of length c_n and $r = 1 + d^{c_n}$. Since there are only d^{c_n} distinct words of length c_n on X, two of the u_i's are identical, and w has a factor uvu with $|u| = c_n$. By the induction hypothesis, $u = au'b$ with u' a quasipower of order n. Thus w has as a factor $u'bvau'$, which is a quasipower of order $n+1$. □

Proof of Theorem 4.1. Let S be a rational series with $L = supp(S)$, let (λ, μ, γ) be a linear representation of S, with dimension n. Set $N = c_n$, where c_n has the meaning of Lemma 4.2. Consider a word $w = aub \in L$ with $|u| \geqq N$. Then u contains a quasipower of order n. Thus there exist words $1 \neq u_0, u_1, \ldots, u_n, v_1, \ldots, v_n$ such that u_n is a factor of u and for each $i=1, \ldots, n$, $u_i = u_{i-1} v_i u_{i-1}$. Next

$$n \geqq rank(\mu u_{i-1}) \geqq rank(\mu u_{i-1} v_i u_{i-1}) \geqq rank(\mu u_i)$$

Consequently, there is an integer i such that $rank(\mu u_{i-1}) = rank(\mu u_{i-1} v_i u_{i-1})$. Set $p = \mu u_{i-1}$ and $q = \mu v_i$. These matrices act on the right on $K^{1 \times n}$. From $rank(p) = rank(pqp)$, it follows that

$$Im(p) \cap Ker(qp) = 0 \tag{4.1}$$

Moreover,

$$rank(p) \geqq rank(qp) \geqq rank(qpq) = rank(p)$$

showing that $rank(p) = rank(qp)$, and since $Im(qp) \subset Im(p)$, it follows that $Im(p) = Im(qp)$. By Eq. (4.1), this gives

$$Im(qp) \cap Ker(qp) = 0$$

Since $n = dim\, Ker(qp) + dim\, Im(qp)$, the space $K^{1 \times n}$ is the direct sum of $Im(qp)$ and $Ker(qp)$. In a base adapted to this direct sum, the matrix qp has the form

$$\begin{pmatrix} m & 0 \\ 0 & 0 \end{pmatrix}$$

where m is an invertible matrix. Consequently the minimal polynomial $P(\lambda)$ of qp is not divisible by λ^2. This shows that u can be factorized into $u = fgh$, with $g \neq 1$ and where the characteristic polynomial

$$P(\lambda) = \lambda^r - a_1 \lambda^{r-1} - \ldots - a_{r-1} \lambda - a_r$$

of μg has at least one of the coefficients a_{r-1} or a_r nonnull. Consider the sequence of numbers (b_k) defined by

$$b_k = (S, afg^k hb) = \lambda \mu a f (\mu g)^k \mu h b \gamma$$

For all $k \geqq 0$, the following relation holds:

$$b_{k+r} = a_1 b_{r+k-1} + \ldots + a_{r-1} b_{k+1} + a_r b_k$$

Since $w \in L$, one has $b_1 = (S, afghb) = (S, w) \neq 0$. The condition $a_{r-1} \neq 0$ or $a_r \neq 0$ in turn implies that there exist infinitely many integers k for which $b_k \neq 0$, whence $afg^k hb \in L$. □

5 Complementation

In this section K is a *commutative field.* We have seen that the complement of the support of a rational series is not the support of a rational series, in general. However, the following result holds.

Theorem 5.1 (Restivo and Reutenauer 1984). *If the complement of the support of a rational series is also the support of a rational series, then it is a rational language.*

For the proof, we use the following theorem.

Theorem 5.2 (Ehrenfeucht, Parikh and Rozenberg 1981). *Let L be a language and let n be an integer such for any word w and any factorization $w = au_1 \dots u_n b$, there exist i, j with $0 \leqq i < j \leqq n$ such that*

$$w \in L \Leftrightarrow au_1 \dots u_i u_{j+1} \dots u_n b \in L$$

Then L is a rational language.

Proof of Theorem 5.1. Let $L = supp(S)$ and $L' = X^* \backslash L = supp(T)$ be two complementary languages which are supports of the rational series S and T respectively. Consider linear representations (λ, μ, γ) and $(\lambda', \mu', \gamma')$ of S and of T. Further, let n be an integer greater then the dimension of both representations.

Let $w = au_1 \dots u_n b \in X^*$.

(i) Assume that w is in L. Then $0 \neq \lambda \mu a u_1 \dots u_n b \gamma$ and in particular $\lambda \mu a \neq 0$. The $n+1$ vectors

$$\lambda \mu a,\ \lambda \mu a u_1,\ \dots,\ \lambda \mu a u_1 \dots u_n$$

belong to a space of dimension at most n. Consequently, there is an integer j with $1 \leqq j \leqq n$ such that $\lambda \mu a u_1 \dots u_j$ is a linear combination of the vectors $\lambda \mu a u_1 \dots u_i$, $0 \leqq i < j$, say

$$\lambda \mu a u_1 \dots u_j = \sum_{0 \leqq i < j} \alpha_i \lambda \mu a u_1 \dots u_i$$

for $\alpha_i \in K$. Multiplying on the right by $\mu u_{j+1} \dots u_n b \gamma$, one gets

$$(S, w) = \sum_{0 \leqq i < j} \alpha_i (S, au_1 \dots u_i u_{j+1} \dots u_n b)$$

Since $(S, w) \neq 0$, there exists i, with $0 \leqq i < j$, such that

$$(S, au_1 \dots u_i u_{j+1} \dots u_n b) \neq 0$$

and hence $au_1 \dots u_i u_{j+1} \dots u_n \in L$.

(ii) Assume now that $w \notin L$, i.e. $w \in L'$. A similar proof, this time with $(\lambda', \mu', \gamma')$, shows that there are integers i, j, $0 \leqq i < j \leqq n$ such that $(T, au_1 \dots u_i u_{j+1} \dots u_n b) \neq 0$, showing that $au_1 \dots u_i u_{j+1} \dots u_n b \in L'$, whence

$$au_1 \dots u_i u_{j+1} \dots u_n b \notin L$$

Thus we have shown that the language L satisfies the conditions of Theorem 5.2. Consequently, L is rational. □

For the proof of Theorem 5.2, we use without proof a well-known theorem of Ramsey. In order to state it simply, we introduce the following notation. For any set E, we denote by $E(p)$ the set of subsets of p elements of E.

Theorem 5.3 (Ramsey; see e.g. Ryser 1963 or Harrison 1978). *For any integers m, p, r, there exists an integer $N = N(m, p, r)$ such that for any set E of N elements and for any partition $E(p) = A_1 \cup \dots \cup A_r$, there exists a subset F of E with m elements, such that $F(p)$ is contained in one of the A_i's.*

Proof of Theorem 5.2. Let n be a fixed integer and let $\mathbf{L}$ be the set of all languages L over X satisfying the hypotheses of Theorem 5.2 with this n. We shall prove that $\mathbf{L}$ is finite. It is not difficult to show that for any $L \in \mathbf{L}$ and any word w, the language

$$w^{-1}L = \{u \in X^* \mid wu \in L\}$$

is still in $\mathbf{L}$. In view of Corollary 1.6, any language in $\mathbf{L}$ is rational.

In order to show that $\mathbf{L}$ is finite, we use Ramsey's theorem for $m = 1 + n$, $p = 2$, $r = 2$. Let $N = N(m, 2, 2)$. Let L and K be two languages in $\mathbf{L}$ such that for all w of length $< N - 1$,

$$w \in L \Leftrightarrow w \in K \tag{5.1}$$

We prove that then $L = K$. This clearly implies that $\mathbf{L}$ is finite. To prove the equality, we argue by induction on the lengths of words in X^*. Let w be a word of length $\geqq N - 1$, let

$$w = x_1 x_2 \dots x_{N-1} u \quad (x_i \in X)$$

and $E = \{0, 1, \dots, n-1\}$. Consider the partition

$$E(2) = A \cup B$$

with

$$A = \{\{i, j\} \mid 0 \leqq i < j \leqq N-1 \quad \text{and} \quad x_1 \dots x_i x_{j+1} \dots x_{N-1} u \in L\},$$

$$B = E(2) \setminus A$$

Observe that, by the induction hypothesis,

$$A = \{\{i, j\} \mid 0 \leqq i < j \leqq N-1 \quad \text{and} \quad x_1 \dots x_i x_{j+1} \dots x_{N-1} u \in K\}$$

By Ramsey's theorem, there exists a subset F of E with $m=n+1$ elements such that

$$F(2)\subset A \quad \text{or} \quad F(2)\subset B$$

Cutting w into $m+1=n+2$ factors $a, u_1, \ldots, u_n, b$ according to the indices in F, one obtains a factorization

$$w=au_1 \ldots u_n b$$

such that

(i) either, for all $0\leqq i<j\leqq n$, the word $au_1 \ldots u_i u_{j+1} \ldots u_n b$ is in both L and K;
(ii) or, for all $0\leqq i<j\leqq n$, the word $au_1 \ldots u_i u_{j+1} \ldots u_n b$ is neither in L nor in K.

Since L and K are in **L**, the first condition implies that $w\in L$ and $w\in K$, and the second condition that $w\notin L$ and $w\notin K$. Thus Eq. (5.1) is satisfied and the proof is complete. □

Theorem 5.1 is a special case of the following conjecture.

Conjecture. Let L and K be disjoint languages which are both support of some rational series. Then there exist two disjoint rational languages L' and K' such that

$$K\subset K',\ L\subset L'$$

(i.e. K and L are *rationally separated*).

Exercises for Chapter III

1.1 Show that a subset of x^* (where x is a letter) is rational iff it is the union of a finite set and of a finite set of arithmetic progressions (we identify $x^*=\{x^n \mid n\in\mathbf{N}\}$ with $\mathbf{N}$).

1.2. Let L be a language. The *syntactic congruence* of L, denoted by $\sim$, is the congruence on X^* defined by

$$u\sim v \quad \text{iff} \quad \forall a, b\in X^*,\ aub\in L \Leftrightarrow avb\in L$$

a) Show that $\sim$ is the coarsest congruence on X^* that saturates L (i.e. such that $u\sim v$ and $u\in L$ imply $v\in L$). The monoid $M=X^*/\sim$ is called the *syntactic monoid* of L.

b) Let K be a commutative ring and let S be the characteristic series of L. Let I be the syntactic ideal of S. Show that $u\sim v$ if and only if $u-v\in I$. Show that the canonical morphism of $K\langle X\rangle$ into $N=K\langle X\rangle/I$ admits the natural factorization

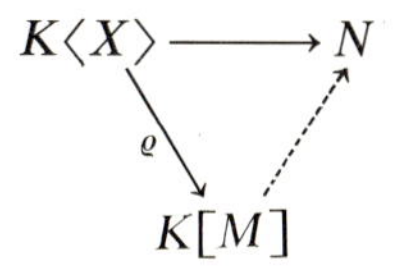

where ϱ is the extension by linearity of the canonical monoid morphism $X^* \to M$ and where $K[M]$ is the *K-algebra of the monoid M*. Show that N is a quotient of $K[M]$. Using for example the language

$$L = (1 + x^3)(x^4)^*$$

show that the dotted arrow is not an isomorphism in general (show that $M = \mathbf{Z}/4\mathbf{Z}$ and $1 - x + x^2 - x^3 \in I$) (see Reutenauer 1980a).

2.1. Let K be a commutative field. The set of rational series of $K\langle\langle X\rangle\rangle$, equipped with the sum and the Hadamard product, is a K-algebra (Theorem I.5.3). Show that the *idempotents* of this algebra are precisely the characteristic series of the rational languages.

3.1. Denote by R_K the set of supports of rational series with coefficients in the semiring K. Thus $R_{\mathbf{N}}$ is the set of rational languages (cf. Sect. 1).

a) Show that if K and L are (commutative) fields and L is an algebraic extension of K, then $R_K = R_L$.
b) Show that if K is a finite field and t is a variable, then the support of the series

$$\sum_{n \geq 0} ((t+1)^n - t^n - 1)x^n$$

is not a rational language (use Exercise 1.1).
c) Show that, given a commutative field K, one has $R_K = R_{\mathbf{N}}$ if and only if K is an algebraic extension of a finite field (use Example 3.1) (see Fliess 1971).

3.2. Let $f, g: X^* \to Y^*$ be two morphisms of a free monoid into another. Define the *equality set* of f and g as the language

$$E(f, g) = \{w \in X^* \mid f(w) = g(w)\}$$

Show that the complement of $E(f, g)$ is the support of some rational series over $\mathbf{Z}$ (see Turakainen 1985).

4.1. Let u_p be a quasipower of order p, with $u_0 \neq 1$ and $u_i = u_{i-1} v_i u_{i-1}$ for $i = 1, \ldots, p$.
a) Show that there exist words $w_1, \ldots, w_p$ such that for all $i = 1, \ldots, p$,

$$u_i = u_0 w_i w_{i-1} \ldots w_1$$

b) Use question (a) to prove that for all integers n and p, there is an integer l such that for every morphism

$$\mu: X^* \to K^{n \times n}$$

and for any word w of length at least l, there exist nonempty words $w_1, \ldots, w_p$ such that $w_p w_{p-1} \ldots w_1$ is a factor of w and all the μw_i's have the same kernel N and the same image I with $N \cap I = 0$ (and consequently belong to the same group contained in the multiplicative monoid $K^{n \times n}$) (see Jacob 1978; Reutenauer 1980b).

Notes to Chapter III

Theorem 2.7 is due to Schützenberger (1961a) for fields, and to Sontag (1975) for rings. Theorem 3.1 is from Schützenberger (1961a), except for the closure under direct morphism which is due to Fliess (1971) for $K = \mathbf{R}$, and to Reutenauer (1980b) for the general case.

The proof of Jacob's theorem (Theorem 4.1) is from Reutenauer (1980c); in this paper, another argument makes it possible to extend the result to infinite alphabets, and also to give a smaller bound N which depends only on the rank of the series (and not on the size of the alphabet).

The *cancellation property* of Theorem 5.2 characterizes the rationality of a language: indeed, each rational language prossesses this property, for some n, as may be easily verified.

Let us mention the following open problem (Salomaa and Soittola 1978). Does there exist a language which is support of a **R**-rational series without being support of any **Q**-rational series?

Chapter IV

Rational Series in One Variable

This chapter gives a short introduction to some striking arithmetic properties of the expansion of rational fractions.

In the first section, the notions of rational series, Hankel matrix and rank are shown to coincide, in the case of series in one variable, with the classical definitions. A new presentation of the exponential polynomial, emphasizing its algebraic aspects, is given in Sect. 2. As an application, we obtain Benzaghou's theorem on the invertible series in the Hadamard algebra (Theorem 2.3).

Section 3 is devoted to a theorem of G. Pólya concerning arithmetic properties of the coefficients of a rational series.

In the final section, we give an elementary proof, due to G. Hansel, of the famous Skolem-Mahler-Lech theorem on the positions of vanishing coefficients of a rational series.

1 Rational Functions

We consider a commutative field K and an alphabet consisting of a single letter x. We write, as usual, $K[x]$ and $K[\![x]\!]$ instead of $K\langle x\rangle$ and $K\langle\!\langle x\rangle\!\rangle$. An element S of $K[\![x]\!]$ is written as

$$S = \sum_{n \geqq 0} a_n x^n$$

Proposition 1.1. *A series S is rational if and only if there exist polynomials P and Q in $K[x]$ with $Q(0)=1$ such that S is the power series expansion of the rational function P/Q.*

Proof. Let **E** be the set of series which are the power series expansion of the form described. Then clearly **E** is contained in the algebra of rational series. Moreover, **E** is a subalgebra of $K[\![x]\!]$ closed under inversion, since if $S \in \mathbf{E}$, and $S = P(x)/Q(x)$ is invertible in $K[\![x]\!]$, then its constant term is invertible in K. This constant term is $P(0)/Q(0) = P(0) = \lambda$. Thus $\lambda \neq 0$ and

$$S^{-1} = \frac{\lambda^{-1}Q(x)}{\lambda^{-1}P(x)} \in \mathbf{E}$$

This shows that any rational series is in **E**. □

Let S be a rational series corresponding to the rational function $P(x)/Q(x)$. The quotient is called *normalized* if P and Q have no common factor in $K[x]$ and if $Q(0)=1$. In this case, Q is called the *minimal denominator* of S. The roots of Q, which are the poles of the function, are called the *poles* of S.

What about the syntactic ideal of S? Set $S=\sum_{n\geqq 0} a_n x^n$, and let

$$R=x^k+\alpha_1 x^{k-1}+\ldots+\alpha_k \in K[x]$$

be a polynomial. Since K is commutative, the syntactic ideal I of S and the syntactic right ideal coincide. Thus $R\in I$ if and only if $S\circ R=0$ by Proposition II.1.3. Since

$$S\circ x^i=\sum_{n\geqq 0} a_{n+i} x^n$$

this gives the equivalence

$$R\in I \Leftrightarrow \quad \text{for all } n\in \mathbf{N},\ a_{n+k}+\alpha_1 a_{n+k-1}+\ldots \alpha_k a_n=0$$

Observe that in view of Theorem II.1.1, the series S is rational if and only if its syntactic ideal is not null, since a nonnull ideal in $K[x]$ always has a finite codimension. This yields the classical result stating that *a series is rational if and only if it satisfies a linear recurrence relation.* The syntactic ideal of S thus precisely the ideal of polynomials associated with the linear recurrence relations satisfied by S. We refer to the generator of the syntactic ideal of S having a leading coefficient equal to 1 as the *minimal polynomial* of S. It is the polynomial associated with the shortest linear recurrence relation. The *roots* of S are the roots of its minimal polynomial, and their *multiplicities* are defined similarly.

Proposition 1.2. *Let*

$$S=\sum_{n\geqq 0} a_n x^n=P(x)/Q(x)$$

be a rational series with an associated normalized rational function. Let $k=\sup(\deg(P)-\deg(Q)+1, 0)$ *and let* (λ, μ, γ) *be a reduced linear representation of* S. *Then the characteristic polynomial of* μx *is equal to the minimal polynomial of* S, *and is also equal to* $x^k\bar{Q}(x)$, *where* $\bar{Q}$ *is the reciprocal polynomial of* Q. *In particular,* Q *is equal to the reciprocal polynomial of the minimal polynomial of* S.

Recall that the *reciprocal polynomial* of a polynomial

$$\alpha_0 x^p+\alpha_1 x^{p-1}+\ldots+\alpha_q x^{p-q}$$

with $\alpha_0\alpha_q \neq 0$, $p\geqq q$ is the polynomial $\alpha_q x^q+\ldots+\alpha_1 x+\alpha_0$ obtained by replacing x by $1/x$, and then multiplying the resulting expression by x^p.

Proof. The rank r of S is equal to the degree of the characteristic polynomial $R(x)$ of μx (because (λ, μ, γ) has dimension r), and it is also equal to the degree of the minimal polynomial, say $R_1(x)$, of S, since $dim(K[x]/R_1)=deg(R_1)$ (cf. Theorem II.1.5). Let

$$R(x)=x^r+\alpha_1 x^{r-1}+\ldots+\alpha_r$$

Then $R(\mu x)=0$. Consequently, by multiplying this equation on the left by $\lambda\mu x^n (n\in\mathbf{N})$, and on the right by γ, one obtains

$$a_{n+r}+\alpha_1 a_{n+r-1}+\ldots+\alpha_r a_n=0, \ (n\geqq 0) \tag{1.1}$$

In other words, and using the notations of Sect. II.1,

$$S\circ R=0$$

Thus R is in the syntactic ideal of S, and therefore is a multiple of R_1. Since they have the same degree and leading coefficient 1, they are equal. Let p be such that

$$R(x)=x^r+\alpha_1 x^{r-1}+\ldots+\alpha_p x^{r-p}, \ \alpha_p\neq 0, \ p\leqq r$$

Then the reciprocal polynomial of R is

$$\bar{R}(x)=1+\alpha_1 x+\ldots+\alpha_p x^p$$

Let $P_1=\bar{R}S$. Then for all $n\geqq r$ (and consequently for $n\geqq p$), one has, in view of Eq. (1.1),

$$(P_1, x^n)=a_n+\alpha_1 a_{n-1}+\ldots+\alpha_p a_{n-p}=0$$

Thus P_1 is a polynomial of degree at most $r-1$, and since $S=P_1/\bar{R}$, the polynomial $\bar{R}$ is a denominator of S. Consequently Q divides $\bar{R}$. Let

$$Q=1+\beta_1 x+\ldots+\beta_q x^q, \ \beta_q\neq 0$$

Then $q\leqq p$. Since $QS=P$ is a polynomial of degree $deg(P)$, and since by definition of k, $q+k>deg(P)$, one has, for all $n\in\mathbf{N}$,

$$0=(P, x^{n+q+k})=a_{n+q+k}+\beta_1 a_{n+q+k-1}+\ldots+\beta_q a_{n+k}$$

Thus, since $\bar{Q}(x)=x^q+\beta_1 x^{q-1}+\ldots+\beta_q$,

$$S\circ(x^k\bar{Q})=0$$

This shows that $x^k\bar{Q}$ is in the syntactic ideal of S, and consequently R divides $x^k\bar{Q}$. Thus $r\leqq q+k$.

If $k=0$, then $r\leqq q$, $q\leqq p$ and $p\leqq r$ imply that all these numbers are equal, whence $\bar{R}=Q$ and $Q=\bar{R}$.

If $k\neq 0$, then $k=deg\,P-deg\,Q+1$ and since $P_1Q=P\bar{R}$,

$$k=deg\,P_1-deg\,\bar{R}+1\leqq r-deg\,\bar{R}$$

whence $k+q\leqq k+p\leqq r$. Thus $r=k+q$ and $p=q$, showing that $R=x^k\bar{Q}$ and $\bar{Q}=\bar{R}$. □

The *Hankel matrix* of $S=\sum a_n x^n$ has a very special form, which is classical. It is the matrix

$$(a_{i+j})_{i,j\in N}$$

Corollary 1.3. *Let $S=\sum a_n x^n$ be a rational series with associated irreducible fraction $P(x)/Q(x)$. Its rank is equal to $\sup(\deg Q, 1+\deg P)$, to the degree of its minimal polynomial, to the length of the shortest linear recurrence relation satisfied by S, and to the rank of its Hankel matrix.* □

Observe that the set of roots $\neq 0$ of S is precisely the set of inverses of its poles, with the same multiplicities.

Definition. A rational series S is *regular* if it admits a linear representation (λ, μ, γ) such that μx is an invertible matrix.

Regular rational series can be defined in several ways. Indeed, the following assertions concerning a rational series $S=\sum a_n x^n$ are equivalent.

(i) S is regular.
(ii) Any reduced linear representation (λ, μ, γ) of S is *regular*, i.e. the matrix μx is invertible.
(iii) The sequence (a_n) satisfies a *proper* linear recurrence relation, i.e.

$$a_{n+k}=\alpha_1 a_{n+k-1}+\ldots+\alpha_k a_n,\ n\geqq 0,\ \alpha_k\neq 0$$

(iv) The shortest linear recurrence relation satisfied by S is proper.
(v) There exists a polynomial P such that $S\circ P=0$ and $P(0)\neq 0$.
(vi) The minimal polynomial of S has a nonvanishing constant term.
(vii) $S=P(x)/Q(x)$ with $\deg P<\deg Q$.
(viii) The rank of S is equal to the degree of its minimal denominator.

The equivalence of these assertions is a consequence of the preceding propositions and of the following observation: if (a_n) satisfies some proper linear recurrence relation and if m the companion matrix of this relation, then $\det(m)\neq 0$ and there exist λ, γ such that $a_n=\lambda m^n \gamma$.

Proposition 1.4. *For every rational series S, there exists a unique couple (T, P), where T is a regular rational series and P is a polynomial, such that $S=P+T$.*

This proposition is a direct consequence of the decomposition of the rational fraction associated with S into simple elements. Then P is just the *integral part* of the fraction. We give here a different proof.

Observe that, as a consequence of this result, a regular rational series which is a polynomial is null.

Proof. Let $x^q R(x)$, with $R(0)\neq 0$, be the minimal polynomial of S. Then

$$(S\circ R)\circ x^q=S\circ(x^q R)=0$$

which shows that $S \circ R$ is polynomial. Consider the linear function

$$Q \mapsto Q \circ R$$

$$K[x] \to K[x]$$

Since $R(0) \neq 0$, one has $deg\,(Q \circ R) = deg\,(Q)$, and this function is consequently a linear automorphism of $K[x]$. Thus there is some P in $K[x]$ such that

$$P \circ R = S \circ R$$

Let $T = S - P$. Then

$$T \circ R = S \circ R - P \circ R = 0$$

showing that T is regular rational.

If $T + P = T' + P'$, where T and T' are regular rational series and P, P' are polynomials, then

$$T - T' = P' - P$$

In view of condition (vii) above, the series $T - T'$ is regular. Thus it suffices to show that if S is regular and is a polynomial, then $S = 0$. For this, set $S = \sum a_n x^n$. There exist coefficients α_i in K such that for all $n \geqq 0$

$$a_{n+k} = \alpha_1 a_{n+k-1} + \ldots + \alpha_k a_n \tag{1.2}$$

with $\alpha_k \neq 0$. Assume $S \neq 0$, and let n be the greatest index such that $a_n \neq 0$. For this n, Eq. (1.2) gives $\alpha_k a_n = 0$, whence $a_n = 0$, a contradiction. □

In view of Proposition 1.4, it suffices for many purposes to study regular rational series. We will restrict ourselves to these series in the following.

Proposition 1.5. *The subset of regular rational series of* $K[\![x]\!]$ *is closed under linear combination, product, and Hadamard product.*

Observe that this set does not contain any nonvanishing polynomials.

Proof. Let $S_1 = P_1/Q_1$ and $S_2 = P_2/Q_2$ be regular rational series with $deg(P_1) < deg(Q_1)$ and $deg(P_2) < deg(Q_2)$. Then $S_1 + S_2 = (P_1Q_2 + P_2Q_1)/Q_1Q_2$ and $S_1S_2 = P_1P_2/Q_1Q_2$. Since $deg(P_1Q_2 + P_2Q_1) < deg(Q_1Q_2)$ and $deg(P_1P_2) < deg(Q_1Q_2)$, the series $S_1 + S_2$ and S_1S_2 are regular. Moreover, if $(S_1, x^n) = \lambda_1 \mu_1 x^n \gamma_1$ and $(S_2, x^n) = \lambda_2 \mu_2 x^n \gamma_2$ where $\mu_1 x$ and $\mu_2 x$ are invertible matrices, then

$$(S_1 \odot S_2, x^n) = (S_1, x^n)\,(S_2, x^n) = (\lambda_1 \otimes \lambda_2)\,(\mu_1 \otimes \mu_2)\,(x^n)\,(\gamma_1 \otimes \gamma_2)$$

and since $(\mu_1 \otimes \mu_2)\,(x)$ is invertible, this shows that $S_1 \odot S_2$ is regular. □

The set of regular rational series equipped with the structure of vector space and with the Hadamard product is the *Hadamard algebra of regular rational series.* Its neutral element is the series $\sum x^n = 1/(1-x)$.

2 The Exponential Polynomial

We assume from now to that K has *characteristic zero.* Let Λ be the multiplicative group $K\backslash 0$, and let t be an indeterminate. We consider the algebra

$$K[t][\Lambda]$$

of the group Λ over the ring $K[t]$. It is in particular an algebra over K. An element of $K[t][\Lambda]$ is called an *exponential polynomial.*

Theorem 2.1. *Let K be algebraically closed. The function which associates to an exponential polynomial*

$$\sum_{\lambda \in \Lambda} P_\lambda(t)\lambda$$

of $K[t][\Lambda]$ *the regular rational series*

$$\sum_{n \geq 0} a_n x^n$$

defined by

$$a_n = \sum_{\lambda \in \Lambda} P_\lambda(n)\lambda^n$$

(with this sum computed in K) is an isomorphism of K-algebra from $K[t][\Lambda]$ *onto the Hadamard algebra of regular rational series.*

Proof. Let φ be the function of the statement. Let $E = \sum P_\lambda(t)\lambda$ and $F = \sum Q_\lambda(t)\lambda$ be two exponential polynomials, and let $G = E + F = \sum R_\lambda(t)\lambda$, $H = EF = \sum S_\lambda(t)\lambda \in K[t][\Lambda]$. Then

$$R_\lambda = P_\lambda + Q_\lambda,\ S_\lambda = \sum_{\mu\nu = \lambda} P_\mu Q_\nu$$

Consequently

$$(\varphi(G), x^n) = \sum R_\lambda(n)\lambda^n = \sum P_\lambda(n)\lambda^n + \sum Q_\lambda(n)\lambda^n$$

$$= (\varphi(E), x^n) + (\varphi(F), x^n)$$

$$(\varphi(H), x^n) = \sum S_\lambda(n)\lambda^n = \sum_\lambda \lambda^n \sum_{\mu\nu = \lambda} P_\mu(n) Q_\nu(n)$$

$$= \left(\sum_\mu P_\mu(n)\mu^n\right)\left(\sum_\nu Q_\nu(n)\nu^n\right)$$

$$= (\varphi(E), x^n)(\varphi(F), x^n)$$

Thus

$$\varphi(E+F)=\varphi(E)+\varphi(F),\ \varphi(EF)=\varphi(E)\varphi(F)$$

Let us now verify that φ is a bijection. Let $\alpha_1, \ldots, \alpha_k$ be elements of K with $\alpha_k \neq 0$, and let V be the set of all (regular rational) series $S=\sum a_n x^n$ satisfying the relation

$$a_{n+k}=\alpha_1 a_{n+k-1}+\ldots+\alpha_k a_n \ (n \geqq 0)$$

Clearly V is a vector space of dimension k. Let $\lambda_1, \ldots, \lambda_p$ be the roots of the polynomial

$$R(x)=x^k-\alpha_1 x^{k-1}-\ldots-\alpha_k$$

with multiplicities $n_1, \ldots, n_p$ respectively. Consider the subspace V' of $K[t][\Lambda]$ of dimension k

$$V'=\left\{\sum_{1 \leqq i \leqq p} P_i(t)\lambda_i \mid deg(P_i) \leqq n_i-1\right\}$$

We show that φ induces a surjection $V' \to V$ (and consequently an injection) and this will prove the theorem.

Any $S=\sum a_n x^n$ in V can be written as $P(x)/Q(x)$, with $deg(P)<deg(Q)$ and Q being the reciprocal polynomial of R. Decomposing P/Q into simple elements shows that S is a linear combination of series

$$\frac{1}{(1-\lambda_i x)^j},\ 1 \leqq i \leqq p,\ 1 \leqq j \leqq n_i$$

Next, it is straightforward that

$$\frac{1}{(1-\lambda x)^j}=\sum_{n \geqq 0}\binom{n+j-1}{j-1}\lambda^n x^n$$

Since $\binom{n+j-1}{j-1}$ is a polynomial of degree $j-1$ in th variable n, the surjectivity of $\varphi: V' \to V$ is proved. □

Observe that in the bijection described in the theorem and its proof, the *support* of an exponential polynomial $E=\sum P_\lambda(t)\lambda$ (i.e. the set of $\lambda \in \Lambda$ such that $P_\lambda \neq 0$) is exactly the set of roots (i.e. inverses of poles) of S, and that the multiplicity of a root λ is equal to $1+deg(P_\lambda)$. Furthermore, if the coefficients and the roots of S are in some subfield K_1 of K, then the corresponding exponential polynomial is in $K_1[t][\Lambda_1]$, with $\Lambda_1=K_1 \backslash 0$.

Corollary 2.2. *Let $S=\sum a_n x^n$ be a rational series over an algebraically closed field K of characteristic 0.*

(i) *The coefficients a_n are given, for large enough n, by*

$$a_n = \sum_{1 \leq i \leq r} \lambda_i^n P_i(n) \tag{2.1}$$

where $\lambda_1, \ldots, \lambda_r \in K \setminus 0$, and $P_i(t) \in K[t]$.

(ii) *The expression (2.1) is unique if the λ_i's are distinct; in particular, the nonzero roots of S are the λ_i's with $P_i \neq 0$.*

Proof. (i) By Proposition 1.4, $S = P + T$ for some polynomial P and some rational regular series T. Thus, it suffices to use Theorem 2.1.

(ii) Let

$$T = \sum_{n \geq 0} \left(\sum_{1 \leq r \leq n} \lambda_i P_i(n) x^n \right)$$

Then, in view of Theorem 2.1, T is rational regular, moreover, $S = T + P$ for some polynomial P (because S and T have by assumption the same coefficients for large enough n). By Proposition 1.4, T depends only on S, and by Theorem 2.1, the exponential polynomial of T is unique. By the remark following the proof of Theorem 2.1, the λ_i's with $P_i \neq 0$ are exactly the roots of T. Now, it is clear that T and S have the same poles, so they have the same nonzero roots. □

Definition. Let $S_0, \ldots, S_{p-1}$ be formal series in $K[[x]]$. The *merge* of these series is the formal series S defined for $m \in \mathbf{N}$ and $i \in \{0, \ldots, p-1\}$ by

$$(S, x^{mp+i}) = (S_i, x^m)$$

In other words, if $n = mp + i$ (Euclidean division of n by p), then $(S, x^n) = (S_i, x^m)$. This can also be written as

$$S(x) = \sum_{0 \leq i < p} x^i S_i(x^p)$$

with notation that is clear.

An example. If $p = 2$, and $S_0 = \sum a_n x^n$, $S_1 = \sum b_n x^n$, then the *merge* of S_0 and S_1 is the series $\sum c_n x^n$, where the sequence (c_n) is

$$a_0, b_0, a_1, b_1, a_2, b_2, a_3, \ldots$$

Observe that for any series $S = \sum a_n x^n \in K[[x]]$ and any p, there is a unique p-tuple of series $(S_0, \ldots, S_{p-1})$ whose merge is S. These series are indeed

$$S_i = \sum_{n \geq 0} a_{i+np} x^n$$

Definition. A series $\sum a_n x^n$ is *geometric* if there exist b, c in K such that $a_n = bc^n$.

Theorem 2.3 (Benzaghou 1970). *If a regular rational series is invertible in the Hadamard algebra of regular rational series, then it is a merge of geometric series.*

The conclusion can also be formulated as follows: there exist an integer p and elements $a_0, \ldots, a_{p-1}, b_0, \ldots, b_{p-1}$ in K such that the series is

$$\sum_{0 \leqq i \leqq p-1} \frac{a_i x^i}{1-b_i x^p}$$

Proof. (i) Let i and p be natural numbers and consider the K-linear function $\psi: K[t][\Lambda] \to K[t][\Lambda]$ defined on monomials by

$$\psi(P(t)\lambda) = (\lambda^i P(i+pt))\lambda^p$$

where $P(t) \in K[t]$, $\lambda \in \Lambda$ and where $\lambda^i P(i+pt)$ is an element of $K[t]$. The function ψ is a morphism of K-algebra. To see this, it suffices to compute ψ on products of monomials, and indeed

$$\psi(P(t)Q(t)\lambda\mu) = (\lambda^i \mu^i P(i+tp)Q(i+tp))\lambda^p \mu^p$$
$$= \psi(P(t)\lambda)\psi(Q(t)\mu)$$

(ii) Consider now two exponential polynomials $E, F \in K[t][\Lambda]$ and let Λ_1 be the subgroup of Λ generated by $supp(E) \cup supp(F)$. The group Λ_1 is a *finitely generated abelian group*, thus is isomorphic to the product of a finite group (of p elements, say) and of a finitely generated free abelian group. Consequently the subgroup Λ_2 of Λ_1 generated by the λ^p, for $\lambda \in \Lambda_1$, is free.

By construction, the supports of $\psi(E)$ and $\psi(F)$ are in Λ_2 (for any i, and for the fixed p), and $\psi(E), \psi(F) \in K[t][\Lambda_2]$. Assume now $EF=1$. Then $\psi(E)\psi(F)=1$. Since Λ_2 is free, the only invertible elements of $K[t][\Lambda_2]$ have the form $a\lambda$, with $a \in K$, $\lambda \in \Lambda_2$. Indeed, this is an easy consequence of the fact that the only invertible elements of an algebra of commutative polynomials are the constant polynomials.

(iii) Consider now two regular rational series S and T such that $S \odot T = \sum_{n \geqq 0} x^n$ (the neutral element of the Hadamard algebra). Let $E, F \in K[t][\Lambda]$ be such that $\varphi(E) = S$, $\varphi(F) = T$, where φ is the isomorphism of Theorem 2.1. Then $EF=1$.

Set $S = \sum a_n x^n$. If $E = \sum P_\lambda(t)\lambda$ and $\psi(E) = \sum \lambda^i P_\lambda(i+tp)\lambda^p$, then

$$\varphi(\psi(E)) = \sum_{n \geqq 0} \left(\sum_{\lambda} \lambda^i P_\lambda(i+pn)\lambda^{pn} \right) x^n = S_i$$

where

$$S_i = \sum_{n \geqq 0} a_{i+pn} x^n$$

In view of the conclusion of (ii), $\psi(E) = a\lambda$ for some $a \in K$, $\lambda \in \Lambda$. Consequently

$$S_i = \sum_{n \geqq 0} a\lambda^n x^n$$

This proves the theorem because S is the merge of the S_i's. □

The proof of the theorem suggests the following definition and proposition which will be of use later.

Definition. A regular rational series is *simple* if the abelian multiplicative subgroup of $K\backslash 0$ generated by its roots is free. Similarly, a set of regular rational series is *simple* if the set of all its roots generates a free abelian group.

Proposition 2.4. *Let* $\mathbf{S}$ *be a finite set of regular rational series. There exists an integer* $p \geqq 1$ *such that the set of series of the form*

$$\sum_{n \geqq 0} a_{i+pn} x^n$$

for $i \in \mathbf{N}$ *and* $\sum a_n x^n \in \mathbf{S}$ *is simple.*

Proof. Since $\mathbf{S}$ is finite, there exists an invertible matrix $m \in K^{q \times q}$ such that each $S \in \mathbf{S}$ can be written as

$$S = \sum_{n \geqq 0} \varphi_S(m^n) x^n$$

for some linear form φ_S on $K^{q \times q}$. Let Λ_1 be the set of eigenvalues of m. The group generated by Λ_1 in $K\backslash 0$ is finitely generated, and consequently there is an integer $p \geqq 1$ such that the group G generated by the λ^p, for $\lambda \in \Lambda_1$, is free abelian. Let P be the characteristic polynomial of m^p. For each $i \in \mathbf{N}$ and $S = \sum a_n x^n \in \mathbf{S}$, the series $S_i = \sum a_{i+np} x^n$ has the form

$$S_i = \sum_n \varphi_S(m^i (m^p)^n) x^n$$

showing that $S_i \circ P = 0$. Consequently, the roots of S_i are in G. □

3 A Theorem of Pólya

In this section, we consider series with coefficients in $\mathbf{Q}$. Recall that for any prime number p, the *p-adic valuation* v_p over $\mathbf{Q}$ is defined by $v_p(0) = \infty$ and $v_p(p^n a/b) = n$ for $n, a, b \in \mathbf{Z}$, $b \neq 0$ and p dividing neither a nor b.

Definition Let $S = \sum a_n x^n \in \mathbf{Q}[[x]]$. The *set of prime factors* of S is the set of prime numbers

$$P(S) = \{p \mid \exists n \in \mathbf{N},\ v_p(a_n) \neq 0, \infty\}$$

Theorem 3.1 (Pólya 1921). *The set of prime factors of a rational series* S *is finite if and only if* S *is the sum of a polynomial and of a merge of geometric series.*

We first prove a lemma of independent interest.

Lemma 3.2 (Benzaghou 1970). *Let $S=\sum a_n x^n$ be a rational series which is not a polynomial, and let p be a prime number. There exist integers $n_0 \geqq 0$ and $q \geqq 1$ such that the function $n \mapsto v_p(a_{n_0+qn})$ is affine.*

Proof. (i) We start by proving a preliminary result. Let K be a commutative field with a discrete valuation v: $K \to \mathbf{N} \cup \{\infty\}$. Let A be its valuation ring, $A=\{x \in K \mid v(x) \geqq 0\}$, let I be the maximal ideal of A, $I=\{x \in K \mid v(x) \geqq 1\}$ and let $U=A \backslash I=\{x \in K \mid v(x)=0\}$ be the group of invertible elements of A. Suppose further that the residual field $F=A/I$ is finite. Since v is discrete, I is a principal ideal, and consequently $I=\pi A$ for some $\pi \in A$ with $v(\pi)=1$. [For a systematic exposition of these concepts, see, e.g. Amice (1975), Koblitz (1974).] Let $\lambda_1, \ldots, \lambda_k$ be elements of $A \backslash 0$, let $P_1, \ldots, P_k \in K[t]$ be polynomials and let (a_n) be a sequence of elements in A defined by

$$a_n = \sum_{1 \leqq i \leqq k} P_i(n) \lambda_i^n \tag{3.1}$$

Then we claim that there exist integers n_0 and q such that the function $n \mapsto v(a_{n_0+qn})$ is affine.

The proof of the claim is in 3 steps.

1. One may assume that all the P_i are in $A[t]$ (by multiplying the polynomials by a common denominator, if necessary).
2. Assuming that $\lambda_i \in I$ for all $i=1, \ldots, k$, set

$$r=\inf\{v(\lambda_i) \mid i=1, \ldots, k\}$$

Then $r \geqq 1$. Since each P_i has coefficients in A and $v(\lambda_i) \geqq r$ for all i, it follows that $v(a_n) \geqq rn$. Consequently $v(a_n/\pi^{rm}) \geqq 0$ and the sequence (b_n) defined by $b_n=a_n/\pi^{rn}$ has its elements in A. Further

$$b_n = \sum_{1 \leqq i \leqq k} P_i(n) \left(\frac{\lambda_i}{\pi^r}\right)^n$$

Thus we may assume in addition that $\lambda_i \in U$ for at least one index i.
3. Let $l \geqq 1$ be such that $\lambda_1, \ldots, \lambda_l \in U$ and $\lambda_{l+1}, \ldots, \lambda_k \in I$ (possibly $l=k$). Set

$$b_n = \sum_{i=1}^{l} P_i(n) \lambda_i^n, \quad c_n = \sum_{i=l+1}^{k} P_i(n) \lambda_i^n$$

($c_n=0$ if $l=k$). We prove that there is an arithmetic progression of integers n where $v(b_n)$ is constant. For this, observe that the minimal polynomial of the regular series $\sum b_n x^n$ is

$$P(x) = \prod_{i=1}^{l} (x-\lambda_i)^{deg(P_i)+1}$$

(cf. Theorem 2.1 and the observation following its proof). By setting

$$P(x) = x^h - \alpha_1 x^{h-1} - \ldots - \alpha_h$$

one has $\alpha_h \in U$. Let

$$s = \inf\{v(b_0), \ldots, v(b_{h-1})\}$$

Since the sequence (b_n) satisfies the recurrence relation associated with P, and since the coefficients of P are in A, it follows that $v(b_n) \geqq s$ for all n. Consequently, the sequence (b'_n) defined by

$$b'_n = b_n/\pi^s$$

is also in A. It has the same minimal polynomial as (b_n) and there is an integer j such that

$$v(b'_j) = 0$$

i.e. $b'_j \in U$. Next

$$b'_n = \lambda m^n \gamma$$

where

$$\lambda = (1, 0, \ldots, 0), \qquad m = \begin{pmatrix} 0 & 1 & 0 & . & 0 \\ 0 & 0 & 1 & . & 0 \\ . & & . & & . \\ . & & . & & 1 \\ \alpha_h & . & . & . & \alpha_1 \end{pmatrix} \qquad \gamma = \begin{pmatrix} b'_0 \\ b'_1 \\ . \\ . \\ b'_{h-1} \end{pmatrix}.$$

Since the determinant of the matrix m is $\pm\alpha_h \in U$, and since $F = A/I$ is finite, there is an integer q such that $m^q \equiv 1 \ mod.\ I$ (with I the identity matrix). This shows that the sequence (b'_n) is periodic modulo I and in particular for all $n \geqq 0$,

$$b'_{j+qn} \equiv b'_j \ mod\ I$$

Thus $v(b'_{j+qn}) = v(b'_j) = 0$, and consequently

$$v(b_{j+qn}) = s \quad \text{for} \quad n \geqq 0$$

Finally, observe that $v(c_n) \geqq n$. Thus if n is large (more precisely if $j + qn > s$) then

$$v(a_{j+qn}) = v(b_{j+qn}) = s$$

Thus is suffices to set $n_0 = j + qn'$, where n' is chosen so that $n_0 > r$. This proves the preliminary claim.

(ii) Since the series S is rational over $\mathbf{Q}$, there exists an integer $d \geqq 1$ such that

$$\sum d^{n+1} a_n x^n$$

is rational over $\mathbf{Z}$. Thus one may assume that S is rational over $\mathbf{Z}$, and even that S is regular rational nonvanishing (by Proposition 1.4).

(iii) Let $P(x)=x^r-\alpha_1x^{r-1}-\ldots-\alpha_r$ be the minimal polynomial of S. Then the coefficients of P are integers by the lemma of Fatou (Corollary V.1.2) and Proposition 1.2. Its roots $\lambda_1, \ldots, \lambda_k$ are algebraic integers. Let K be the number field $K=\mathbf{Q}[\lambda_1, \ldots, \lambda_k]$. By Theorem 2.1, the a_n admit the expression given by Eq. (3.1). Moreover, for any prime ideal $\mathbf{p}$ of K, the α_i and a_n are in the valuation ring of K for the valuation $v_{\mathbf{p}}$, and by our preliminary result (i), there exist integers j and l such that

$$n \mapsto v_p(a_{j+ln})$$

is an affine function.

(iv) Let B be the ring of algebraic integers of K, and let p be a prime number. The ideal pB of B decomposes as

$$pB=\mathbf{p}_1^{m_1}\ldots\mathbf{p}_s^{m_s}$$

where $\mathbf{p}_1, \ldots, \mathbf{p}_s$ are distinct prime ideals of K. By applying the preceding argument for $\mathbf{p}=\mathbf{p}_1$ one obtains integers j, l such that the function

$$n \mapsto v_{\mathbf{p}_1}(a_{j+ln})$$

is affine. By iteration of this computation for $\mathbf{p}_2, \ldots, \mathbf{p}_s$, one gets successive subsequences and finally one obtains an arithmetic progression $n'_0+q'\mathbf{N}$ such that for each $i=1, \ldots, s$, the function

$$n \mapsto v_{\mathbf{p}_i}(a_{n'_0+q'n})$$

is affine. Thus there exist integers x_i and y_i such that

$$v_{\mathbf{p}_i}(a_{n'_0+q'n})=x_i+y_in$$

Now observe that for all $a \in \mathbf{Z}$

$$v_p(a)=\inf\left\{\left\lfloor\frac{v_{\mathbf{p}_i}(a)}{m_i}\right\rfloor; i=1, \ldots, s\right\}$$

(where $\lfloor z \rfloor$ denotes the integral part of z). Since the functions

$$n \mapsto \frac{v_{\mathbf{p}_i}(a_{n'_0+q'n})}{m_i}$$

also are affine, there exists an integer i_0 such that for all $i=1, \ldots, s$ and all sufficiently large n,

$$\frac{1}{m}(x_i+y_in) \geqq \frac{1}{m_{i_0}}(x_{i_0}+y_{i_0}n)$$

showing that

$$v_p(a_{n'_0}+q'n)=\left\lfloor\frac{x_{i_0}+y_{i_0}n}{m_{i_0}}\right\rfloor$$

for sufficiently large n. Since the function

$$n \mapsto \left\lfloor \frac{x_{i_0} + y_{i_0} m_{i_0} n}{m_{i_0}} \right\rfloor$$

also is affine, the constants $q = q' m_{i_0}$ and n_0 are now clear. □

Proof of Theorem 3.1. Let S be a rational series having a finite set of prime factors. Clearly we may assume that S is regular (Proposition 1.4). In view of Proposition 2.4, we may even assume that S is simple.

Let $S = \sum a_n x^n$ and let $p_1, \ldots, p_l$ be the prime factors of S. Applying Lemma 3.2 successively to $p_1, \ldots, p_l$, one obtains integers n_0 and q such that, for every $i = 1, \ldots, l$, the function

$$n \mapsto v_{p_i}(a_{n_0 + qn})$$

is affine. Set $\varepsilon_n = -1, 0, 1$ according to $a_n < 0$, $a_n = 0$, $a_n > 0$. Then for $n \geqq 0$, one has

$$a_{n_0 + qn} = \theta_n b c^n$$

with $\theta_n = \varepsilon_{n_0 + qn}$.

Now let $\lambda_1, \ldots, \lambda_k$ ($k \geqq 1$) be the distinct roots of S. In view of Theorem 2.1, there are nonvanishing polynomials $P_1, \ldots, P_k$ such that

$$a_n = \sum_{i=1}^{k} P_i(n) \lambda_i^n \tag{3.2}$$

Thus, setting

$$b_n = a_{n_0 + qn}, \quad Q_i(t) = P_i(n_0 + qt) \lambda_i^{n_0}, \quad \mu_i = \lambda_i^q$$

one has

$$b_n = \theta_n b c^n = \sum_{i=1}^{k} Q_i(n) \mu_i^n$$

Since the group generated by the λ_i's is free, all the μ_i are distinct. Moreover, the polynomials $Q_i(t)$ do not vanish, and thus $\sum b_n x^n$ is not a polynomial. Thus $\theta_n \neq 0$ for infinitely many n, and we may suppose that $\theta_n = 1$ for infinitely many n. The series

$$\sum \frac{b_n}{c^n} x^n$$

has a finite image. By Theorem III.2.7, (and Exercise III.1.1), there exists an arithmetic progression $n_1 + r\mathbf{N}$ such that $\theta_n = 1$ for $n \in n_1 + r\mathbf{N}$. Thus

$$b_{n_1 + rn} = b c^{n_1} (c^r)^n = \sum_{i=1}^{k} Q_i(n_1 + rn) \mu_i^{n_1} (\mu_i^r)^n$$

As before, the μ_i^r are pairwise distinct. In view of the unicity of the exponential polynomial, one has $k=1$, and $Q_1(n_1+rt)=C$, for some constant. Thus Q_1 is a constant and also P_1. By Eq. (3.2), $a_n=P_1\lambda_1^n$. This completes the proof. □

4 A Theorem of Skolem, Mahler and Lech

The following result describes completely the supports of rational series in one variable with coefficients in a field of characteristic zero. They are exactly the rational one-letter languages. This does not hold for more than one variable (see, e.g. Example III.3.1).

Theorem 4.1 (Skolem 1934; Mahler 1935; Lech 1953). *Let K be a field of characteristic 0, and let $S=\sum a_n x^n$ be a rational series with coefficients in K. Then the set*

$$\{n\in\mathbf{N} \mid a_n=0\}$$

is the union of a finite set and of a finite number of arithmetic progressions.

In fact, this result has been proved for $K=\mathbf{Z}$ by Skolem, it has been extended to algebraic number fields by Mahler and to fields of characteristic 0 by Lech. This author also gives the following example showing that the theorem does not hold in characteristic $p\neq 0$. Indeed, let θ be transcendent over the field $\mathbf{F}_p$ with p elements. Then the series $\sum a_n x^n$, with

$$a_n=(\theta+1)^n-\theta^n-1$$

is rational over $F_p(\theta)$, and, however,

$$\{n \mid a_n=0\}=\{p^r \mid r\in\mathbf{N}\}$$

The proof we give here is elementary and does not use p-adic analysis. It requires several definitions and lemmas, and goes through three steps. First, the result is proved for series with integral coefficients. Then it is extended to transcendental extensions and finally to the general case.

Definitions. A set A of nonnegative integers is called *purely periodic* if there exist an integer $N\geqq 0$ and integers $k_1, k_2, \ldots, k_r\in\{0, 1, \ldots, N-1\}$ such that

$$A=\{k_i+nN \mid n\in\mathbf{N},\ 1\leqq i\leqq r\}$$

The integer N is *a period* of A. A *quasiperiodic* set (of period N) is a subset of $\mathbf{N}$ which is the union of a finite set and of a purely periodic set (of period N).

Lemma 4.2. *The intersection of a family of quasiperiodic sets of period N is quasiperiodic of period N.*

Proof. Let $(A_i)_{i\in I}$ be a family of quasiperiodic sets, all having period N. Given a $j\in\{0, 1,\dots,N-1\}$, for any $i\in I$, the set $(j+N\mathbf{N})\cap A_i$ is either finite or equal to $j+N\mathbf{N}$. Thus the same holds for $(j+N\mathbf{N})\cap(\cap A_i)$. □

Definition. Given a series $S=\sum a_n x^n$ with coefficients in a semiring K, the *annihilator* of S is the set

$$ann(S)=\{n\in\mathbf{N}\mid a_n=0\}$$

Thus the annihilator is the complement of the support. With these definitions the first (and most difficult) step in the proof of Theorem 4.1 can be formulated as follows.

Proposition 4.3. *Let $S=\sum a_n x^n\in\mathbf{Q}[\![x]\!]$ be a regular rational series with rational coefficients. Then the annihilator of S is quasiperiodic.*

Let p be a fixed prime number. The p-adic valuation v_p is defined at the beginning of Sect. 3. Observe that

$$v_p(q_1\cdots q_n)=\sum_{1\leqq i\leqq n} v_p(q_i)$$

$$v_p(q_1+\dots+q_n)\geqq\inf\{v_p(q_1),\dots,v_p(q_n)\}$$

Observe also that for $n\in\mathbf{N}$

$$v_p(n!)\leqq n/(p-1) \tag{4.1}$$

since indeed (Exercise!)

$$v_p(n!)=\lfloor n/p\rfloor+\lfloor n/p^2\rfloor+\dots+\lfloor n/p^k\rfloor+\dots$$

$$\leqq n/p+n/p^2+\dots+n/p^k+\dots\leqq n/(p-1)$$

We shall use later the inequality

$$v_p\left(\frac{p^n}{n!}\right)\geqq n\frac{p-2}{p-1} \tag{4.2}$$

which follows immediately from Eq. (4.1).

Next, consider an arbitrary polynomial

$$P(x)=a_0+a_1x+\dots+a_nx^n$$

with integral coefficients. For any integer $k\geqq 0$, let

$$\omega_k(P)=inf\{v_p(a_j)\mid j\geqq k\}$$

Clearly

$$\omega_0(P) \leqq \omega_1(P) \leqq \ldots \leqq \omega_k(P) \leqq \ldots$$

and

$$\omega_k(P) = \infty \quad \text{for } k > n$$

Observe also that $v_p(P(t)) \geqq \inf\{a_0, a_1 t, \ldots, a_n t^n\}$ for any integer $t \in \mathbf{Z}$, and consequently

$$v_p(P(t)) \geqq \omega_0(P) \tag{4.3}$$

Lemma 4.4. *Let P and Q be two polynomials with rational coefficients such that*

$$P(x) = (x-t)Q(x)$$

for some $t \in \mathbf{Z}$. Then for all $k \in \mathbf{N}$

$$\omega_{k+1}(P) \leqq \omega_k(Q)$$

Proof. Set

$$Q(x) = a_0 + a_1 x + \ldots + a_n x^n$$

$$P(x) = b_0 + b_1 x + \ldots + b_{n+1} x^{n+1}$$

Then $b_{j+1} = a_j - t a_{j+1}$ $(0 \leqq j \leqq n-1)$, $b_{n+1} = a_n$, whence for $j = 0, \ldots, n$,

$$a_j = b_{j+1} + t b_{j+2} + \ldots + t^{n-j} b_{n+1}$$

This shows that $v_p(a_j) \geqq \omega_{j+1}(P)$ for any $j \in \mathbf{N}$. Thus, given any $k \in \mathbf{N}$, one has for $j \geqq k$

$$v_p(a_j) \geqq \omega_{j+1}(P) \geqq \omega_{k+1}(P)$$

and consequently

$$\omega_k(Q) \geqq \omega_{k+1}(P)$$

□

Corollary 4.5. *Let Q be a polynomial with rational coefficients, let $t_1, t_2, \ldots, t_k \in \mathbf{Z}$, and let*

$$P(x) = (x-t_1)(x-t_2)\ldots(x-t_k)Q(x)$$

Then

$$\omega_k(P) \leqq \omega_0(Q)$$

The main argument is the following lemma.

Lemma 4.6. *Let $(d_n)_{n\in\mathbf{N}}$ be any sequence of integers and let $(b_n)_{n\in\mathbf{N}}$ be the sequence defined by*

$$b_n = \sum_{i=0}^{n} \binom{n}{i} p^i d_i$$

where p is an odd prime number. If $b_n = 0$ for infinitely many indices n, then the sequences $(b_n)_{n\in\mathbf{N}}$ vanishes.

Proof. For $n \in \mathbf{N}$, let

$$R_n(x) = \sum_{i=0}^{n} d_i p^i \frac{x(x-1)\ldots(x-i+1)}{i!}$$

Then for $t \in \mathbf{N}$,

$$R_n(t) = \sum_{i=0}^{n} \binom{t}{i} p^i d_i$$

and since $\binom{t}{i} = 0$ for $i > t$, it follows that

$$b_t = R_t(t) = R_n(t) \quad (n \geqq t) \tag{4.4}$$

Next, we show that for all k, $n \geqq 0$,

$$\omega_k(R_n) \geqq k\frac{p-2}{p-1}$$

For this, let

$$R_n(x) = \sum_{k=0}^{n} c_k^{(n)} x^k$$

Each $c_k^{(n)} x^k$ is a linear combination, with integral coefficients, of numbers $d_i \frac{p^i}{i!}$, for indices i with $k \leqq i \leqq n$. Consequently

$$v_p(c_k^{(n)}) \geqq \inf_{k \leqq i \leqq n} \left(v_p\left(d_i \frac{p^i}{i!} \right) \right)$$

In view of Eq. (4.2), this implies

$$v_p(c_k^{(n)}) \geqq \inf\left(i\frac{p-2}{p-1} \right) \geqq k\frac{p-2}{p-1}$$

which in turn shows that

$$\omega_k(R_n) \geqq k\frac{p-2}{p-1} \tag{4.5}$$

Consider now any coefficient b_t of the sequence $(b_n)_{n\in\mathbf{N}}$. We shall see that

$$v_p(b_t) \geqq k\frac{p-2}{p-1}$$

for any integer k, which of course shows that $b_t = 0$. For this, let $t_1 < t_2 < \ldots < t_k$ be the first k indices with $b_{t_1} = \ldots = b_{t_k} = 0$, and let $n \geqq sup(t, t_k)$. By Eq. (4.1), $R_n(t_i) = b_{t_i} = 0$ for $i = 1, \ldots, k$. Thus

$$R_n(x) = (x-t_1)(x-t_2)\ldots(x-t_k)Q(x) \tag{4.6}$$

for some polynomial $Q(x)$ with integral coefficients. By Corollary 4.5, one has

$$\omega_k(R_n) \leqq \omega_0(Q) \tag{4.7}$$

Next, by Eq. (4.4) $v_p(b_t) = v_p(R_n(t))$ and by Eqs. (4.6), (4.3) and (4.7)

$$v_p(R_n(t)) \geqq v_p(Q(t)) \geqq \omega_0(Q) \geqq \omega_k(R_n)$$

Thus, in view of Eq. (4.5),

$$v_p(b_t) \geqq k\frac{p-2}{p-1}$$

for all $k \geqq 0$. □

Remark. Set

$$B(x) = \sum_{n=0}^{\infty} b_n x^n, \; D(x) = \sum_{n=0}^{\infty} d_n x^n$$

with the integers b_n, d_n related as in Lemma 4.6. Then it is easily verified that

$$B(x) = \sum_{n=0}^{\infty} d_n \frac{p^n x^n}{(1-x)^{n+1}}$$

Lemma 4.7. *Let $S = \sum a_n x^n \in \mathbf{Z}[\![x]\!]$ be a regular rational series and let $\lambda, \mu, \gamma)$ be a linear representation of S of dimension k with integral coefficients. For any odd prime p not dividing $det(\mu(x))$, the annihilator $ann(S)$ is quasiperiodic of period at most p^{k^2}.*

Proof. Let p be an odd prime that does not divide $det(\mu(x))$. Let

$$n \mapsto \bar{n}$$

be the canonical morphism from $\mathbf{Z}$ onto $\mathbf{Z}/p\mathbf{Z}$. Since $\overline{det(\mu(x))} = det(\overline{\mu(x)}) \neq 0$, the matrix $\overline{\mu(x)}$ is invertible over $\mathbf{Z}/p\mathbf{Z}$, and there is an integer $N < p^{k^2}$ with

$$\overline{\mu(x^N)} = \bar{I}$$

Reverting to the original matrix, this means that

$$\mu(x^N) = I + pM$$

for some matrix M with integral coefficients.

Consider now a fixed integer $j \in \{0, \ldots, N-1\}$, and set for $n \geqq 0$,

$$b_n = a_{j+nN}$$

Then

$$b_n = \lambda\mu(x^{j+nN})\gamma = \lambda\mu(x^j)(I+pM)^n\gamma = \sum_{i=0}^{n} \binom{n}{i} p^i \lambda\mu(x^j) M^i \gamma$$

Thus, setting $d_i = \lambda\mu(x^j) M^i \gamma$, one obtains

$$b_n = \sum_{i=0}^{n} \binom{n}{i} p^i d_i$$

In view of Lemma 4.6, the sequence $(b_n)_{n \geqq 0}$ either vanishes or contains only finitely many vanishing terms. Thus, the annihilator of S is quasiperiodic with period less than p^{k^2}. □

Proof of Proposition 4.3. Let (λ, μ, γ) be a regular linear representation of S, and let q be a common multiple of the denominators of the coefficients in λ, μ and γ. Then $(q\lambda, q\mu, q\gamma)$ is a linear representation of the regular rational series $S' = \sum q^{n+2} a_n x^n$. Clearly $ann(S) = ann(S')$. By Lemma 4.7, the set $ann(S')$ is quasiperiodic. Thus $ann(S)$ is quasiperiodic. □

We now turn to the second part of the proof. For this, we consider the ring $\mathbf{Z}[y_1, \ldots, y_m]$ of polynomials over $\mathbf{Z}$ in commutative variables $y_1, \ldots, y_m$, and the quotient field $\mathbf{Q}(y_1, \ldots, y_m)$ of rational functions. An element in either one of these sets will be denoted indistinctly without or with an enumeration of the variables. As usual, if $P \in \mathbf{Q}(y_1, \ldots, y_m)$ and $a_1, \ldots, a_m \in \mathbf{Q}$, then $P(a_1, \ldots, a_m)$ is the value of P at that point. The result to be proved is the following.

Proposition 4.8. *Let $S = \sum a_n x^n$ be a regular rational series with coefficients in the field $\mathbf{Q}(y_1, \ldots, y_m)$. Then $ann(S)$ is quasiperiodic.*

We start by recalling the following well-known property of polynomials.

Lemma 4.9. *Let K be a (commutative) field, and let $P \in K[y_1, \ldots, y_m]$. Let δ_i be the degree of P in the variable y_i. Assume that there exists subsets $A_1, \ldots, A_m$ of K with $Card(A_i) > \delta_i$ for $i = 1, \ldots, m$, such that $P(a_1, \ldots, a_m) = 0$ for all $(a_1, \ldots, a_m) \in A_1 \times \ldots \times A_m$. Then $P = 0$.*

Proof. Straightforward induction on m. □

Corollary 4.10. *Let $S=\sum a_n x^n$ be any series with coefficients in $K[y_1,\dots,y_m]$, and let $H_1, \dots, H_m$ be arbitrary infinite subsets of K. For each $(h_1,\dots,h_m)\in K^m$, let*

$$S_{h_1,\dots,h_m}=\sum a_n(h_1,\dots,h_m)x^n$$

Then

$$ann(S)=\bigcap_{(h_1,\dots,h_m)\in H_1\times\dots\times H_m} ann(S_{h_1,\dots,h_m})$$

Proof. It follows immediately from Lemma 4.9 that $a_n=0$ iff $a_n(h_1,\dots,h_m)=0$ for all $(h_1,\dots,h_m)\in H_1\times\dots\times H_m$. □

Lemma 4.11. *Let $P\in\mathbf{Z}[y_1,\dots,y_m]$, $P\neq 0$. For all but a finite number of prime numbers p, there exists a subset $H\subset\mathbf{Z}^m$ of the form*

$$H=(k_1,\dots,k_m)+p\mathbf{Z}^m \tag{4.8}$$

such that for all $(h_1,\dots,h_m)\in H$,

$$P(h_1,\dots,h_m)\neq 0 \bmod p$$

Proof. Let

$$P=\sum c_{i_1i_2\dots i_m}y_1^{i_1}y_2^{i_2}\dots y_m^{i_m}$$

Let δ_i be the degree of P in the variable y_i, and let p be any prime number strictly greater than the δ_i's and not dividing all the coefficients $c_{i_1i_2}\dots_{i_m}$. Again let $n\mapsto\bar{n}$ be the morphism from $\mathbf{Z}$ onto $\mathbf{Z}/p\mathbf{Z}$. The polynomial

$$\bar{P}=\sum\bar{c}_{i_1i_2\dots i_m}y_1^{i_1}y_2^{i_2}\dots y_m^{i_m}$$

is a nonvanishing polynomial with coefficients in $\mathbf{Z}/p\mathbf{Z}$. Since $p>\delta_i$ for $i=1,\dots,m$, it follows from Lemma 4.9 that there exists $(k_1,\dots,k_m)\in\mathbf{Z}^m$ such that $\bar{P}(\bar{k}_1,\dots,\bar{k}_m)\neq 0$. This proves the lemma. □

Proof of Proposition 4.8. Let (λ,μ,γ) be a linear representation of S of dimension k. As in the proof of Proposition 4.3, consider a common multiple $q\in\mathbf{Z}[y_1,\dots,y_m]$ of the denominators of the coefficients of λ, μ and γ. Then $(q\lambda, q\mu, q\gamma)$ is a linear representation of the series $S'=\sum q^{n+2}a_nx^n$ and $ann(S')=ann(S)$. Thus we may suppose that the coefficients of λ, μ, and γ are in $\mathbf{Z}[y_1,\dots,y_m]$.

Let $P=det(\mu(x))\in\mathbf{Z}[y_1,\dots,y_m]$. Since S is regular, $P\neq 0$, and by Lemma 4.11, there exists a prime number p and an infinite $H\subset\mathbf{Z}^m$ of the form Eq. (4.8) such that

$$det(\mu(x)(h_1,\dots,h_m))\neq 0 \bmod p$$

for all $(h_1,\dots,h_m)\in H$. Setting

$$S_{h_1,\dots,h_m}=\sum_n a_n(h_1,\dots,h_m)x^n$$

this implies, in view of Lemma 4.7, that for all $(h_1, \ldots, h_m) \in H$, the set $ann(S_{h_1, \ldots, h_m})$ is quasiperiodic with a period at most p^{k^2}. Thus $r = (p^{k^2})!$ is a period for all these annihilators. In view of Lemma 4.2, the set

$$\bigcap_{(h_1, \ldots, h_m) \in H} ann(S_{h_1, \ldots, h_m})$$

is quasiperiodic. By Corollary 4.10, this intersection is the set $ann(S)$. Thus the proof is complete. □

It is convenient to introduce the following

Definition. A (commutative) field K is a *SML field* (Skolem-Mahler-Lech field) if K satisfies Theorem 4.1.

We have already seen that the field $\mathbf{Q}$ of rational numbers, and the field $\mathbf{Q}(y_1, \ldots, y_m)$ are *SML* fields.

Proposition 4.12. *Let K and L be fields. If L is an SML field and K is a finite algebraic extension of L, then K is a SML field.*

Proof. Let $S = \sum a_n x^n$ be a rational series over K. Let k be the dimension of K over L, and let $\varphi_1, \ldots, \varphi_k$ be L-linear functions $K \to L$ such that, for any $h \in K$

$$k = 0 \Leftrightarrow \varphi_i(h) = 0, \; i = 1, \ldots, k$$

Define

$$S_i = \sum_n \varphi_i(a_n) x^n \in L[\![x]\!]$$

Then, by the choice of the function φ_i, one has

$$ann(S) = \bigcap_{1 \leqq i \leqq k} ann(S_i) \tag{4.9}$$

Thus, it suffices to prove that the series S_i are rational over L. Indeed, by hypothesis, each set $ann(S_i)$ is the union of a finite set and of a finite set of arithmetic progressions. Since the intersection (4.9) is finite, the set $ann(S)$ has the same form.

By Proposition I.5.1, there exists a finite dimensional subvector space M of $K[\![x]\!]$, containing S and which is stable, i.e. closed for the operation $T \mapsto T \circ x$. Since K has finite dimension over L, the space M also has finite dimension over L.

The functions φ_i extended to series

$$\varphi_i \colon K[\![x]\!] \to L[\![x]\!]$$

by

$$\varphi_i\Big(\sum_n b_n x^n\Big) = \sum_n \varphi_i(b_n) x^n$$

are L-linear. Consequently $\varphi_i(M)$ is a finite dimensional vector space over L. Since $\varphi_i(T \circ x) = \varphi_i(T) \circ x$, the space $\varphi_i(M)$ is stable. Moreover, it contains the series $S_i = \varphi_i(S)$. Thus, using again Proposition I.5.1, each series S_i is rational over L. □

Proof of Theorem 4.1. Let S be a rational series with coefficients in K. Then by Proposition 1.4, there is a polynomial P such that $S-P$ is regular. Since $ann(S-P)$ and $ann(S)$ differ only by a finite set, it suffices to prove the result for $S-P$. Thus we may assume that S is regular.

Let (λ, μ, γ) be a linear representation of S, and let K' be the subfield of K over $\mathbf{Q}$ generated by the set Z of coefficients of λ, $\mu(x)$, γ. Then S has coefficients in K' and we may assume that K is a finite extension of $\mathbf{Q}$, i.e. $K = \mathbf{Q}(Z)$ for a finite set Z.

Let Y be a maximal subset of Z that is algebraically independent over $\mathbf{Q}$. The field $\mathbf{Q}(Y)$ is isomorphic to the field of rational functions $\mathbf{Q}(y_1, \ldots, y_m)$ with $Y = \{y_1, \ldots, y_m\}$. In view of Proposition 4.8, the field $\mathbf{Q}(Y)$ is a *SML* field. Next K is a finite algebraic extension of $\mathbf{Q}(Y)$. By Proposition 4.12, the field K is an *SML* field. This concludes the proof. □

Notes to Chapter IV

The notion of an exponential polynomial is a classical one. The formalism we use here is from Reutenauer (1982). It allows us to give an algebraic proof of Benzaghou's theorem. His proof was based on analytic techniques. The algebraic method makes it possible to prove Benzaghou's theorem in characteristic p. Some modifications are necessary, since in that case, the exponential polynomial may not exist nor be unique. Pólya's theorem is extended to general fields by Bezivin (1984).

There are a great number of arithmetic and combinatorial properties of linear recurrence sequences. The use of symmetric functions to derive divisibility properties is illustrated by Duboué (1983). Lascoux (1986) gives numerous applications of expressions of the exponential polynomial by means of symmetric functions. For a rich collection of formulas and results about symmetric functions, see Lascoux and Schützenberger (1985).

The proof of the Skolem-Mahler-Lech theorem given here is due to Hansel (1986). The original proofs, by Skolem (1934), Mahler (1935), and Lech (1953) depend on p-adic analysis. An open problem, stated by C. Pisot, is the following: Is it decidable, for a rational series $\sum a_n x^n$, whether there exists an n such that $a_n = 0$? It is decidable whether there exist infinitely many n with $a_n = 0$ (Berstel and Mignotte 1976).

An extension of Pólya's theorem to several noncommutative variables is studied in Reutenauer (1980b). For this, define as follows the *unambiguous rational operations* on languages (see Eilenberg and Schützenberger 1969):

The union $L_1 \cup L_2$ is unambiguous if the set are disjoint. The product $L_1 L_2$ is unambiguous if $u, u' \in L_1$, $v, v' \in L_2$, and $uv = u'v'$ imply $u = u'$, $v = v'$. The star operation $L \mapsto L^*$ is unambiguous if L is the basis of a free submonoid of X^*.

It can be shown that any rational language is obtained from finite languages by unambiguous operations (Eilenberg 1974).

The *unambiguous rational operations* on series are defined as follows. A rational operation (sum, product, star) on series is unambiguous if the corresponding operation on the support (union, product, star) is unambiguous. A rational series $S \in \mathbf{Q}\langle\langle X \rangle\rangle$ is *unambiguous* if it is obtained from polynomials using only unambiguous rational operations.

It is not very difficult to see that any unambiguous rational series has only finitely many prime factors. The problem is the converse property, which we state as a conjecture.

Conjecture. If a rational series has only finitely many prime factors, then it is unambiguous.

According to Pólya's theorem, this holds for one variable. Partial results are proved in Reutenauer (1980b).

Chapter V

Changing the Semiring

The main problem considered in this chapter is the following: how to determine which of the rational series over an extension of some semiring are rational over this semiring. This leads to the study of semirings of a special type, and also shows the existence of remarkable families of rational series.

In the first section, we examine principal rings from this aspect. Fatou's Lemma is proved and the rings satisfying this lemma are characterized.

Section 2 contains several results on rational series with nonnegative coefficients. The main theorem (Theorem 2.10) is a characterization of $\mathbf{R}_+$-rational series.

In the last section, Fatou extensions are introduced. We show in particular that $\mathbf{Q}_+$ is a Fatou extension of $\mathbf{N}$ (Theorem 3.3).

1 Rational Series over a Principal Ring

Let K be a commutative principal ring and let F be its quotient field. Let $S \in K\langle\langle X \rangle\rangle$ be a formal series over X with coefficients in K. If S is a rational series over F, is it also rational over K? This question admits a positive answer, and there is an even stronger result, namely that S has a linear representation of minimal dimension (i.e. equal to its rank) with coefficients in K.

Theorem 1.1 (Fliess 1974a). *Let $S \in K\langle\langle X \rangle\rangle$ be a series which is rational of rank n over F. Then S is rational over K and has a linear representation over K of dimension n.*

Proof. Let (λ, μ, γ) be a reduced linear representation of S over F. According to Corollary II.2.3, there exist polynomials $P_1, \dots, P_n, Q_1, \dots, Q_n \in F\langle X \rangle$ such that for $w \in X^*$,

$$\mu w = ((S, P_i w Q_j))_{1 \leq i, j \leq n}$$

Let d be an element in $K - \{0\}$ such that $dP_i, dQ_j \in K\langle X \rangle$ and $d\lambda \in K^{1 \times n}$. Then for any polynomial $P \in K\langle X \rangle$

$$d^3 \lambda \mu P = (d\lambda)((S, dP_i P dQ_j))_{i,j} \in K^{1 \times n}$$

since $(S, R) \in K$ whenever $R \in K\langle X \rangle$. Consequently,

$$\lambda\mu(K\langle X \rangle) \subset \frac{1}{d^3} K^{1 \times n}$$

This shows that $\lambda\mu(K\langle X\rangle)$, considered as a submodule of a free K-module of rank n, is also free and has rank $\leqq n$. It suffices now to apply Lemma II.1.2. □

This theorem admits the following corollary, known as *Fatou's Lemma.*

Corollary 1.2 (Fatou 1904). *Let $P(x)/Q(x)\in\mathbf{Q}(x)$ be an irreducible rational function such that the coefficient of the term of lowest degree of Q is 1. If the coefficients of its series expansion are integers, then P and Q have integral coefficients.*

Proof. It suffices to consider the case where $Q(0)=1$. Then $S=\sum a_n x^n = P(x)/Q(x)$ is a rational series. Let (λ, μ, γ) be a reduced linear representation of S. Since $\mathbf{Z}$ is principal, this representation is similar, by Theorem 1.1 and Theorem II.2.4, to a representation over $\mathbf{Z}$. In particular, the characteristic polynomial of $\mu(x)$ has integral coefficients. Now, $Q(x)$ is the reciprocal polynomial of this polynomial (Proposition IV.1.2). Thus $Q(x)$ has integral coefficients, and so does $P=SQ$. □

The previous result holds for rings other than the ring $\mathbf{Z}$ of integers. We shall characterize these rings completely.

Let K be a commutative integral domain and let F be its quotient field. Let M be an F-algebra. An element $m\in M$ is *quasi-integral* over K if there exists an injection of the K-module $K[m]$ into a finitely generated K-module.

Proposition 1.3. *If $m\in M$ is quasi-integral over K, then there exists a finitely generated K-submodule of M containing $K[m]$.*

Proof. There exists a finitely generated K-module N and a K-linear injection $K[m]\to N$. Since $K[m]$ is contained in some F-algebra, it is torsion-free over K. Thus the injection extends to an F-linear injection $i{:}F[m]\to N\otimes_K F$. Consequently $F[m]$ has finite dimension over K and m is algebraic over F. Let $p{:}N\otimes F\to i(F[m])$ be an F-linear projection. Then $p(N)=p(N\otimes 1)$ is a finitely generated K-module containing $i(K[m])$ and contained in $i(F[m])$. Consequently, its inverse image by i, say N_1, is a finitely generated K-module and

$$K[m]\subset N_1\subset F[m]\subset M$$ □

Corollary 1.4. *An element $m\in F$ is quasi-integral over K if and only if there exists $d\in K-\{0\}$ such that $dm^n\in K$ for all $n\in\mathbf{N}$.* □

Corollary 1.5. *If M is a commutative algebra, then the set of elements of M which are quasi-integral over K is a subring of M.* □

Definition. The domain K is called *completely integrally closed* if any m in F which is quasi-integral over K is already in K.

Observe that an element in F which is integral over K is also quasi-integral over K. Thus, if K is completely integrally closed, it is integrally closed.

Theorem 1.6 (Chabert 1972). *The following two conditions are equivalent.*
(i) *The domain K is completely integrally closed.*
(ii) *For any irreducible rational function $P(x)/Q(x) \in F(x)$ whose series expansion has coefficients in K, and such that the coefficient of the term of lowest degree of Q is 1, both P and Q have coefficients in K.*

We use the following lemma.

Lemma 1.7. *Let m be a matrix in $F^{n\times n}$ which is quasi-integral over K. Then the coefficients of the characteristic polynomial of m are quasi-integral over K.*

Proof. Let $P(t)=t^n+a_1t^{n-1}+\ldots+a_n \in F[t]$ be the characteristic polynomial of m. Since m is quasi-integral over K, there exists, by Proposition 1.3, a finitely generated K-submodule of $F^{n\times n}$ containing all powers of m. Thus there exists some $d\in K-\{0\}$ such that

$$dm^k \in K^{n\times n}$$

for all $k\in \mathbf{N}$. Consequently, since $\pm a_i$ is a sum of products of i entries of m,

$$da_1,\ d^2a_2,\ \ldots,\ d^na_n \in K$$

Let λ be an eigenvalue of m. Then $d\lambda$ is integral over K. Indeed, $0=d^nP(\lambda) = (d\lambda)^n+da_1(d\lambda)^{n-1}+\ldots+d^na_n$. Consequently, the K-algebra $L=K[d\lambda]$ is a finitely generated K-module. The element λ is in the quotient field E of L, and there exists $q\in GL_n(E)$ such that

$$m'=q^{-1}mq=\begin{pmatrix} \lambda & * & . & . & * \\ 0 & * & . & . & * \\ . & . & . & . & . \\ . & . & . & . & . \\ 0 & * & . & . & * \end{pmatrix}.$$

Let d' be a common denominator of the coefficients of q and q^{-1}, i.e. such that $d'q$ and $d'q^{-1}$ have coefficients in L. Then for all $k\in\mathbf{N}$

$$(d'^2d)m'^k=(d'q^{-1})dm^k(d'q)\in L^{n\times n}$$

Thus $(d'^2d)\lambda^k\in L$, whence $K[\lambda]\subset(d'^2d)^{-1}L$. This shows that λ is quasi-integral over K.

Since all eigenvalues of m are quasi-integral, the same holds for the coefficients a_i by Corollary 1.5. □

Proof of Theorem 1.6. Assume that K is completely integrally closed. Let $P(x)/Q(x)$ be a function satisfying the hypotheses of (ii). One may assume that $Q(0)=1$. The series

$$S=\sum a_nx^n=P(x)/Q(x)$$

is F-rational and has coefficients in K. Let (λ, μ, γ) be a reduced linear representation of S. By Corollary II.2.3, the matrix $\mu(x)$ is quasi-integral over K. In view of Lemma 1.7, the characteristic polynomial of $\mu(x)$ has coefficients in K, and since Q is its reciprocal polynomial (Proposition IV.1.2), the polynomial Q has coefficients in K, and the same holds for $P=SQ$.

Assume conversely that (ii) holds. Let $m \in F$ be quasi-integral over K. Then there exists $d \in K-\{0\}$ such that

$$dm^n \in K$$

for all $n \in \mathbf{N}$. Set $P(x)=d$, $Q(x)=1-mx$. Then

$$P(x)/Q(x)=d\sum m^n x^n \in K[\![x]\!]$$

Thus $Q(x) \in K[x]$, whence $m \in K$. This shows that K is completely integrally closed. □

2 Positive Rational Series

In this section, we study series with nonnegative coefficients. We start with the following result.

Theorem 2.1 (Schützenberger 1970). *If $S \in \mathbf{N}\langle\langle X\rangle\rangle$ is an $\mathbf{N}$-rational series, then*

$$S-\underline{supp(S)} \in \mathbf{N}\langle\langle X\rangle\rangle \tag{2.1}$$

is $\mathbf{N}$-rational.

Recall that $\underline{L}$ is the characteristic series of the language L. Observe that the series (2.1) can also be written as

$$S \dot{-} 1$$

where

$$(S \dot{-} 1, w)=\begin{cases}(S,w)-1 & \text{if } (S,w) \geqq 1\\ 0 & \text{otherwise}.\end{cases}$$

Proof (Salomaa and Soittola 1978). In view of Proposition I.5.1, there exist rational series $S_1, \ldots, S_n$ such that the $\mathbf{N}$-submodule of $\mathbf{N}\langle\langle X\rangle\rangle$ they generate is stable and contains S. By Lemma III.1.4, the supports $supp(S_1), \ldots, supp(S_n)$ are rational languages. Let $\mathbf{L}$ be the family of languages obtained by taking all intersections of $supp(S_1), \ldots, supp(S_n)$. Then $\mathbf{L}$ is a finite set of rational languages. The set $\mathbf{L}'=\{u^{-1}L \mid u \in X^*, L \in \mathbf{L}\}$ is also a finite set of rational languages (Corollary III.1.6). Let $\mathbf{T}$ be the set of characteristic series of the languages in $\mathbf{L}'$.

Let M be the finitely generated $\mathbf{N}$-submodule of $\mathbf{N}\langle\langle X\rangle\rangle$ generated by $\mathbf{T}$ and by the series

$$S_i'=S_i-\underline{supp(S_i)}$$

for $i=1, \dots, n$. We claim that M is stable. Indeed, let $u \in X^*$. By construction, for all $T \in \mathbf{T}$, the series $u^{-1}T$ is still in $\mathbf{T}$. Next, for any $i=1, \dots, n$,

$$u^{-1}S_i' = u^{-1}S_i - \underline{supp(u^{-1}S_i)}$$

Moreover, there exist coefficients $a_j \in \mathbf{N}$ such that

$$u^{-1}S_i = \sum_j a_j S_j$$

whence

$$u^{-1}S_i = \sum a_j S_j' + T$$

where

$$T = \sum_j a_j \underline{supp(S_j)} \tag{2.2}$$

Thus

$$u^{-1}S_i' = \sum_j a_j S_j' + T - \underline{supp(u^{-1}S_i)} \tag{2.3}$$

Observe that

$$supp(T) = supp(u^{-1}S_i)$$

Consequently, in order to show that $u^{-1}S_i' \in M$, it suffices to prove, in view of Eq. (2.3), that the series $T - \underline{supp(T)}$ is in M. The definition (2.2) of T can be rewritten as

$$T = \sum_{k=1}^{h} b_k T_k$$

where each integer $b_k \geqq 1$, and $T_k \in \mathbf{T}$ have disjoint supports. This is done by keeping only the a_j's greater than 0, by making the necessary intersections of supports. Consequently

$$T - \underline{supp(T)} = \sum_{k=1}^{h} (b_k - 1) T_k$$

is in M. Thus M is stable.

In order to prove that $S - \underline{supp(S)}$ is in M, it suffices to write S as a linear combination of the S_i and to proceed as above. In view of Proposition I.5.1, the series $S - \underline{supp(S)}$ is rational. □

We now consider series of the form

$$\sum a_n x^n$$

with all coefficients in $\mathbf{R}_+$. If such a series is the expansion of a rational function, it does not imply in general that it is $\mathbf{R}_+$-rational (see Exercise 2.2). We shall characterize those rational functions over **R** whose series expansion is $\mathbf{R}_+$-rational. We call them $\mathbf{R}_+$-*rational functions.*

Theorem 2.2 (Berstel 1971). *Let $f(x)$ be an $\mathbf{R}_+$-rational function which is not a polynomial, and let ϱ be the minimum of the moduli of its poles. Then ϱ is a pole of f, and any pole of f of modulus ϱ has the form $\varrho\theta$, where θ is a root of unity.*

Observe that the minimum of the moduli of the poles of a rational function is just the radius of convergence of the associated series. We start with a lemma.

Lemma 2.3. *Let $f(x)$ be a rational function which is not a polynomial and with a series expansion $\sum a_n x^n$ having nonnegative coefficients. Let ϱ be the minimum of the moduli of the poles of f. Then ϱ is a pole of f, and the multiplicity of any pole of f of modulus ϱ is at most that of ϱ.*

Proof. Let $z \in \mathbf{C}$, $|z| < \varrho$. Then

$$|f(z)| = |\sum a_n z^n| \leqq \sum a_n |z|^n = f(|z|) \tag{2.4}$$

Let z_0 be a pole of modulus ϱ, and let n be its multiplicity. Assume that the multiplicity of ϱ as a pole of f is less than n. Then the function

$$g(z) = (\varrho - z)^n f(z)$$

is analytic in the neighborhood of ϱ, and $g(\varrho) = 0$, whence

$$\lim_{r \to 1,\ r < 1} (\varrho - \varrho r)^n f(\varrho r) = 0 \tag{2.5}$$

The function

$$h(z) = (z_0 - z)^n f(z)$$

is analytic at z_0 and $h(z_0) \neq 0$. Thus

$$\lim_{z \to z_0,\ |z| < \varrho} |(z_0 - z)^n f(z)| > 0$$

In particular, setting $z = r z_0$, with $r \in [0, 1[$, this implies

$$\lim_{r \to 1,\ r < 1} |z_0^n (1 - r)^n f(r z_0)| > 0$$

In view of Eq. (2.4), this shows that

$$\lim_{r \to 1,\ r < 1} \varrho^n (1 - r)^n f(r\varrho) > 0$$

contradicting (2.5). □

Proof of Theorem 2.2. Let **S** be the set of polynomials with nonnegative coefficients and of rational functions with series expansions having nonnegative coefficients and satisfying the conclusions of the statement. It suffices to show that **S** is closed for sum, product and star. Recall that the star operation is

$$f \mapsto f^* = \sum_{n \geq 0} f^n = (1-f)^{-1}$$

Let $f = \sum a_n x^n$ and g be in **S**. Let ϱ_f be the radius of convergence of f. Recall that $\varrho_f = sup\{r \in \mathbf{R}_+ | \sum a_n r^n < \infty\}$. Since the associated series has nonnegative coefficients,

$$\varrho_{f+g} = \inf(\varrho_f, \varrho_g)$$

and, if $f, g \neq 0$,

$$\varrho_{fg} = \inf(\varrho_f, \varrho_g)$$

Thus, according to Lemma 2.3, $f+g$ and fg are in **S**, since each pole of $f+g$ and of fg is a pole of f or g.

Now let $f(x) = \sum_{n \geq 1} a_n x^n \in \mathbf{S}$, and assume $f \neq 0$. The poles of $f^* = (1-f)^{-1}$ are the zeros of $1-f$. Observe that $\sum a_n \varrho_f^n = \infty$ since otherwise $\lim_{r \to \varrho_f} f(r)$ would exist (Abel's lemma) and this is impossible because f has a pole in ϱ_f. The coefficients a_n being nonnegative, the function $r \mapsto \sum a_n r^n$ is strictly increasing from 0 to ∞ when r ranges from 0 to ϱ_f, and consequently there is a unique real number r with $0 < r < \varrho_f$ such that $f(r) = 1$. Thus r is a pole of f^*. Let z be a pole of f^* of modulus $\leqq r$. We prove that $z = r\theta$ for some root of unity θ. Indeed, the relations

$$1 = \sum a_n z^n = Re\left(\sum a_n z^n\right) = \sum a_n Re(z^n)$$

$$\leqq \sum a_n |z|^n \leqq \sum a_n r^n = 1$$

show that equality holds everywhere, whence $a_n Re(z^n) = a_n r^n$ for all $n \geqq 0$. Let n be an integer with $a_n \neq 0$ (it exists because $f \neq 0$). Then $Re(z^n) = r^n$ and $|z| \leqq r$ imply $z^n = r^n$ whence $z = r\theta$ for θ a nth root of unity. Thus f^* is in **S**. □

The previous theorem gives a necessary condition for a rational function to be $\mathbf{R}_+$-rational. We now give a sufficient condition. For this, we go back to the vocabulary of formal series.

A rational series with complex coefficients is said to have a *dominating root* if there exists, among its roots (in the sense of Sect. IV.1) a unique root having maximal modulus. It is equivalent to say that the associated rational function is either a polynomial or has a unique pole of minimal modulus.

Theorem 2.4 (Katayama et al. 1978; Soittola 1976). *Let $S \in \mathbf{R}[\![x]\!]$ be a rational series with nonnegative coefficients and having a dominating root. Then S is $\mathbf{R}_+$-rational.*

We shall use several lemmas.

Lemma 2.5. *Let K be a semiring and let $S=\sum a_n x^n \in K[\![x]\!]$ be a series.*
(i) *The series S is rational if and only if there exists an integer $k \geqq 0$ such that $T=\sum_{n\geqq k} a_n x^n$ is rational. Moreover, if $K=\mathbf{C}$, then S and T have the same nonzero roots with the same multiplicities.*
(ii) *The series S is rational if and only if there exist rational series $S_0, S_1, \ldots, S_{p-1} K[\![x]\!]$ whose merge is S.*

Proof. (i) Let $T=\sum_{n\geqq k} a_n x^n$. Then $S=P+T$ where P is a polynomial. Thus if T is rational, then S is rational. Conversely, T is rational as Hadamard product of S and of $x^k x^*$. The last assertion is obvious, because $S-T$ is a polynomial and therefore S and T have the same minimal denominator.

(ii) Let $S_i=\sum a_{i+np} x^n$. If S is rational and has a linear representation (λ, μ, γ), then S_i has a linear representation $(\lambda(\mu x)^i, \mu', \gamma)$, with $\mu'(x)=\mu(x)^p$. Thus each S_i is rational. To show the converse, observe first that

$$S_i'=\sum_n a_{i+np} x^{np}$$

is rational as image under the morphism $x \mapsto x^p$ (Proposition I.4.2). Thus the sum of products

$$S=\sum_{i=0}^{p-1} x^i S_i'$$

is rational. □

Lemma 2.6. *Let S be a rational series having the root $\lambda_0 \neq 0$ with multiplicity $d+1 \geqq 2$, and let R be a polynomial having the simple root $\dfrac{1}{\lambda_0}$ and $T=RS$. Then T has the root λ_0 at multiplicity d. More precisely, if $S=\sum a_n x^n$, $T=\sum b_n x^n$ with exponential polynomials*

$$a_n=\sum_{0\leqq i\leqq r} P_i(n)\lambda_i^n, \qquad b_n=\sum_{0\leqq i\leqq r} Q_i(n)\lambda_i^n \tag{2.6}$$

(n large enough), where $\deg(P_0)=d$, $\deg(Q_0)=d-1$ and α is the coefficient of t^d in $P_0(t)$, then the coefficient β of t^{d-1} in $Q_0(t)$ is

$$d\alpha\left(\frac{\alpha_1}{\lambda_0}+2\frac{\alpha_2}{\lambda_0^2}+\ldots+k\frac{\alpha_k}{\lambda_0^k}\right) \neq 0$$

with $R=1-\alpha_1 x-\ldots-\alpha_k x^k$.

Proof. Recall that the nonzero roots of a rational series are the inverses of its poles, with the same multiplicities (see Sect. IV.1). Thus the first assertion follows.

Now, for n large enough, one has

$$b_n=a_n-\alpha_1 a_{n-1}-\ldots-\alpha_k a_{n-k}=\sum_{i=0}^{r} P_i(n)\lambda_i^n-\sum_{j=1}^{k}\alpha_j\sum_{i=0}^{r} P_i(n-j)\lambda_i^{n-j} \tag{2.7}$$

In order to compute β, note that

$$n^q\lambda^n - \alpha_1(n-1)^q\lambda^{n-1} - \ldots - \alpha_k(n-k)^q\lambda^{n-k}$$

$$= n^q\lambda^n\left(1 - \frac{\alpha_1}{\lambda} - \ldots - \frac{\alpha_k}{\lambda^k}\right) + qn^{q-1}\lambda^n\left(\frac{\alpha_1}{\lambda} + \ldots + k\frac{\alpha_k}{\lambda^k}\right) + Q(n)\lambda^n \qquad (2.8)$$

where $Q(n)$ is some polynomial of degree $\leqq q-2$ in n.

Note that if $1/\lambda$ is a root of R, then the first term on the right-hand side of (2.8) vanishes, which easily implies the lemma. □

Definition. Let $\lambda_0, \ldots, \lambda_r$ be the roots of a rational series S. The root λ_0 is *strictly dominating* if $\lambda_0 \in \mathbf{R}$, $\lambda_0 > 1$ and $|\lambda_0\lambda_i| < 1$ for $i = 1, \ldots, r$.

Lemma 2.7. *Let $S = \sum a_n x^n$ be a rational series with nonnegative coefficients which is not a polynomial and which has a dominating root. Then for some real number $s > 0$, the series $\sum \frac{a_n}{s^n} x^n$ has a strictly dominating root.*

Proof. Since S has a dominating root, one has, for large enough n,

$$a_n = P(n)\lambda^n + \sum_{i=1}^{r} P_i(n)\lambda_i^n$$

with $|\lambda| > |\lambda_i|$ for $i = 1, \ldots, r$ and polynomials $P, P_1, \ldots, P_r$. If a is the leading coefficient of P, then for $n \to \infty$

$$a_n \sim a n^d \lambda^n$$

with $d = deg(P)$. Thus $a > 0$ and λ is real, $\lambda > 0$.

Set $\lambda_0 = \lambda$. Let $s' > 0$ be a real number with $\lambda > s' > \lambda_i$ for $i = 1, \ldots, r$, and set $\lambda_i' = \lambda_i/s'$. Then of course $\lambda_0' > 1 > |\lambda_i'|$. Next, let s'' be such that

$$1 < s'' < \lambda_0' < s''^2$$

Setting $\lambda_i'' = \lambda_i'/s''$, it follows that

$$|\lambda_0''\lambda_i''| = \frac{|\lambda_0'\lambda_i'|}{s''^2} < \frac{\lambda_0'}{s''^2} < 1$$

and $\lambda_0'' > 1$. Thus the number $s = s's''$ gives the desired result. □

Lemma 2.8. *Let $S = \sum a_n x^n \in \mathbf{R}_+[\![x]\!]$ be a rational series having a strictly dominating root. Then for large enough n*

$$a_{n+1} > a_n \qquad (2.9)$$

Proof. For large enough n, one has

$$a_n = P(n)\lambda^n + \sum_{i=1}^{r} P_i(n)\lambda_i^n \tag{2.10}$$

with $\lambda \in \mathbf{R}$, $\lambda > 1$ and $|\lambda\lambda_i| < 1$, hence also $|\lambda_i| < \frac{1}{\lambda} < 1 < \lambda$. This shows that

$$a_n \underset{n\to\infty}{\sim} \alpha n^d \lambda^n$$

where d is the degree of P and α the coefficient of t^d in $P(t)$. This implies that

$$\frac{a_{n+1}}{a_n} \underset{n\to\infty}{\sim} \lambda$$

Since $\lambda > 1$ and $a_n \in \mathbf{R}_+$, this shows that $a_{n+1} > a_n$ for large enough n. □

Lemma 2.9. *Let U be a rational series having a strictly dominating root with multiplicity m. Then there exists an integer p such that U is the merge of p rational series such that if $S = \sum a_n x^n$ is any one of them, then*

(i) *S has a dominating root λ with multiplicity m.*
(ii) *There exists a polynomial $R = 1 - \alpha_1 x - \ldots - \alpha_k x^k$ in $\mathbf{R}[x]$ which has the simple root $1/\lambda$ and such that*

$$\alpha_1 > 1,\ \alpha_1 + \alpha_2 > 1,\ \ldots,\ \alpha_1 + \ldots + \alpha_k > 1 \tag{2.11}$$

$$\frac{\alpha_1}{\lambda} + \frac{2\alpha_2}{\lambda^2} + \ldots + \frac{k\alpha_k}{\lambda^k} > 0$$

Moreover, if $m = 1$, then R is a denominator for S.

Proof 1. Let $\lambda_0, \ldots, \lambda_r$ be the distinct nonzero roots of U. Then for large enough n

$$u_n = \sum_{0 \le i \le r} \lambda_i^n P_i(n)$$

where $U = \sum u_n x^n$, $P_i(t) \in \mathbf{C}[t] \setminus 0$ and, by hypothesis,

$$\lambda_0 \in \mathbf{R},\ \lambda_0 > 1,\ \lambda_0 |\lambda_i| < 1 \quad \text{for } i = 1, \ldots, r$$

2. Define a polynomial R as follows: if λ_0 is a simple root of U, then R is the minimal denominator of U, otherwise, let R be a divisor of the minimal denominator of U in $\mathbf{R}[x]$ such that R has the simple root $1/\lambda_0$.

3. Let $R^{(p)} = 1 - \alpha_1^{(p)} x - \ldots - \alpha_k^{(p)} x^k$ be the polynomial whose roots are the p-th powers of those of R, with the same multiplicities. We show that for some p, we have Eq. (2.11) (with α_i replaced by $\alpha_i^{(p)}$).

Let $\lambda_0=\mu_0, \ldots, \mu_k$ be the inverses of the roots of R. Then, by assumption,

$$\mu_0>1>\mu_0|\mu_i| \quad \text{for } i=1, \ldots, k$$

Let $\sigma_i^{(p)}$ be the ith elementary symmetric function of the μ_i^p's. Then

$$\sigma_1^{(p)}=\mu_0^p+\ldots+\mu_k^p>\mu_0^p-k$$

and for $i=2, \ldots, k$

$$\sigma_i^{(p)}=\sum_{0\leqq j_1<\ldots<j_i\leqq k} \mu_{j_1}^p\mu_{j_2}^p\ldots\mu_{j_i}^p<\binom{k+1}{i}$$

since each monomial has modulus less than 1. Thus, for large enough p, $\sigma_1^{(p)}>1$ and $\sigma_1^{(p)}\pm\sigma_i^{(p)}>1$ for $i=2,\ldots,k$. Now, observe that $\alpha_1^{(p)}=\sigma_1^{(p)}$, and $\alpha_i^{(p)}=\pm\sigma_i^{(p)}$ for $i=2,\ldots,k$. Hence

$$\alpha_1^{(p)}>1,\ \alpha_1^{(p)}+\alpha_2^{(p)}>1,\ \ldots,\ \alpha_1^{(p)}+\ldots+\alpha_k^{(p)}>1$$

Moreover, since $\alpha_1^{(p)}=\sigma_1^{(p)}$ is equivalent to μ_0^p, $\mu_0>1$ and the $\alpha_i^{(p)}\,(i=1, \ldots, k)$ are bounded, we obtain, for large enough p,

$$\frac{\alpha_1^{(p)}}{\mu_0^p}+2\frac{\alpha_2^{(p)}}{\mu_0^{2p}}+\ldots+k\frac{\alpha_k^{(p)}}{\mu_0^{kp}}>0$$

4. Let p be as in 3, and define S_j by

$$S_j=\sum_n u_{j+np}x^n$$

Then U is the merge of $S_0, \ldots, S_{p-1}$. We have for large enough n

$$u_{j+np}=\sum_{0\leqq i\leqq r}(\lambda_i^p)^n\lambda_i^jP_i(j+np) \tag{2.12}$$

This shows that the roots of S_j are among $\lambda_0^p, \ldots, \lambda_r^p$ (by unicity of the exponential polynomial, see Corollary IV.2.2). Moreover, $\lambda_0^p\neq\lambda_i^p$ for $i=1,\ldots,k$, hence λ_0^p is a root of S_j, and hence S_j has the dominating root λ_0^p. Since the polynomials $P_0(t)$ and $P_0(j+nt)$ have the same degree, the multiplicity of λ_0^p for S_j is $m=deg(P_0)+1$. Now, it is clear that $R^{(p)}$ has the simple root $1/\mu_0^p=1/\lambda_0^p$, with multiplicity 1 (because $\lambda_0^p\neq\lambda_i^p$ if $i\neq 0$) and that the relations (2.11) hold.

If $m=1$, then R was chosen to be the minimal denominator of U, hence $R^{(p)}$ is a multiple of the minimal denominator of S_j. Indeed, by Eq. (2.12) and Corollary IV.2.2, each root of S_j is one of the λ_i^p, with multiplicity $\leqq deg(P_i)$. Now, $R(x)=\prod_i(1-\lambda_ix)^{deg(P_i)+1}$ (see Sect. IV.2), hence $R^{(p)}(x)=\prod_i(1-\lambda_i^px)^{deg(P_i)+1}$ by definition. □

Proof of Theorem 2.4. 1. We argue by induction on the multiplicity m of the dominating root λ of S. By Lemma 2.7 we may assume that S has a strictly dominating root. Hence, by Lemma 2.8 and Lemma 2.5 (i), we may assume that

$$a_{n+1} > a_n$$

for any n. Now, by Lemma 2.9 and Lemma 2.5 (ii), we may further assume that there exists a polynomial $R = 1 - \alpha_1 x - \ldots - \alpha_k x^k$ having $1/\lambda$ as a simple root, satisfying Eq. (2.11), and which is a denominator of S if $m = 1$.

2. Let $S = \dfrac{P}{Q} = \dfrac{T}{R}$, with $P, Q \in \mathbf{R}[x]$, $T \in \mathbf{R}[\![x]\!]$. The series $T = \sum b_n x^n$ is of course rational, and with the notation of Lemma 2.6, we obtain (λ_0 being dominating)

$$b_n \underset{n \to \infty}{\sim} d\alpha \left(\frac{\alpha_1}{\lambda_0} + \ldots + k \frac{\alpha_k}{\lambda_0^k} \right) \lambda_0^n$$

Since $a_n \geqq 0$, we must have $\alpha \geqq 0$, hence $b_n \geqq 0$ for large n.

Let $T^{[h]} = \sum_{n > h} b_n x^h$. If $m = 1$, then R is a denominator of S, hence $T^{[h]} = 0$ for large h. If $m \geqq 2$, then, as $1/\lambda_0$ is a simple root of R, λ_0 is a root of T and the other roots are among those of S. Hence T has a dominating root of multiplicity $m - 1$. The same holds for $T^{[h]}$. Thus, in both cases, $T^{[h]}$ is $\mathbf{R}_+$-rational by induction, for large h.

3. Before going into the technicalities of the proof, we consider, from a heuristic point of view, the case where $b_n \geqq 0$ for any n. Then T is $\mathbf{R}_+$-rational by induction and $S = T \dfrac{1}{R}$. Thus we only have to show that $\dfrac{1}{R}$ is $\mathbf{R}_+$-rational. Now $\dfrac{1}{R} = x^* \dfrac{1}{Rx^*}$ (where $x^* = \sum x^n = \dfrac{1}{1-x}$) and

$$Rx^* = (1 - \alpha_1 x - \ldots - \alpha_k x^k)(1 + x + x^2 + \ldots + x^n + \ldots)$$

$$= 1 + (1 - \alpha_1)x + (1 - \alpha_1 - \alpha_2)x^2 + \ldots + (1 - \alpha_1 - \ldots - \alpha_{k-1})x^{k-1}$$

$$+ (1 - \alpha_1 - \ldots - \alpha_k)(x^k + x^{k+1} + \ldots + x^n + \ldots)$$

$$= 1 - \gamma_1 x - \ldots - \gamma_{k-1} x^{k-1} - \gamma_k x^k x^*$$

where

$$\gamma_1 = \alpha_1 - 1$$

$$\gamma_2 = \alpha_2 + \alpha_1 - 1$$

$$\vdots$$

$$\gamma_k = \alpha_k + \ldots + \alpha_1 - 1$$

By Eq. (2.11), the γ's are nonnegative, so that $\frac{1}{Rx^*} = (\gamma_1 x + \ldots + \gamma_{k-1}x^{k-1} + \gamma_k x^k x^*)^*$ is $\mathbf{R}_+$-rational. Hence $\frac{1}{R}$ is also $\mathbf{R}_+$-rational, which concludes the proof in this special case.

4. There remains the problem of treating the case $h \geqq 0$. We may suppose $h \geqq k$. We show that for some polynomial R_h with nonnegative coefficients, one has

$$S^{[h]} = a_h \frac{x^{h+1}}{1-x} + \frac{1}{R}\left(T^{[h]} + \frac{\gamma_k a_h x^{h+k}}{1-x} + R_h\right) \tag{2.13}$$

where the γ's are defined by 3. Note that $T^{[h]}$ and $\frac{1}{R}$ are $\mathbf{R}_+$-rational (by 2 and 3), so $S^{[h]}$ is $\mathbf{R}_+$-rational. Thus

$$S = a_0 + \ldots + a_h x^h + S^{[h]}$$

is also $\mathbf{R}_+$-rational.

5. Let $C = \sum c_n x^n$ with

$$c_0 = a_0, \; c_n = a_n - a_{n-1} \; (n \geqq 1)$$

Of course

$$C = (1-x)S$$

and by a previous remark, C has nonnegative coefficients. As before, let

$$C^{[h]} = \sum_{n>h} c_n x^n$$

We shall see that

$$C^{[h]} = \frac{1-x}{R}\left(T^{[h]} + \gamma_k a_h \frac{x^{k+h}}{1-x} + R_h\right) \tag{2.14}$$

Since, as is easily verified

$$S^{[h]} = \frac{1}{1-x}\left(C^{[h]} + a_h x^{h+1}\right)$$

the formula (2.13) follows easily from Eq. (2.14).

6. Since $T = SR$, we have for $n > h$ (hence $n \geqq k$, because $h \geqq k$)

$$\begin{aligned} b_n &= a_n - \alpha_1 a_{n-1} - \ldots - \alpha_{k-1} a_{n-k+1} - \alpha_k a_{n-k} \\ &= a_n - (1+\gamma_1) a_{n-1} - \ldots - (\gamma_{k-1} - \gamma_{k-2}) a_{n-k-1} - (\gamma_k - \gamma_{k-1}) a_{n-k} \\ &= a_n - a_{n-1} - \gamma_1 (a_{n-1} - a_{n-2}) - \ldots - \gamma_{k-1}(a_{n-k+1} - a_{n-k}) - \gamma_k a_{n-k} \\ &= c_n - \gamma_1 c_{n-1} - \ldots - \gamma_{k-1} c_{n-k+1} - \gamma_k a_{n-k} \end{aligned}$$

This relation can be developed further, when $n \geq h+k$, since $a_p = c_p + a_{p-1}$. We obtain

$$b_n = c_n - \gamma_1 c_{n-1} - \dots - \gamma_{k-1} c_{n-k+1} - \gamma_k c_{n-k} - \gamma_k c_{n-k-1}$$
$$- \dots - \gamma_k c_{h+1} - \gamma_k a_h$$

Summing up these relations, we get

$$\sum_{n>h} b_n x^n = \left(\sum_{n>h} c_n x^n \right) (1 - \gamma_1 x - \dots - \gamma_k x^k - \gamma_k x^{k+1} - \dots) - \frac{\gamma_k a_h x^{h+k}}{1-x} - R_h$$

with

$$R_h = (\gamma_1 c_h + \gamma_2 c_{h-1} + \dots + \gamma_{k-1} c_{h-k+2} + \gamma_k a_{h-k+1}) x^{h+1}$$
$$+ (\gamma_2 c_h + \dots + \gamma_{k-1} c_{h-k+3} + \gamma_k a_{h-k+2}) x^{h+2}$$
$$+ \dots$$
$$+ (\gamma_{k-1} c_h + \gamma_k a_{h-1}) x^{h+k-1}$$

This polynomial has nonnegative coefficients. We have

$$T^{[h]} = C^{[h]} \left(1 - \gamma_1 x - \dots - \gamma_{k-1} x^{k-1} - \frac{\gamma_k x^k}{1-x} \right) - \gamma_k \frac{a_h x^{h+k}}{1-x} - R_h$$

Formula (2.14) follows immediately because

$$\frac{1-x}{R} = \left(1 - \gamma_1 x - \dots - \gamma_{k-1} x^{k-1} - \gamma_k \frac{x^k}{1-x} \right)^{-1}$$

(see 3). The proof of the theorem is complete. □

The two preceding theorems give the following characterization of $\mathbf{R}_+$-rational series.

Theorem 2.10. *A series $S \in \mathbf{R}_+[\![x]\!]$ is $\mathbf{R}_+$-rational if and only if it is a merge of rational series having a dominating root.*

Proof. Let S be a $\mathbf{R}_+$-rational series and let m be the number of its roots. We argue by induction on m, the case $m=1$ being clear. If $m>1$, then S is not a polynomial, since the only root of a polynomial is 0. Since the nonvanishing roots of S are the inverses of the poles of the associate function (see Sect. IV.2), there exists, by Theorem 2.2, a real number $\varrho > 0$ such that any root of S with maximal modulus has the form $\varrho\theta$, where θ is a root of unity. Let p be a common order of all these roots of unity and let $S_0, S_1, \dots, S_{p-1}$ be the series whose merge is S. By Lemma 2.5, each S_i is $\mathbf{R}_+$-rational and their roots are λ^p, with λ a root of S. Each S_i has strictly fewer roots than S, and is $\mathbf{R}_+$-rational. This concludes the proof of the direct part. For the converse, it suffices to use Theorem 2.4 and Lemma 2.5. □

3 Fatou Extensions

According to Fatou's Lemma (Corollary 1.2) any rational series in $\mathbf{Q}[\![x]\!]$ with integral coefficients is rational in $\mathbf{Z}[\![x]\!]$. The same result still holds for an arbitrary alphabet X, by Theorem 1.1. This leads to the following definition.

Definition. Let $K \subset L$ be two semirings. Then L is a *Fatou extension* of K if every L-rational series with coefficients in K is K-rational.

Theorem 3.1 (Fliess 1974a). *If $K \subset L$ are commutative fields, then L is a Fatou extension of K.*

Proof. This follows immediately from the expression of rationality by means of the rank of the Hankel matrix (Theorem II.1.5). □

Theorem 3.2. *Let K be a commutative Noetherian integral domain, and let F be its quotient field. Then F is a Fatou extension of K.*

Proof. Let S be an F-rational series with coefficients in K and let (λ, μ, γ) be a reduced linear representation of S. According to Corollary II.2.3, there exists $d \in K \backslash 0$ such that

$$d\mu X^* \subset K^{n \times n}$$

Consequently, the algebra $\mu(K\langle X\rangle)$ is contained in $d^{-1}K^{n\times n}$, which is a Noetherian K-module. It follows that $\mu(K\langle X\rangle)$ is a finitely generated K-module and this in turn shows that the syntactic algebra of S over K (which is equal to $\mu(K\langle X\rangle)$) is a finitely generated K-module. By Theorem II.1.1, the series S is rational. □

Theorem 3.3 (Fliess 1975). *The semiring $\mathbf{Q}_+$ is a Fatou extension of $\mathbf{N}$.*

We need some preliminary lemmas.

Lemma 3.4 (Eilenberg and Schützenberger 1969). *The intersection of two finitely generated submonoids of an abelian group is still a finitely generated monoid.*

Proof. Let M_1 and M_2 be two finitely generated submonoids of an abelian group G, with law denoted by $+$. There exist integers k_1, k_2 and surjective monoid morphisms φ_i: $\mathbf{N}^{k_i} \to M_i$, $i=1, 2$. Let $k=k_1+k_2$ and let S be the submonoid of $\mathbf{N}^k = \mathbf{N}^{k_1} \times \mathbf{N}^{k_2}$ defined by

$$S = \{x = (x_1, x_2) \in \mathbf{N}^k \mid \varphi_1 x_1 = \varphi_2 x_2\}$$

Let p_1: $\mathbf{N}^k \to \mathbf{N}^{k_1}$ be the projection. Then

$$M_1 \cap M_2 = \varphi_1 \circ p_1(S)$$

Thus, it suffices to prove that S is finitely generated. Observe that S satisfies the following condition

$$x,\ x+y\in S \Rightarrow y\in S \tag{3.1}$$

Indeed, since $\varphi_1 x_1=\varphi_2 x_2$ and $\varphi_1 x_1+\varphi_1 y_1=\varphi_2 x_2+\varphi_2 y_2$ and since all these elements are in G, it follows that $\varphi_1 y_1=\varphi_2 y_2$, whence $y\in S$.

Let A be the set of minimal elements of S (for the natural ordering of $\mathbf{N}^k$). For all $z\in S$, there is $x\in A$ such that $x\leqq z$. Thus $z=x+y$ for some $y\in\mathbf{N}^k$, and by Eq. (3.1), $y\in S$. This shows by induction that A generates S. In view of the following well-known lemma, the set A is finite. □

Lemma 3.5. *Every infinite sequence in* $\mathbf{N}^k$ *contains an infinite increasing subsequence.*

Proof. By induction on k. Let (u_n) be a sequence of elements of $\mathbf{N}^k$. If $k=1$, either the sequence is bounded, and one can extract a constant sequence, or it is unbounded, and one can extract a strictly increasing subsequence. For $k>1$, one first extracts a sequence that is increasing in the first coordinate, and then uses induction for this subsequence. □

Lemma 3.6 (Eilenberg and Schützenberger 1969). *Let I be a set and let M be a finitely generated submonoid of* $\mathbf{N}^I$. *Then the submonoid M' of* $\mathbf{N}^I$ *given by*

$$M'=\{x\in\mathbf{N}^I \mid \exists n\geqq 1,\ nx\in M\}$$

is finitely generated.

Proof. Let $x_1, \ldots, x_p$ be generators of M. Let

$$C=\{x\in\mathbf{N}^I \mid \exists\lambda_1,\ldots,\lambda_p\in\mathbf{Q}_+\cap[0,1]:\ x=\textstyle\sum\lambda_i x_i\}$$

Then $C\cup\{x_1,\ldots,x_p\}$ is a set of generators for M'. Indeed, if $nx=\sum\lambda_i x_i\in M$ for some $n\geqq 1$, then

$$x=\sum\left\lfloor\frac{\lambda_i}{n}\right\rfloor x_i+\sum\left(\frac{\lambda_i}{n}-\left\lfloor\frac{\lambda_i}{n}\right\rfloor\right)x_i,$$

where $\lfloor a\rfloor$ is the integral part of a. Thus, it suffices to show that C is finite.

Let E be the subvector space of $\mathbf{R}^I$ generated by M'. Since E has finite dimension, there exists a finite subset J of I such that the $\mathbf{R}$-linear function

$$p_J\colon E\to\mathbf{R}^J$$

(p_J is the projection $\mathbf{R}^I\to\mathbf{R}^J$) is injective. The image of C by p_J is contained in $\mathbf{N}^J$, and it is also contained in the set

$$K=\{y\in\mathbf{R}^J \mid \exists\lambda_1,\ldots,\lambda_p\in[0,1]:\ y=\textstyle\sum\lambda_i y_i\}$$

where $y_i = p_J(x_i)$. Now K is compact and $\mathbf{N}^J$ is discrete and closed. Thus $K \cap \mathbf{N}^J$ is finite. It follows that C is finite. □

Proof of Theorem 3.3. Let S be a $\mathbf{Q}_+$-rational series with coefficients in $\mathbf{N}$. We use systematically Proposition I.5.1. There exists a finitely generated stable $\mathbf{Q}_+$-submodule in $\mathbf{Q}_+\langle\langle X\rangle\rangle$ that contains S. Denote it by $M_{\mathbf{Q}_+}$. Similarly, the series S is $\mathbf{Q}$-rational with coefficients in $\mathbf{Z}$, and therefore S is $\mathbf{Z}$-rational. Thus, there is a finitely generated stable $\mathbf{Z}$-submodule in $\mathbf{Z}\langle\langle X\rangle\rangle$ that contains S, say $M_{\mathbf{Z}}$. Then $M = M_{\mathbf{Q}_+} \cap M_{\mathbf{Z}}$ is a stable $\mathbf{N}$-submodule of $\mathbf{N}\langle\langle X\rangle\rangle$ containing S, and it suffices to show that M is finitely generated.

Let $T_1, \ldots, T_r$ be series in $M_{\mathbf{Q}_+}$ generating it as a $\mathbf{Q}_+$-module, and let

$$M'_{\mathbf{Q}_+} = \sum \mathbf{N} T_i$$

This is a finitely generated $\mathbf{N}$-module. Since $M_{\mathbf{Z}}$ is also a finitely generated $\mathbf{N}$-module, the $\mathbf{N}$-module

$$M' = M_{\mathbf{Z}} \cap M'_{\mathbf{Q}_+} \subset \mathbf{N}\langle\langle X\rangle\rangle$$

is finitely generated (this is Lemma 3.4, noting that $\mathbf{N}$-module = commutative monoid). Consequently

$$\bar{M} = \{T \in \mathbf{N}\langle\langle X\rangle\rangle \mid n \geq 1,\ nT \in M'\}$$

is, in view of Lemma 3.6, a finitely generated $\mathbf{N}$-module. Finally the $\mathbf{N}$-module $\bar{M} \cap M_{\mathbf{Z}}$ is finitely generated, by Lemma 3.4. Since

$$M = \bar{M} \cap M_{\mathbf{Z}}$$

this proves the theorem. □

We now give two examples of extensions which are not Fatou extensions.

1. The ring $\mathbf{Z}$ is not a Fatou extension of $\mathbf{N}$.

Consider the series

$$S = \sum_{w \in \{x,\, y\}^*} (|w|_x - |w|_y)^2 w$$

This series is $\mathbf{Z}$-rational (it is the Hadamard square of the series considered in Example III.3.1) and has coefficients in $\mathbf{N}$. However, it is not $\mathbf{N}$-rational, since otherwise its support would be a rational language (Sect. III.1), and also the complement of its support. In Example III.3.1, it was shown that this set is not the support of any rational series.

2. The semiring $\mathbf{R}_+$ is not a Fatou extension of $\mathbf{Q}_+$ (Reutenauer 1977a).

Let $\alpha = \frac{1}{2}(1+\sqrt{5})$ be the golden ratio and let S be the series

$$S = \sum_{w \in \{x,\, y\}^*} \left(\alpha^{2(|w|_x - |w|_y)} + \alpha^{-2(|w|_x - |w|_y)}\right) w$$

Since $S=(\alpha^2x+\alpha^{-2}y)^*+(\alpha^{-2}x+\alpha^2y)^*$, the series S is $\mathbf{R}_+$-rational. Moreover, since α is an algebraic integer over $\mathbf{Z}$ and $-\frac{1}{\alpha}$ is its conjugate, for all $n\in\mathbf{N}$

$$\alpha^{2n}+\alpha^{-2n}\in\mathbf{Z}$$

Consequently, S has coefficients in $\mathbf{N}$. Assume that S is $\mathbf{Q}_+$-rational. Then by Theorem 3.3, it is $\mathbf{N}$-rational. However, the languages $S^{-1}(2)=\{w\mid(S,w)=2\}$ is

$$S^{-1}(2)=\{w\in\{x,y\}^*\mid |w|_x=|w|_y\}$$

since $a+\frac{1}{a}>2$ for all $a>0, a\neq 1$. Since the language $S^{-1}(2)$ is not rational, the series S is not $\mathbf{N}$-rational (Corollary III.2.5). Thus S is not $\mathbf{Q}_+$-rational.

Exercises for Chapter V

2.1. a) Let $P(x)=x^k-\alpha_1x^{k-1}-\ldots-\alpha_k$ $(\alpha_k\neq 0)$ be a polynomial with integral coefficients, and suppose that all its roots have modulus $\leqq 1$. Show that these roots are roots of unity. (Consider the series $S=\sum a_nx^n$ with

$$a_n=\lambda_1^n+\ldots+\lambda_k^n$$

where the λ_i's are the roots of P with their multiplicities. The minimal polynomial Q of S has the same roots as P, but with multiplicity 1. The sequence (a_n) takes only a finite number of distinct values, and thus Q has a multiple of the form x^p-x^q.)

b) Let $S=\sum a_nx^n$ be a rational series with coefficients in $\mathbf{Z}$, and with *polynomial growth* (i.e. there exist a constant C and an integer q such that $|a_n|\leqq Cn^q$ for all $n\geqq 1$). Show that there exist an integer p, and polynomials $P_i\in\mathbf{Q}[t]$ for $0\leqq i\leqq p-1$, such that for all $i\in\{0,\ldots,p-1\}$

$$a_{i+np}=P_i(n)$$

for all but a finite number of n.

c) Show that if a polynomial $P\in\mathbf{Q}[t]$ satisfies

$$P(n)\in\mathbf{Z}\quad\text{for } n\in\mathbf{N}$$

then P is a linear combination with integral coefficients, of polynomials $\binom{t}{q}=\frac{t(t-1)\ldots t-q+1}{q!}$. Show that if moreover $P(n)\in\mathbf{N}$ for all $n\in\mathbf{N}$, then the series $\sum P(n)x^n$ is $\mathbf{N}$-rational.

d) Use the previous questions to show that any $\mathbf{Z}$-rational series in one variable with nonnegative coefficients and with polynomial growth is $\mathbf{N}$-rational.

(See Pólya, Szegö 1964, Exercise 200 in Chapter 4 and Exercise 85 in Chapter 2.)

2.2. a) Let Θ be a real number. Show that the series $S = \sum_{n \geq 0} (\cos^2 n\Theta) x^n$ is a $\mathbf{C}$-rational series. (Give an expression for S as a rational function by using the formula $\cos n\Theta = 1/2(e^{in\Theta} + e^{-in\Theta})$.) Show that the poles of the rational function are $1, e^{2i\Theta}, e^{2i\Theta}$.

b) Let $0 < a < c$ be integers and let Θ be a real number with $0 < \Theta < \pi/2$, such that $\cos \Theta = a/c$. Show that the numbers $c^n \cos n\Theta$ are integers. Show that the series $T = \sum (c^{2n} \cos^2 n\Theta) x^n$ is $\mathbf{Z}$-rational with coefficients in $\mathbf{N}$.

c) Show that if $c \neq 2a$, then $z = e^{i\Theta}$ is not a root of unity (use the fact that z is an algebraic number of degree $\leqq 2$, and that the assumption that z is a root of unity of order p implies that $\varphi(p) \leqq 2$, where φ is Euler's function). Show that T is not $\mathbf{R}_+$-rational (use Theorem 2.4) (see Berstel 1971, and also Eilenberg 1974).

3.1. Show that for any rational series $S \in K\langle\langle X \rangle\rangle$ where K is a commutative field, the field generated by its coefficients is a finitely generated field.

Notes to Chapter V

Fliess (1974a) calls a *strong Fatou ring* a ring K satisfying Theorem 1.1. Sontag and Rouchaleau (1977) show that for a principal ring K, the ring $K[t]$ is a strong Fatou ring. In the case of one variable, the class of strong Fatou rings is completely characterized by Theorem 1.6. (The formulation is different, but is equivalent by the results of Sect. IV.1.) For several variables, a complete characterization of strong Fatou rings is still lacking.

A slightly different proof of Theorem 2.4 (which makes no use of Lemma 2.7) shows that if $S = \sum a_n x^n$ is a rational series with nonnegative coefficients in a subfield K of $\mathbf{R}$, then S is K_+-rational. Thus Theorem 2.10 and Theorem 3.3 give a complete characterization of $\mathbf{N}$-rational series. The proof also shows that any $\mathbf{R}_+$-rational series has *star-height* at most 2 (over $\mathbf{R}_+$). The star-height of a rational series $S \in K\langle\langle X \rangle\rangle$ is defined as follows. Consider the sequence

$$R_0 \subset R_1 \subset \ldots \subset R_n \subset \ldots$$

of sets of series, such that the union of the R_n is the set of all rational series. The set R_0 is the set of polynomials, and for $S, T \in R_i$, both $S + T$ and ST are in R_i; if $S \in R_i$ is proper, then $S^* \in R_{i+1}$. The star-height of a series S is the least integer n with $S \in R_n$.

The *weak Fatou rings* (i.e. the rings whose quotient fields are a Fatou extension) are completely characterized in Reutenauer (1980a). These rings have a property which is analogous to the case of one variable, as shown by Cahen and Chabert (1975).

J. Karhumäki (1977) has characterized those polynomials $P \in \mathbf{Z}[x_1, \ldots, x_n]$ such that the rational series over $X = \{x_1, \ldots, x_n\}$

$$\sum_{w \in X^*} P(|w|_{x_1}, \ldots, |w|_{x_n}) w$$

is $\mathbf{N}$-rational.

Chapter VI

Decidability

Basically, any operation or property of series can be examined from the aspect of effectivity. In this chapter, we present the positive result, i.e. those concerning decidable properties, and we limit ourselves to the most striking ones.

The first section shows that the most fundamental properties concerning supports (emptiness, finiteness) are decidable. However, most of the other standard questions, such as equality of supports, are undecidable.

In the second section, we show first that the size of a finite semigroup of matrices can be bounded (Theorem 2.1). This implies that finiteness is decidable for a matrix semigroup. As a consequence, one can decide whether the image of a rational series is finite. To complete the chapter, series with polynomial growth are studied. A beautiful characterization (Corollary 2.11) is given, and this property is shown to be decidable.

1 Problems of Supports

We start by showing that several problems concerning the support of rational series are decidable. An instance of these problems is a language $L = supp(S)$, where S is a rational series given either by a linear representation (λ, μ, γ) or by a rational expression. The proof of Schützenberger's Theorem I.6.1 shows indeed that a linear representation of a rational series can be effectively computed from one of its rational expressions, and conversely, that a rational expression denoting a recognizable series can be derived from a linear representation.

Here we assume that the semiring of coefficients is the field **Q** (any other "computable" field is also convenient).

Proposition 1.1. *It is decidable whether the support of a rational series is empty.*

Proof. This proposition is just a restatement of Corollary II.3.6. Indeed, if $L = supp(S)$, with S a rational series given by a linear representation of dimension n, then the rank of S is less than or equal to n. By the corollary, the series S vanishes if and only if $(S, w) = 0$ for all words w of length at most $n-1$. This condition is easy to test. Finally, it suffices to note the equivalence

$$L = \emptyset \Leftrightarrow S = 0$$ □

Remark. An analogous proof shows that the equality of two rational series is decidable. It suffices to test whether their difference vanishes.

Proposition 1.2. *It is decidable whether the support of a rational series is finite.*

Proof. Let $L = supp(S)$. Then L is finite if and only if S is a polynomial.

We prove that given a reduced linear representation (λ, μ, γ) of S of dimension $n = rank(S)$, the series S is a polynomial if and only if $\mu w = 0$ for all words w of length n. This will prove the proposition since a reduced linear representation is effectively computable as shown in Sect. II.3.

Assume first that $\mu w = 0$ for all words w of length n. Then the same relation holds for any word w of length $\geqq n$. Consequently $(S, w) = \lambda \mu w \gamma = 0$ for all these words, showing that S is a polynomial of degree $\leqq n-1$.

Conversely, assume that S is a polynomial of degree d, and let $w \in supp(S)$ be a word of length d. For any left factor u of w, of length i, the polynomial $u^{-1}S$ (see Sect. II.1) has degree $d-i$. Indeed, $w = uv$ for some word v with $|v| = d-i$, and $(u^{-1}S, v) = (S, uv) = (S, w) \neq 0$, showing that the degree of $u^{-1}S$ is at least $d-i$. Moreover, if a word t has length $> d-i$, then $(u^{-1}S, t) = (S, ut) = 0$, since $|ut| > d$. This shows that $u^{-1}S$ has degree $d-i$.

It follows that the $d+1$ polynomials of the form $u^{-1}S$, where u runs through the left factors of w, are linearly independent. Consequently $dim(S \circ \mathbf{Q}\langle X \rangle) \geqq d+1$. This dimension is precisely the rank n of the series, by Theorem II.1.5 and Corollary II.1.4. Thus $n \geqq d+1$.

Consider now a word w of length n. Since $|w| > d$, one has $(S, uwv) = 0$ for all words u, v. Consequently the ideal of $\mathbf{Q}\langle X \rangle$ generated by w is contained in $Ker\, S$, and therefore is contained in the syntactic ideal I of S. In particular, $w \in I$. Since $I = Ker\, \mu$ by Corollary II.2.2, it follows that $\mu w = 0$. □

We now consider an *undecidable* problem: *It is undecidable whether the support of a rational series is the whole free monoid* X^*. Indeed, setting $L = supp(S)$, one has the equivalence

$$L \neq X^* \Leftrightarrow (S, w) = 0 \quad \text{for some } w \in X^*$$

The claim then follows from the undecidability of the following problem (Tenth problem of Hilbert; theorem of Davis, Putman, Robinson, Matijacevic, Cudnowskii; see Manin 1977, Theorem VI.1.2 et seq.): given a (commutative) polynomial $P \in \mathbf{Z}[x_1, \ldots, x_n]$, does there exist an n-tuple $(\alpha_1, \ldots, \alpha_n) \in \mathbf{N}^n$ such that $P(\alpha_1, \ldots, \alpha_n) = 0$?

To such a polynomial P, we indeed associate the series $S \in \mathbf{Q}\langle\langle x_1, \ldots, x_n \rangle\rangle$ defined for a word w by

$$(S, w) = P(|w|_{x_1}, \ldots, |w|_{x_n})$$

This series is rational (see Example I.5.2). Clearly, there exists a word w with $(S, w) = 0$ if and only if P vanishes for some n-tuple of nonnegative integers.

The undecidability of this problem also implies the undecidability of the following question: Given two supports of rational series, are they equal?

See Exercise 1.2 for a proof of these undecidability results using the Post correspondence problem instead of Hilbert's tenth problem.

2 Growth

We first give a result concerning finite monoids of matrices. Recall that for a given word w, we denote by w^* the submonoid generated by w.

Theorem 2.1 (Jacob 1978; Mandel and Simon 1977). *Let $\mu: X^* \to \mathbf{Q}^{n \times n}$ be a monoid morphism such that, for all $w \in X^*$, the monoid μw^* is finite. Then there exists an effectively computable integer N depending only on $|X|$ and n such that $|\mu(X^*)| \leqq N$.*

As we shall see, the function

$$(|X|, n) \mapsto N$$

grows extremely rapidly. There exists, however, one case where there is a reasonable bound, namely the case described in the lemma below.

A set E of matrices in $\mathbf{Q}^{n \times n}$ is called *irreducible* if there is no subspace of $\mathbf{Q}^{1 \times n}$ other than 0 and $\mathbf{Q}^{1 \times n}$ stable for all matrices in E (the matrices act on the right on $\mathbf{Q}^{1 \times n}$).

Lemma 2.2. *Let $M \subset \mathbf{Q}^{n \times n}$ be an irreducible monoid of matrices such that all nonvanishing eigenvalues of matrices in M are roots of unity. Then $|M| \leqq (2n+1)^{n^2}$.*

Proof. Let $m \in M$. The eigenvalues $\neq 0$ of m are roots of unity, whence algebraic integers over $\mathbf{Z}$. The same holds for $tr(m)$. Since $tr(m) \in \mathbf{Q}$ and $\mathbf{Z}$ is integrally closed, this implies that $tr(m) \in \mathbf{Z}$. The norm of each eigenvalue is 0 or 1. Thus $|tr(m)| \leqq n$. This shows that $tr(m)$ takes at most $2n+1$ distinct values for $m \in M$.

Let $m_1, \ldots, m_k \in M$ be a basis of the subspace N of $\mathbf{Q}^{n \times n}$ generated by M. Clearly $k \leqq n^2$. Define an equivalence relation $\sim$ on M by

$$m \sim m' \Leftrightarrow tr(mm_i) = tr(m'm_i) \quad \text{for} \quad i=1, \ldots, k$$

The number of equivalence classes of this relation is at most $(2n+1)^k$. In order to prove the lemma, it suffices to show that $m \sim m'$ implies $m = m'$.

Let $m, m' \in M$ be such that $m \sim m'$. Set $p = m - m'$, and assume $p \neq 0$. There exists a vector $v \in \mathbf{Q}^{1 \times n}$ such that $vp \neq 0$. It follows that the subspace vpN of $\mathbf{Q}^{1 \times n}$ is not the null space. Since it is stable under M and M is irreducible, one has $vpN = \mathbf{Q}^{1 \times n}$. Consequently, there exists some $q \in N$ such that $vpq = v$. This shows that pq has the eigenvalue 1. Now for all integers $j \geqq 1$,

$$tr((pq)^j) = tr(pq(pq)^{j-1}) = 0$$

because $q(pq)^{j-1}$ is a linear combination of the matrices $m_1, \ldots, m_k$, and by assumption $tr(pr) = 0$ for $r \in M$. Newton's formulas show that all eigenvalues of pq vanish. The yields a contradiction. □

For the proof Theorem 2.1, we need another lemma.

Lemma 2.3 (Schützenberger 1962c). *Let μ: $X^* \to \mathbf{Q}^{n \times n}$ be a morphism into a monoid of matrices which are triangular by blocks*

$$\mu = \begin{pmatrix} \mu' & \nu \\ 0 & \mu'' \end{pmatrix}$$

Assume that $\mu' X^*$ and $\mu'' X^*$ are finite, and that μw^* is finite for any word w. Then

$$|\nu X^*| \leqq \sum_{0 \leqq i < |\mu' X^*|^2 |\mu'' X^*|^2} |X|^i$$

Proof. Let $\mu_1 = (\mu', \mu'')$, and set

$$T = \{(v', v, v'') \in X^* \times X^+ \times X^* | \mu_1 v' v = \mu_1 v', \ \mu_1 v v'' = \mu_1 v''\}$$

(i) Let w be a word of length $\geqq H^2$, with $H = |\mu' X^*| |\mu'' X^*|$. Then there exists a factorization $w = v' v v''$ such that $(v', v, v'') \in T$.

Indeed, the set $\{(a, b) | w = ab\}$ has at least $1 + H^2$ elements, and since $\mu_1 X^* \times \mu_1 X^*$ has H^2 elements, there are two distinct factorizations

$$w = ab = a'b'$$

such that

$$\mu_1 a = \mu_1 a' \quad \text{and} \quad \mu_1 b = \mu_1 b'$$

Assume for instance $|a| < |a'|$. Then there is a word $v \neq 1$ such that $a' = av$, $b = vb'$. Thus $w = avb$ with $(a, v, b) \in T$.

(ii) For any $t = (v', v, v'') \in T$, one has

$$\nu(v' v^n v'') = \nu(v' v'') + n \cdot \nu t$$

where

$$\nu t = \mu' v' \cdot \nu v \cdot \mu'' v''$$

Indeed, the identity

$$\begin{pmatrix} a & b \\ 0 & c \end{pmatrix}^n = \begin{pmatrix} a^n & \sum_{k+l=n-1} a^k b c^l \\ 0 & c^n \end{pmatrix}$$

shows that

$$\nu v^n = \sum_{k+l=n-1, \ 0 \leqq k, l} \mu' v^k \nu v \mu'' v^l$$

Since $(v', v, v'') \in T$, this equation implies

$$\mu' v' \nu v^n \mu'' v'' = n \cdot \nu t$$

Finally

$$\nu(v'v^n v'') = \nu v'\mu''(v^n v'') + \mu' v'\nu(v^n)\mu'' v'' + \mu'(v'v^n)\nu v''$$

$$= \nu v'\mu'' v'' + n\nu t + \mu' v'\nu v''$$

$$= \nu(v'v'') + n\nu t$$

(iii) Consider now a word $w \in X^*$ with $|w| \geq H^2$. In view of (i), the word w admits a factorization $w = v'vv''$ with $t = (v', v, v'') \in T$. By (ii), for all $n \geq 0$

$$\nu(v'v^n v'') = \nu(v'v'') + n\nu t$$

Since μv^* is finite, $\mu(v'v^*v'')$ is also finite, and consequently also $\nu(v'v^*v'')$. This implies that $\nu t = 0$ and $\nu(w) = \nu(v'vv'') = \nu(v'v'')$. Since $|v'v''| < |w|$, the lemma follows. □

Proof of Theorem 2.1. Assume first that the monoid μX^* is irreducible, and consider any matrix $\mu w \in \mu X^*$. Since μw^* is finite, there are integers $0 \leq i < j$ with $\mu w^i = \mu w^j$. But this implies that the eigenvalues of w are 0 or roots of unity. The theorem thus follows from Lemma 2.2.

If μX^* is not irreducible, there is some subspace V of $\mathbf{Q}^{1\times n}$ which is stable under μX^*. Consider a supplementary space W of V. In a basis which is adapted to the decomposition $\mathbf{Q}^{1\times n} = W \oplus V$, the morphism μ admits the form described in Lemma 2.3. Arguing by induction on the dimension of the representation, the result follows from Lemma 2.3. □

Corollary 2.4 (McNaughton and Zalcstein 1975). *If every matrix of a finitely generated monoid M of matrices over $\mathbf{Q}$ generates a finite monoid, then the monoid M is finite.* □

Recall that a *ray* is a subset of X^* of the form uv^*w, with $u, v, w \in X^*$.

Corollary 2.5 (Reutenauer 1977b). *Let $S \in \mathbf{Q}\langle\langle X \rangle\rangle$ be a rational series such that for any ray R, the set $\{(S, w) \mid w \in R\}$ is finite. Then the set of coefficients of S is finite.*

Proof. Let (λ, μ, γ) be a reduced linear representation of S. By Corollary II.2.3, there exist polynomials $P_1, \ldots, P_n, Q_1, \ldots, Q_n$ such that for all words w,

$$\mu w = ((S, P_i w Q_j))_{1 \leq i, j \leq n}$$

By assumption, the set $\{(S, uw^m v) \mid m \in \mathbf{N}\}$ is finite for all words u, v, w. The same holds for sets $\{(S, Pw^m Q) \mid m \in \mathbf{N}\}$ where P, Q are polynomials. This shows that μw^* is finite for any word w. By Corollary 2.4, the monoid μX^* is finite, and in particular

$$\{(S, w) \mid w \in X^*\}$$

is finite, since $(S, w) = \lambda \mu w \gamma$. □

Corollary 2.6 (Jacob 1978). *It is decidable whether a finite set of matrices over* **Q** *generates a finite monoid.*

Proof. By Theorem 2.1, there is an upper bound on the size of such a monoid if it is finite. Let E be the finite set of matrices, M the monoid generated by E, and let N be the upper bound given in Theorem 2.1. Then M is finite if and only if every product of N matrices in E equals a product of at most $N-1$ matrices in E. This last condition is clearly easy to check. □

Corollary 2.7 (Jacob 1978). *It is decidable whether a rational series has a finite image.* □

Recall that the image of a series is the set of its coefficients.

We now turn our attention to questions concerning growth of rational series over **Z**. A series $S \in \mathbf{Z}\langle\langle X \rangle\rangle$ has *polynomial growth* if there exist an integer $q \geqq 0$ and a real number C such that

$$|(S, w)| \leqq C|w|^q$$

for all nonempty words w. The smallest q satisfying the inequality, provided it exists, is called the *degree of growth* of S. Observe that series with degree of growth zero are precisely the series with finite image.

Theorem 2.8. *Let $S \in \mathbf{Z}\langle\langle X \rangle\rangle$ be a rational series and let (λ, μ, γ) be a reduced linear representation of S. Then S has polynomial growth if and only if the set $\{tr(\mu w) \mid w \in X^*\}$ is finite.*

Proof. Suppose first that S has polynomial growth. Then there exist, by Corollary II.2.3, real numbers C, q such that $|\mu w| \leqq C|w|^q$ for all words w. Consequently, for every eigenvalue λ of μw one has

$$|\lambda|^r \leqq C' r^q$$

for some constant C'. Thus $|\lambda| \leqq 1$. This implies that $-n \leqq tr(\mu w) \leqq n$, where n is the dimension of μ. Since S is **Z**-rational, there exists a reduced linear representation with coefficients in **Z** (Theorem V.1.1). This representation is similar to (λ, μ, γ) by Theorem II.2.4 and consequently, the trace of a matrix μw is an integer. Thus each $tr(\mu w)$ is in $\{-n, \ldots, n\}$.

Conversely, suppose that the set $\{tr(\mu w) \mid w \in X^*\}$ is finite. Let w be a word and let $\lambda_1, \ldots, \lambda_n$ be the eigenvalues of μw with their multiplicities. The sequence

$$a_p = \sum_{1 \leqq i \leqq n} \lambda_i^p = tr(\mu w^p)$$

takes only a finite number of distinct values. Since it satisfies a linear recurrence relation, it is ultimately periodic, and there is a relation

$$a_{p+h} = a_{p+k} \quad p \geqq 0$$

for some $h, k \in \mathbf{N}, h > k$. The minimal polynomial (see Sect. IV.1) of the rational series $\sum_{p \in \mathbf{N}} a_p x^p$ divides the polynomial $x^h - x^k$. Consequently, the roots of this series (in the sense defined in Sect. IV.1) are roots of unity or 0. In view of the unicity of the exponential polynomial (Sect. IV.2), the λ_i are roots of unity or 0.

Next, if the monoid μX^* is not irreducible, then μ can be put, by changing the basis, into the form

$$\mu = \begin{pmatrix} \mu' & v \\ 0 & \mu'' \end{pmatrix}$$

Arguing by induction, μ is equivalent to a morphism that is triangular by blocks

$$\begin{pmatrix} \mu_1 & * & * & . & * \\ & \mu_2 & & & * \\ & & . & & * \\ & & & . & * \\ 0 & 0 & & & \mu_n \end{pmatrix}$$

where each $\mu_i X^*$ is irreducible. By Lemma 2.2, and according to our computations, all monoids $\mu_i X^*$ are finite. To complete the proof, it suffices to apply the following lemma iteratively, observing that the product of series with polynomial growth also has polynomial growth. □

Lemma 2.9. *Let*

$$\mu = \begin{pmatrix} \mu' & v \\ 0 & \mu'' \end{pmatrix}$$

be a morphism $X^* \to K^{n \times n}$, where K is a commutative semiring. Every series recognized by μ is a linear combination of series recognized by μ' or by μ'' and of series of the form $S'xS''$ where S' is recognized by μ', $x \in X$ and S'' is recognized by μ''.

Proof. A series recognized by μ is a linear combination of series of the form

$$\sum_w (\mu w)_{i,j} w \tag{2.1}$$

with $0 \leqq i, j \leqq n$. It suffices to show that when i, j are coordinates of v, the corresponding series (2.1) is a linear combination of series of the form $S'xS''$. This is an immediate consequence of the formula

$$vw = \sum_{w = uxv} \mu' u \cdot vx \cdot \mu'' v$$ □

Corollary 2.10. *It is decidable whether a rational series $S \in \mathbf{Z}\langle\langle X \rangle\rangle$ has polynomial growth.*

Proof. A reduced linear representation (λ, μ, γ) of S can be computed effectively. Then according to Theorem 2.8, the series S has polynomial growth if and only if the series

$$\sum_w tr(\mu w) w$$

has a finite image. This series is rational (Lemma II.1.2) and it is decidable, by Corollary 2.7, whether a rational series has a finite image. □

Corollary 2.11 (Schützenberger 1962c). *The set of* $\mathbf{Z}$*-rational series of polynomial growth is equal to the* $\mathbf{Z}$*-subalgebra of* $\mathbf{Z}\langle\langle X\rangle\rangle$ *generated by the characteristic series of rational languages.*

Proof. Let $S \in \mathbf{Z}\langle\langle X\rangle\rangle$ be a rational series having polynomial growth, and let (λ, μ, γ) be a reduced linear representation of S. We may assume, by Theorem V.1.1, that (λ, μ, γ) has integral coefficients. The second part of the proof of Theorem 2.8 shows that, after a change of the basis of $\mathbf{Q}^{1 \times n}$, μ has a decomposition of the form

$$\begin{pmatrix} \mu_1 & * & * & . & * \\ & \mu_2 & & & * \\ & & . & & * \\ & & & . & * \\ 0 & 0 & & & \mu_r \end{pmatrix}$$

In fact, since $\mathbf{Z}$ is a principal ring, the change of basis can be done in $\mathbf{Z}^{1 \times n}$. Each $\mu_i X^*$ is finite.

Observe now that any series recognized by a morphism $\mu' : X^* \to \mathbf{Q}^{p \times p}$, with $\mu' X^*$ finite, is a linear combination of characteristic series of rational languages. This is a consequence of Theorem III.2.7. To complete the proof, it suffices to apply Lemma 2.9.

Conversely, each characteristic series of a rational language is rational (Proposition III.2.1), and the set of rational series with polynomial growth is indeed a subalgebra of $\mathbf{Z}\langle\langle X\rangle\rangle$. □

Exercises for Chapter VI

1.1. Show that the following problem is undecidable: Given a rational series $S \in \mathbf{Q}\langle\langle X\rangle\rangle$, are there infinitely many words w such that $(S, w) = 0$?

1.2. Use the undecidability of the *Post Correspondence Problem* and Exercise III.3.2 to give another proof of the undecidability property of Sect. 1 (recall that Post's problem is whether or not a given *equality set* is empty).

2.1. Let $S \in \mathbf{Q}\langle\langle X\rangle\rangle$ be a rational series such that for every ray R, almost all coefficients (S, w), $w \in R$, vanish. Show that S is a polynomial.

2.2. Let $S \in \mathbf{N}\langle\langle X \rangle\rangle$ be an $\mathbf{N}$-rational series having polynomial growth. Show that S is in the $\mathbf{N}$-subalgebra of $\mathbf{N}\langle\langle X \rangle\rangle$ generated by the characteristic series of rational languages (use a rational expression for S and the fact that if $T \in \mathbf{N}\langle\langle X \rangle\rangle$ is not the characteristic series of the basis of a free submonoid of X^*, then the growth of T^* is not polynomial).

Notes to Chapter VI

Most of the results of Sect. 2 hold in arbitrary fields. Theorem 2.1 can be extended, but the bound N then also depends on the field considered. Lemma 2.2 and Corollaries 2.4, 2.5 hold in arbitrary fields, and Lemma 2.3 holds in fields of characteristic 0, provided the bound $(2n+1)^{n^2}$ is replaced by r^{n^2}, where r is the size of the set $\{tr(m) \mid m \in M\}$. This set is always finite (under the assumptions of the lemma) for a finite monoid M. Corollaries 2.6, 2.7 extend to "computable" fields. Corollary 2.11 is a special case of a results of Schützenberger (1962c): for any integer $q \geq 0$, the $\mathbf{Z}$-module of rational series S satisfying a condition of the form

$$|(S, w)| \leqq C|w|^q \quad (w \in X^*)$$

is equal to the $\mathbf{Z}$-module generated by the products of at most $q+1$ characteristic series of rational languages. He shows also that the degree of growth of a rational series of $\mathbf{Z}\langle\langle X \rangle\rangle$ is always an integer or ∞.

Chapter VII
Noncommutative Polynomials

This chapter deals with algebraic properties of noncommutative polynomials. They are of independent interest, but most of them will be of use in the final chapter.

In contrast to commutative polynomials, the algebra of noncommutative polynomials is not Euclidean, and not even factorial. However, there are many interesting results concerning factorization of noncommutative polynomials: this is one of the major topics of the present chapter.

The basic tool is Cohn's weak algorithm (Theorem 1.1), which is the subject of Sect. 1. This operation constitutes a natural generalization of the classical Euclidean algorithm.

Section 2 deals with continuant polynomials which describe the multiplicative relations between noncommutative polynomials (Theorem 2.2).

We introduce in Sect. 3 regular modules over the ring of polynomials. We characterize these modules (Theorem 3.1) and obtain, as consequences, results on full matrices, factorization of polynomials, and inertia.

The main result of Sect. 4 is the (easy) extension of Gauss's lemma to noncommutative polynomials.

1 The Weak Algorithm

Let K be a (commutative) field and let X be an alphabet. Recall that the *degree* of a polynomial P in $K\langle X\rangle$ was defined in Sect. I.2; we will denote it by $deg(P)$. We recall also the usual facts about the degree, that is:

$$deg(0) = -\infty$$

$$deg(P+Q) \leqq \max(deg(P), deg(Q)), \tag{1.1}$$

$$deg(P+Q) = deg(P), \qquad \text{if } deg(Q) < deg(P)$$

$$deg(PQ) = deg(P) + deg(Q) \tag{1.2}$$

Note that the last equality shows that $K\langle X\rangle$ is *entire*, that is:

$$PQ = 0 \textit{ implies } P = 0 \textit{ or } Q = 0$$

Definition. A finite family $P_1, \ldots, P_n$ of polynomials in $K\langle X\rangle$ is (right) *dependent* if either some $P_i=0$ or if there exist polynomials $Q_1, \ldots, Q_n$ such that

$$deg\left(\sum_i P_iQ_i\right) < \max_i(deg(P_iQ_i))$$

Definition. A polynomial P is (right) *dependent* on the finite family $P_1, \ldots, P_n$ if either $P=0$ or if there exist polynomials $Q_1, \ldots, Q_n$ such that

$$deg\left(P-\sum_i P_iQ_i\right) < deg(P)$$

and furthermore for any $i=1, \ldots, n$

$$deg(P_iQ_i) \leqq deg(P)$$

Note that if P is dependent on $P_1, \ldots, P_n$, then clearly the family $P, P_1, \ldots, P_n$ is dependent. The converse is given by the following theorem.

Theorem 1.1 (Cohn 1961). *Let $P_1, \ldots, P_n$ be a dependent family of polynomials with*

$$deg(P_1) \leqq \ldots \leqq deg(P_n)$$

Then some P_i is dependent on $P_1, \ldots, P_{i-1}$.

Let P be a polynomial and let w be a word in X^*. We define the polynomial Pu^{-1} as

$$Pu^{-1} = \sum_{w\in X^*} (P, wu)w$$

The operator $P \mapsto Pu^{-1}$ is symmetric to the operator $P \mapsto u^{-1}P$ which was introduced in Sect. I.5. It is easy to verify that this operator is linear, and that the following relations hold:

$$deg(Pu^{-1}) \leqq deg(P) - |u| \tag{1.3}$$

$$P(uv)^{-1} = (Pv^{-1})u^{-1} \tag{1.4}$$

Moreover, for any letter x,

$$(PQ)x^{-1} = P(Qx^{-1}) + (Q, 1)Px^{-1} \tag{1.5}$$

where $(Q, 1)$ denotes as usual the constant term of Q. The last equality is simply the symmetric equivalent of Lemma I.6.2.

Lemma 1.2. *If P, Q are polynomials and w is a word, then there exists a polynomial P' such that*

$$(PQ)w^{-1} = P(Qw^{-1}) + P'$$

with either $P = P' = 0$ or $deg(P') < deg(P)$.

Proof. We may assume $P \neq 0$. If w is the empty word, then $(PQ)w^{-1} = PQ$ and $Qw^{-1} = Q$, so $(PQ)w^{-1} = P(Qw^{-1})$, and the proof is complete.

Let $w = xu$ with x a letter. Then, by induction, one has

$$(PQ)u^{-1} = P(Qu^{-1}) + P'$$

$$deg(P') < deg(P)$$

Now, by Eq. (1.4), one has

$$(PQ)w^{-1} = ((PQ)u^{-1})x^{-1} = (P(Qu^{-1}))x^{-1} + P'x^{-1}$$

Thus, by Eqs. (1.5) and (1.4), we have

$$(PQ)w^{-1} = P((Qu^{-1})x^{-1}) + (Qu^{-1}, 1)(Px^{-1}) + P'x^{-1} = P(Qw^{-1}) + P''$$

with $P'' = (Qu^{-1}, 1)(Px^{-1}) + P'x^{-1}$. Next, by Eq. (1.3), $deg(Px^{-1}) < deg(P)$ and $deg(P'x^{-1}) \leqq deg(P') - |x| < deg(P)$. Hence $deg(P'') < deg(P)$, as desired. □

Proof of Theorem 1.1. We may suppose that no P_i is equal to 0. Hence $deg(\sum P_iQ_i) < \max_i(deg(P_iQ_i))$. Let $r = \max_i(deg(P_iQ_i))$ and let $I = \{i \mid deg(P_iQ_i) = r\}$. The polynomial $R = \sum_{i\in I} P_iQ_i$ has degree $deg(R) < r$. Let $k = sup(I)$; then $i \in I \Rightarrow deg(P_i) \leqq deg(P_k)$. Let w be a word such that $|w| = deg(Q_k)$ and $0 \neq (Q_k, w) = \alpha^{-1} \in K$: such a word exists, because $Q_k \neq 0$ (otherwise $deg(R) < r = deg(P_kQ_k) = -\infty$).

By Lemma 1.2, we have

$$Rw^{-1} = \sum_{i\in I} P_i(Q_iw^{-1}) + \sum_{i\in I} P_i'$$

for some polynomials P_i' with $deg(P_i') < deg(P_i)$. Since $Q_kw^{-1} = \alpha^{-1}$,

$$P_k + \alpha \sum_{i\in I\setminus k} P_i(Q_iw^{-1}) = \alpha Rw^{-1} - \alpha \sum_{i\in I} P_i'. \tag{1.6}$$

Now, by Eq. (1.3),

$$deg(Rw^{-1}) \leqq deg(R) - |w| < r - |w| = deg(P_kQ_k) - deg(Q_k) = deg(P_k).$$

Furthermore, $deg(P_i') < deg(P_i) \leqq deg(P_k)$. Consequently, by Eq. (1.1), the degree of the right-hand side of Eq. (1.6) is $< deg(P_k)$. Moreover,

$$deg(P_i(Q_i w^{-1})) = deg(P_i) + deg(Q_i w^{-1}) \leqq deg(P_i) + deg(Q_i) - deg(Q_k)$$

by Eq. (1.3). So we have $deg(P_i(Q_i w^{-1})) \leqq r - deg(Q_k) = deg(P_k)$. This shows that P_k is dependent on P_i, $i \in I \backslash k$; hence P_k also is dependent on $P_1, \ldots, P_{k-1}$. □

For two polynomials A, B in $K\langle X\rangle$, the (left) *Euclidean division* of A and B (i.e. the problem of finding polynomials Q and R such that $A = BQ + R$ and $deg(R) < deg(B)$) is not always possible. However, the next result gives a necessary and sufficient condition for this.

Corollary 1.3. *Let A, B, P, Q_1, Q_2, R_1 be polynomials such that*

$$AP + Q_1 = BQ_2 + R_1$$

with

$$P \neq 0,\ deg(Q_1) \leqq deg(P),\ deg(R_1) < deg(B).$$

Then there exist polynomials Q and R such that

$$A = BQ + R \quad \text{with} \quad deg(R) < deg(B)$$

(i.e., the Euclidean division of A by B is possible).

Proof. Note that $B \neq 0$ (otherwise $deg(R_1) < -\infty$). If $B \in K$, the corollary is immediate (take $Q = B^{-1}A$, $R = 0$). Otherwise, we prove it by induction on $deg(A)$. If $deg(A) < deg(B)$, the proof is immediate (take $Q = 0$, $R = A$). Suppose that $deg(A) \geqq deg(B)$. Then

$$deg(Q_1) \leqq deg(P) < deg(AP)$$

(because $1 \leqq deg(B) \leqq deg(A)$), and

$$deg(R_1) < deg(B) \leqq deg(A) \leqq deg(AP)$$

(because $0 \leqq deg(P)$). Thus $deg(Q_1)$ and $deg(R_1)$ are both $< \max(deg(AP), deg(BQ_2))$ and by Eq. (1.1), $deg(R_1 - Q_1) < \max(deg(AP), deg(BQ_2))$. In view of Theorem 1.1, A is dependent on B, i.e. there exist two polynomials Q_3 and A_1 such that $A = BQ_3 + A_1$ with $deg(A_1) < deg(A)$.

Put this expression for A into the initial equality. This gives

$$A_1 P + Q_1 = B(Q_2 - Q_3 P) + R_1$$

Since $deg(A_1) < deg(A)$, we have by induction $A_1 = BQ_4 + R$ with $deg(R) < deg(B)$; thus $A = BQ_3 + BQ_4 + R$, which proves the corollary. □

The next result is a particular case of the previous one.

Corollary 1.4. *If A, B, A', B' are nonzero polynomials such that $AB'=BA'$, then there exist polynomials Q, R such that $A=BQ+R$ and $deg(R)<deg(B)$.* □

2 Continuant Polynomials

Definition. Let $a_1, \ldots, a_n$ be a finite sequence of polynomials. We define the sequences $p_0, \ldots, p_n$ of *continuant polynomials* (with respect to $a_1, \ldots, a_n$) in the following way:

$$p_0=1,\ p_1=a_1$$

and for $2 \leqq i \leqq n$,

$$p_i=p_{i-1}a_i+p_{i-2}$$

Example 2.1. The first continuant polynomials are:

$$p_2=a_1a_2+1$$

$$p_3=a_1a_2a_3+a_1+a_3$$

$$p_4=a_1a_2a_3a_4+a_1a_2+a_1a_4+a_3a_4+1$$

Notation. We shall write $p(a_1, \ldots, a_i)$ for p_i.

It is easy to see that the continuant polynomials may be obtained by the "leap-frog construction": consider the "word" $a_1 \ldots a_n$ and all words obtained by repetitively suppressing some factor of the form a_ia_{i+1} in it. Then $p(a_1, \ldots, a_n)$ is the sum of all these "words".

Now, we have by definition

$$p(a_1, \ldots, a_n)=p(a_1, \ldots, a_{n-1})a_n+p(a_1, \ldots, a_{n-2}) \tag{2.1}$$

The combinatorial construction sketched above shows that symmetrically,

$$p(a_1, \ldots, a_n)=a_1p(a_2, \ldots, a_n)+p(a_3, \ldots, a_n) \tag{2.2}$$

An equivalent but useful relation is

$$p(a_n, \ldots, a_1)=a_np(a_{n-1}, \ldots, a_1)+p(a_{n-2}, \ldots, a_1) \tag{2.3}$$

Proposition 2.1 (Wedderburn 1932). *The continuant polynomials satisfy the relation*

$$p(a_1, \ldots, a_n)p(a_{n-1}, \ldots, a_1)=p(a_1, \ldots, a_{n-1})p(a_n, \ldots, a_1) \tag{2.4}$$

Proof. This is surely true for $n=1$. Suppose $n \geqq 2$. Then by Eq. (2.1),

$$p(a_1, \ldots, a_n)p(a_{n-1}, \ldots, a_1)$$

$$=p(a_1, \ldots, a_{n-1})a_n p(a_{n-1}, \ldots, a_1)+p(a_1, \ldots, a_{n-2})p(a_{n-1}, \ldots, a_1)$$

which is equal by induction to

$$p(a_1, \ldots, a_{n-1})a_n p(a_{n-1}, \ldots, a_1)+p(a_1, \ldots, a_{n-1})p(a_{n-2}, \ldots, a_1)$$

This is equal, by Eq. (2.3), to

$$p(a_1, \ldots, a_{n-1})p(a_n, \ldots, a_1)$$

as desired. □

Theorem 2.2 (Cohn 1969). *Let A, B, A', B' be nonzero polynomials such that $AB'=BA'$. Then there exist polynomials $U, V, a_1, \ldots, a_n (n \geqq 1)$ such that*

$$A=Up(a_1, \ldots, a_n),\ B'=p(a_{n-1}, \ldots, a_1)V$$

$$B=Up(a_1, \ldots, a_{n-1}),\ A'=p(a_n, \ldots, a_1)V$$

Moreover, $deg(a_1), \ldots, deg(a_{n-1}) \geqq 1$, and if $deg(A)>deg(B)$, then $deg(a_n) \geqq 1$.

Proof. (i) Suppose first that A is a right multiple of B, i.e. $A=BQ$. Then the theorem is obvious: for $U=B$, $V=B'$, $n=1$, $a_1=Q$; then indeed

$$A=BQ=Up(a_1),\ B'=1.V,\ B=U.1$$

and $BA'=AB'=BQB'$, whence $A'=QB'=p(a_1)V$. Furthermore, if $deg(A)>deg(B)$, then $deg(Q) \geqq 1$.

(ii) Next, we prove the theorem in the case where $deg(A)>deg(B)$, by induction on $deg(B)$. If $deg(B)=0$, then A is a right multiple of B and we may apply (i). Suppose $deg(B) \geqq 1$. By Corollary 1.4, $A=BQ+R$ for some polynomials Q and R such that $deg(R)<deg(B)$. If $R=0$, apply (i). Otherwise, we have $BA'=AB'=BQB'+RB'$, hence $B(A'-QB')=RB'$; note that $B, R, B' \neq 0$, hence $A'-QB' \neq 0$. Furthermore, $deg(R)<deg(B)$, and we may apply the induction hypothesis: there exist polynomials $U, V, a_1, \ldots, a_n$ such that

$$B=Up(a_1, \ldots, a_n),\ A'-QB'=p(a_{n-1}, \ldots, a_1)V$$

$$R=Up(a_1, \ldots, a_{n-1}),\ B'=p(a_n, \ldots, a_1)V \tag{2.5}$$

$$deg(a_1), \ldots, deg(a_n) \geqq 1$$

Hence

$$A = BQ + R = U[p(a_1, \ldots, a_n)Q + p(a_1, \ldots, a_{n-1})]$$

$$= Up(a_1, \ldots, a_n, Q)$$

by Eq. (2.1). Similarly, $A' = p(Q, a_n, \ldots, a_1)V$. Thus A, B, A', B' admit the announced expression. Furthermore, $deg(Q) \geqq 1$: indeed, by Eq. (1.2), $deg(A) = deg(BQ) = deg(B) + deg(Q)$, hence $deg(Q) = deg(A) - deg(B) \geqq 1$.

This proves the theorem in the case where $deg(A) > deg(B)$.

(iii) In the general case, one has again $A = BQ + R$ with $deg(R) < deg(B)$ (Corollary 1.4). If $R = 0$, the proof is completed by (i). Otherwise, as above, $B(A' - QB') = RB'$ with $deg(B) > deg(R)$. Hence we may apply (ii): there exist U, V, $a_1, \ldots, a_n$ such that Eq. (2.5) holds. Then we obtain, as in (ii):

$$A = Up(a_1, \ldots, a_n, Q), \quad B' = p(a_n, \ldots, a_1)V$$

$$B = Up(a_1, \ldots, a_n), \quad A' = p(Q, a_n, \ldots, a_1)V$$

This proves the theorem. □

Proposition 2.3. *Let $a_1, \ldots, a_n$ be polynomials such that $a_1, \ldots, a_{n-1}$ have positive degree, and let Y be a polynomial of degree 1 such that $p(a_{n-1}, \ldots, a_1)$ and $p(a_n, \ldots, a_1)$ are both congruent to a scalar modulo the right ideal $YK\langle X\rangle$. Then for $i = 1, \ldots, n$*

$$p(a_i, \ldots, a_1) \equiv p(a_1, \ldots, a_i) \bmod YK\langle X\rangle$$

We prove first a lemma.

Lemma 2.4. *Let $a_1, \ldots, a_n$ be polynomials such that $a_1, \ldots, a_{n-1}$ have positive degree. Then the degrees of 1, $p(a_1), \ldots, p(a_{n-1}, \ldots, a_1)$ are strictly increasing.*

Proof. Obviously, $deg(1) < deg(a_1)$. Suppose

$$deg(p(a_{i-2}, \ldots, a_1)) < deg(p(a_{i-1}, \ldots, a_1))$$

for $2 \leqq i \leqq n-1$. From the relation

$$p(a_i, \ldots, a_1) = a_i p(a_{i-1}, \ldots, a_1) + p(a_{i-2}, \ldots \ldots, a_1)$$

it follows that the degree of $p(a_i, \ldots, a_1)$ is equal to $deg(a_i p(a_{i-1}, \ldots, a_1))$, and

$$deg(a_i p(a_{i-1}, \ldots, a_1))$$

$$= deg(a_i) + deg(p(a_{i-1}, \ldots, a_1)) > deg(p(a_{i-1}, \ldots, a_1))$$

because $deg(a_i) \geqq 1$. This proves the lemma. □

Proof of Proposition 2.3 (Induction on n). When $n=1$, the result is evident. Suppose $n \geqq 2$. Note that if the condition on the degrees is fulfilled for $a_1, \ldots, a_n$, then *a fortiori* also $a_1, \ldots, a_{n-2}$ have positive degree. By assumption, $p(a_n, \ldots, a_1)$ is congruent to some scalar α and $p(a_{n-1}, \ldots, a_1)$ to some scalar β mod. $YK\langle X \rangle$. Suppose $p(a_{n-1}, \ldots, a_1)=0$. Then by Eq. (2.3), we have $p(a_{n-2}, \ldots, a_1) \equiv \alpha = \alpha - \beta\alpha$ (because $\beta = 0$ in this case).

Suppose $p(a_{n-1}, \ldots, a_1) \neq 0$. Then by Eq. (2.3),

$$a_n p(a_{n-1}, \ldots, a_1) + p(a_{n-2}, \ldots, a_1) = YQ + \alpha$$

for some polynomial Q. As $deg(p(a_{n-2}, \ldots, a_1)) < deg(p(a_{n-1}, \ldots, a_1))$ by Lemma 2.4, we obtain by Corollary 1.3 that $a_n \equiv \gamma$ *mod.* $YK\langle X \rangle$ for some scalar γ. Using Eq. (2.3) again and the fact that $P \equiv \gamma$, $Q \equiv \beta \Rightarrow PQ \equiv \gamma\beta$, we obtain $p(a_{n-2}, \ldots, a_1) \equiv \alpha - \gamma\beta$.

In both cases, the induction hypothesis gives $p(a_1, \ldots, a_{n-2}) \equiv \alpha - \gamma\beta$ and $p(a_1, \ldots, a_{n-1}) \equiv \beta$. Hence, by Eq. (2.1), $p(a_1, \ldots, a_n) \equiv \beta\gamma + \alpha - \gamma\beta \equiv p(a_n, \ldots, a_1)$, as desired. □

Lemma 2.5. *Let $a_1, \ldots, a_n$ be polynomials. Then*

$$p(a_1, \ldots, a_n) = 0 \Leftrightarrow p(a_n, \ldots, a_1) = 0$$

Proof (Induction on n). The lemma is evidently true for $n=0, 1$. Suppose $n \geqq 2$. It is enough to show that $p(a_1, \ldots, a_n) = 0$ implies $p(a_n, \ldots, a_1) = 0$. Now, by Eq. (2.4),

$$p(a_1, \ldots, a_n) p(a_{n-1}, \ldots, a_1) = p(a_1, \ldots, a_{n-1}) p(a_n, \ldots, a_1)$$

Suppose $p(a_1, \ldots, a_n) = 0$. If $p(a_1, \ldots, a_{n-1}) \neq 0$, then $p(a_n, \ldots, a_1) = 0$ because $K\langle X \rangle$ is entire. If $p(a_1, \ldots, a_{n-1}) = 0$, then $p(a_{n-1}, \ldots, a_1) = 0$ by induction. Hence, by Eqs. (2.1) and (2.3). $p(a_1, \ldots, a_n) = p(a_1, \ldots, a_{n-2})$ and $p(a_n, \ldots, a_1) = p(a_{n-2}, \ldots, a_1)$. By induction, $p(a_1, \ldots, a_{n-2})$ and $p(a_{n-2}, \ldots, a_1)$ simultaneously vanish, which proves the lemma. □

3 Inertia

Recall that $K\langle X \rangle^{p \times q}$ denotes the set of p by q matrices over $K\langle X \rangle$. In particular, $K\langle X \rangle^{1 \times n}$ is the set of column vectors of order n over $K\langle X \rangle$; this set has a natural structure of right $K\langle X \rangle$-module. If V is in $K\langle X \rangle^{1 \times n}$, we denote by $(V, 1)$ its *constant term*, that is, setting

$$V = \begin{pmatrix} P_1 \\ \vdots \\ P_n \end{pmatrix}$$

one has

$$(V,1)=\begin{pmatrix}(P_1,1)\\ \vdots\\ (P_n,1)\end{pmatrix}\in K^{1\times n}.$$

Furthermore, if w is a word in X^*, we denote by Vw^{-1} the vector

$$Vw^{-1}=\begin{pmatrix}P_1w^{-1}\\ \vdots\\ P_nw^{-1}\end{pmatrix}.$$

We have the following relation

$$V=(V,1)+\sum_{x\in X}(Vx^{-1})x \tag{3.1}$$

Definition. A (right) submodule E of $K\langle X\rangle^{1\times n}$ is *regular* if, whenever $V\in E$ and $(V, 1)=0$, then $Vx^{-1}\in E$ for any letter $x\in X$.

This property of vectors of polynomials is closely related to (but weaker than) the property of stability introduced in Sect. I.5.

The next result characterizes regular submodules and will be the key to all the results of this section.

Theorem 3.1. *A submodule E of $K\langle X\rangle^{1\times n}$ is regular if and only if it may be generated, as a $K\langle X\rangle$-module, by p vectors $V_1,\dots,V_p$ such that the matrix $((V_1,1),\dots,(V_p,1))\in K^{n\times p}$ is of rank p. In this case $p\leqq n$ and $V_1,\dots,V_p$ are linearly $K\langle X\rangle$-independent.*

Proof. 1. We begin with the easy part: suppose that E is generated by $V_1,\dots,V_p$ as indicated. Let $V\in E$ with $(V,1)=0$. Then

$$V=\sum_{1\leqq i\leqq p}V_iP_i\quad(P_i\in K\langle X\rangle)$$

Taking constant terms, we obtain

$$0=(V,1)=\sum(V_i,1)(P_i,1)$$

Because of the rank condition, we have $(P_i,1)=0$ for any i. Hence $P_i=\sum_{x\in X}(P_ix^{-1})x$, which shows that

$$V=\sum_{i,\ x}V_i(P_ix^{-1})x$$

By Eq. (3.1) we obtain

$$Vx^{-1}=\sum_i V_i(P_ix^{-1})$$

hence $Vx^{-1}\in E$, as desired.

2. Let E be a regular submodule of $K\langle X\rangle$. If $V \in K\langle X\rangle^{1\times n}$, V may be written $V = \sum_{w\in X^*} (V, w)w$ where $(V, w) \in K^{1\times n}$ are almost all zero. Let $deg(V)$ be the maximal length of a word w such that $(V, w) \neq 0$.

Claim. There are vectors $V_1, \ldots, V_p$ in E such that

(i) $deg(V_1) \leqq deg(V_2) \leqq \ldots \leqq deg(V_p)$
(ii) The vectors $(V_i, 1)$ form a K-basis of the K-space $(E, 1) = \{(V, 1) | V \in E\}$.
(iii) If $V \in E$ and $deg(V) < deg(V_i)$, then $(V, 1)$ is a K-linear combination of $(V_1, 1), \ldots, (V_{i-1}, 1)$.

Suppose the claim is true. Then the matrix $((V_1, 1), \ldots, (V_p, 1))$ has rank p. We show by induction on $deg(V)$ that each $V \in E$ is in $E' = \sum_{1\leqq i\leqq p} V_i K\langle X\rangle$.

If $deg(V) = -\infty$, i.e. $V=0$, it is obvious. Let $deg(V) \geqq 0$ and let i be the smallest integer such that $deg(V) < deg(V_i)$ (with $i = p+1$ if such an integer does not exist). Then $deg(V) \geqq deg(V_1), \ldots, deg(V_{i-1})$. Moreover, if $i \leqq p$ then by (iii), $(V, 1)$ is a linear combination of $(V_1, 1), \ldots, (V_{i-1}, 1)$; and if $i = p+1$ then by (ii), $(V, 1)$ is also a linear combination of $(V_1, 1), \ldots, (V_{i-1}, 1)$. Let $V' = V - \sum_{1\leqq j\leqq i-1} \alpha_j V_j$ $(\alpha_j \in K)$ be such that $(V', 1) = 0$. By the regularity of E, $V'x^{-1}$ is in E for any letter x. Now,

$$deg(V') \leqq \max(deg(V), deg(\alpha_1 V_1), \ldots, deg(\alpha_{i-1} V_{i-1})) = deg(V)$$

hence $deg(V'x^{-1}) < deg(V)$. Hence by induction, $V'x^{-1} \in E'$. Now, by Eq. (3.1), $V' = \sum_x (V'x^{-1})x$, and V' is in E'. Thus $V = V' + \sum_j \alpha_j V_j$ is in E' as well.

3. *Proof of the claim.* For $d = -1, 0, 1, 2, \ldots$, let $F(d)$ be the subspace of $K^{1\times n}$ defined by

$$F(d) = \{(V, 1) | V \in E, deg(V) \leqq d\}$$

Then

$$0 = F(-1) \subset F(0) \subset F(1) \subset \ldots \subset F(d) \subset \ldots$$

Let $0 \leqq d_1 < \ldots < d_q$ be such that for any i, $F(d_i - 1) \subsetneqq F(d_i)$ and such that each $F(d)$ is equal to some $F(d_i)$; in other words, one has

$$0 = F(-1) = \ldots = F(d_1 - 1) \subsetneqq F(d_1) = \ldots = F(d_2 - 1)$$

$$\subsetneqq F(d_2) \ldots \subsetneqq F(d_q) = F(d_q + 1) = \ldots$$

In particular, $F(d_q) = (E, 1)$. Now, let B_1 be a basis of $F(d_1)$, B_2 a basis of $F(d_2)$ *mod.* $F(d_1), \ldots$, and B_q a basis of $F(d_q)$ *mod* $F(d_{q-1})$. By definition of the F's we may find for each i in $\{1, \ldots, q\}$ vectors $W_{i,1}, \ldots, W_{i,k_i}$ in E of degree $\leqq d_i$ such that $\{(W_{i,1}, 1), \ldots, (W_{i,k_i}, 1)\} = B_i$; in fact, the degree of each $W_{i,j}$ is exactly d_i, otherwise $(W_{i,j}, 1) \in F(d_i - 1) = F(_{i-1})$, which contradicts the fact that B_i is a basis *mod* $F(d_{i-1})$.

Define $V_1, \ldots, V_p$ by

$$(V_1, \ldots, V_p) = (W_{1,1}, \ldots, W_{1,k_1}, W_{2,1}, \ldots, W_{2,k_2}, \ldots, W_{q,k_q})$$

Then the condition (i) of the claim is clearly satisfied. Moreover, as $F(d_q) = (E, 1)$, condition (ii) is also satisfied. Let $V \in E$ with $deg(V) < deg(V_k)$. Then $V_k = W_{i,j}$ for some i, j, hence $deg(V) < d_i (= deg(W_{i,j}))$, which implies that $(V, 1) \in F(d_i - 1) = F(d_{i-1})$ and $(V, 1)$ is a linear combination of $W_{1,1}, \ldots, W_{i-1,k_{i-1}}$, hence of $V_1, \ldots, V_{k-1}$. This proves the claim.

4. We show the last assertion of the theorem. Clearly $p \leqq n$. Suppose $\sum V_i P_i = 0$ where $P_i \in K\langle X \rangle$ are not all zero; choose such a relation with $sup(deg(P_i))$ minimum. Then $\sum (V_i, 1)(P_i, 1) = 0$, which shows as in (1) that $(P_i, 1) = 0$ for each i. Now some P_j is $\neq 0$, hence $P_j x^{-1} \neq 0$ for some letter x. By Eq. (3.1) we obtain $\sum V_i (P_i x^{-1}) = 0$, which is a new relation contradicting the above minimality. Thus the V's are $K\langle X \rangle$-independent. □

Definition. An n by n matrix M over $K\langle X \rangle$ is *full* if, whenever $M = M_1 M_2$ for some matrices $M_1 \in K\langle X \rangle^{n \times p}$ and $M_2 \in K\langle X \rangle^{p \times n}$, then $p \geqq n$.

Remark. Taking in the above definition a field instead of $K\langle X \rangle$, one obtains exactly the definition of an invertible matrix over this field (consider for instance the rank of M, in order to verify it).

Corollary 3.2 (Cohn 1971). *Let M be an n by n matrix over $K\langle X \rangle$. If $S_1, \ldots, S_n$ in $K\langle\langle X \rangle\rangle$ are formal series, not all zero, such that $(S_1, \ldots, S_n) M = (0, \ldots, 0)$, then M is not full.*

Proof. Let E be the set of vectors $V \in K\langle X \rangle^{n \times 1}$ such that $(S_1, \ldots, S_n) V = 0$. Then E is a right submodule of $K\langle X \rangle^{n \times 1}$. Let $V = {}^t(P_1, \ldots, P_n) \in E$ be such that $(V, 1) = 0$. Then $(P_i, 1) = 0$ for any i. Moreover $\sum_i S_i P_i = 0$, so that if x is a letter, by Eq. (3.1), one has $\sum_i S_i (P_i x^{-1}) = 0$. This means that $V x^{-1} \in E$: thus E is regular. By Theorem 3.1, the right $K\langle X \rangle$-module E admits a basis consisting of p vectors $V_1, \ldots, V_p$ such that $rank((V_1, 1), \ldots, (V_p, 1)) = p$ (and $p \leqq n$).

Now suppose that $p = n$. Then the matrix $N = ((V_1, 1), \ldots, (V_n, 1)) \in K^{n \times n}$ is invertible. But N is the constant matrix of $H = (V_1, \ldots, V_n) \in K\langle X \rangle^{n \times n}$, i.e. $N = (H, 1)$; this implies that H is invertible in $K\langle\langle X \rangle\rangle^{n \times n}$. Now we have $(S_1, \ldots, S_n) H = 0$ (because $(S_1, \ldots, S_n) V_i = 0$ for all i), hence $(S_1, \ldots, S_n) = 0$ (multiply by H^{-1}), a contradiction.

So $p < n$. Let $M = (C_1, \ldots, C_n)$ where C_k is the k-th column of M. Then, by hypothesis, C_k belongs to E, hence $C_k = \sum_{j=1}^{p} V_j P_{jk}$ for some polynomials P_{jk}. Thus

$$M = (V_1, \ldots, V_p)(P_{jk})_{1 \leqq j \leqq p,\ 1 \leqq k \leqq n}$$

and M is not full. □

Corollary 3.3 (Cohn 1982). *Let P_1, P_2, P_3, P_4 be polynomials such that P_2 is invertible as a formal series, i.e. $(P_2, 1) \neq 0$, and such that $P_1 P_2^{-1} P_3 = P_4$. Then there exist polynomials Q_1, Q_2, Q_3, Q_4 such that $P_1 = Q_1 Q_2$, $P_2 = Q_3 Q_2$, $P_3 = Q_3 Q_4$, $P_4 = Q_1 Q_4$.*

Proof. Consider the 2 by 2 matrix over $K\langle X\rangle$:

$$M = \begin{pmatrix} P_1 & P_4 \\ P_2 & P_3 \end{pmatrix}$$

By assumption, we have

$$(1, \; -P_1 P_2^{-1}) M = 0.$$

Hence M is not full by Corollary 3.2, and M may be written as

$$M = \begin{pmatrix} Q_1 \\ Q_3 \end{pmatrix} (Q_2, Q_4)$$

for some polynomials Q_i. This proves the corollary. □

The next result is the *Inertia Theorem*. It will not be used in Chap. VIII. Let $S_1, \ldots, S_n, T_1, \ldots, T_n$ be formal series. We say that

$$\sum_j S_j T_j$$

is trivially a polynomial if for each j, either $S_j = 0$, or $T_j = 0$, or both S_j and T_j are polynomials. Note that one has

$$\sum_i S_i T_i = (S_1, \ldots, S_n) \begin{pmatrix} T_1 \\ \vdots \\ T_n \end{pmatrix}.$$

Corollary 3.4 (Inertia Theorem. Bergmann 1967, Cohn 1971). *Let $(S_{i,j})_{i \in I, 1 \leqq j \leqq n}$ and $(T_{j,k})_{1 \leqq j \leqq n, k \in K}$ be two families of formal series such that for each $i \in I$ and $k \in K$, $\sum_j S_{ij} T_{jk}$ is a polynomial. Then there exists an invertible matrix M over $K\langle\langle X\rangle\rangle$ such that for any i and k*

$$[(S_{i,1}, \ldots, S_{i,n}) M] \left[M^{-1} \begin{pmatrix} T_{1,k} \\ \vdots \\ T_{n,k} \end{pmatrix} \right]$$

is trivially a polynomial.

Proof. 1. We prove the theorem first in the case where each $T_{j,\,k}$ is a polynomial. Let $E=\{V\in K\langle X\rangle^{n\times 1}\,|\,\forall i\in I,\ (S_{i,\,1},\,\dots,\,S_{i,\,n})\,V\in K\langle X\rangle\}$. Then E is a regular right submodule of $K\langle X\rangle^{n\times 1}$, as may be easily verified (cf. the proof of Corollary 3.2). By Theorem 3.1 there exist p vectors $V_1,\dots,V_p$ in E which form a basis of E (as a right $K\langle X\rangle$-module) and such that the constant matrix of $(V_1,\dots,V_p)$ is of rank $p\leqq n$. By performing a permutation of the coordinates, we may assume that

$$(V_1,\dots,V_p)=\begin{pmatrix}A\\B\end{pmatrix}$$

where $(A,1)\in K^{p\times p}$ is invertible. Let

$$M=\begin{pmatrix}A & 0\\ B & I_{n-p}\end{pmatrix}$$

where I_{n-p} is the identity matrix of order $n-p$. Then $(M,1)\in K^{n\times n}$ is invertible, hence M is invertible in $K\langle\langle X\rangle\rangle^{n\times n}$.

Note that the first p columns of M (i.e. the V_i's) are in E: this implies that for any $i\in I$ the first p components of $(S_{i,1},\dots,S_{i,n})\ M$ are polynomials. Moreover, let $1\leqq j\leqq p$: then $M^{-1}V_j$ is equal to the jth column of $M^{-1}M$, that is, to the jth canonical vector $E_j\in K^{n\times 1}$. Now let $k\in K$. Then, by assumption, $V={}^t(T_{1,k},\dots,T_{n,k})$ is in E. Hence $V=\sum_{1\leqq j\leqq p} V_jP_j$ for some polynomials P_j. Thus $M^{-1}V=\sum_j M^{-1}V_jP_j$ is equal, by the previous remark, to $\sum_j E_jP_j={}^t(P_1,\,\dots,\,P_p,\,0,\,\dots,\,0)$. This shows that the product

$$[(S_{i,1},\dots,S_{i,n})M]\left[M^{-1}\begin{pmatrix}T_{1,k}\\ \vdots\\ T_{n,k}\end{pmatrix}\right]$$

is trivially a polynomial.

2. We come to the general case. Let

$$J=\{j\in\{1,\dots,n\}\,|\,\forall k\in K,\ T_{j,k}\in K\langle K\rangle\}$$

If $J=\{1,\dots,n\}$, then we are in case 1. Suppose that $|J|<n$: we may suppose that $J=\{1,\dots,p\}$ with $0\leqq p<n$ (including the case $J=\varnothing$). Suppose that $\forall i\in I,\ \forall j\notin J,\ S_{ij}=0$, Then

$$\sum_{j=1}^{n} S_{ij}T_{jk}=\sum_{j=1}^{p} S_{ij}T_{jk}$$

is a polynomial, so we are also in case 1 (with p instead of n). Otherwise there is some $i_0\in I$ such that for some $j_0\notin J$, $S_{i_0j_0}\neq 0$. Choose $j_0\notin J$ such that $\omega(S_{i_0j_0})\leqq\omega(S_{i_0j})$ for any $j\notin J$ (for the definition of ω, see Sect. I.3). Choose polynomials $R_1,\dots,R_p$ such that for $1\leqq j\leqq p$, $\omega(S_{i_0j}+R_j)\geqq\omega(S_{i_0j_0})$. Define S'_j by: $S'_j=S_{i_0j}+R_j$ if $1\leqq j\leqq p$ and $S'_j=S_{i_0j}$ if $p<j\leqq n$. Then $\omega(S'_{j_0})\leqq\omega(S'_j)$, $S'_{j_0}=S_{i_0j_0}\neq 0$ and

$$\sum_{1\leqq j\leqq n} S'_jT_{jk}=\sum_{j\leqq p}(S_{i_0j}+R_j)\,T_{jk}+\sum_{j>p} S_{i_0j}T_{jk}=\sum_{1\leqq j\leqq n} S_{i_0j}T_{jk}+\sum_{j\leqq p} R_jT_{jk}$$

is a polynomial, by definition of $J=\{1,\ldots,p\}$. Let w be a word of minimal length in the support of S'_{j_0}; then $w^{-1}S'_{j_0}$ is an invertible formal series, and for any j, since $\omega(S'_j)\geqq|w|$, one has $w^{-1}(S'_jT_{jk})=(w^{-1}S'_j)T_{jk}$. Hence $\sum_j(w^{-1}S'_j)T_{jk}$ is a polynomial. Define the matrix $N\in K\langle\langle X\rangle\rangle^{n\times n}$ which coincides with the $n\times n$ identity matrix, except in the j_0th row, where it is equal to $(w^{-1}S'_1,\ldots,w^{-1}S'_n)$; in particular the entry of the coordinates (j_0,j_0) of N is the invertible series $w^{-1}S_{j_0}$, so N is invertible in $K\langle\langle X\rangle\rangle$. Let $M=N^{-1}$. Then for any k, $M^{-1}\,{}^t(T_{1k},\ldots,T_{nk})=N\,{}^t(T_{1k},\ldots,T_{nk})$ is equal to ${}^t(T_{1k},\ldots,T_{nk})$ except in the j_0th component, where it is equal to $\sum(w^{-1}S'_j)T_{jk}$: hence the first p and the j_0th components of $M^{-1t}(T_{1k},\ldots,T_{nk})$ are polynomials and we may conclude the proof because we have increased $|J|$. □

4 Gauss's Lemma

We consider in this section polynomials with integers or rational coefficients. Everything would work, however, with any factorial ring instead of **Z**.

Definition. A polynomial $P\in\mathbf{Q}\langle X\rangle$ is *primitive* if $P\neq 0$, $P\in\mathbf{Z}\langle X\rangle$ and if its coefficients have no nontrivial common divisor in **Z**.

Definition. The *content* of a nonzero polynomial $P\in\mathbf{Q}\langle X\rangle$ is the unique positive rational number $c(P)$ such that $P/c(P)$ is primitive.

Notation. $P/c(P)$ will be denoted by $\bar{P}$.

Example 4.1. $c(4/3+6x-2xy)=2/3$ because $3/2(4/3+6x-2xy)=2+9x-3xy$ is primitive.

Note that for $P\neq 0$

$$P\text{ primitive}\Leftrightarrow c(P)=1 \tag{4.1}$$

$$P\in\mathbf{Z}\langle X\rangle\Leftrightarrow c(P)\in\mathbf{N} \tag{4.2}$$

Theorem 4.1 (Gauss's Lemma).
(i) *If P, Q are primitive, then so is PQ.*
(ii) *If P, Q are nonzero polynomials, then $c(P)=c(P)c(Q)$ and $\overline{PQ}=\bar{P}\bar{Q}$.*

Proof. (i) Suppose PQ is not primitive. Then there is some prime number n which divides each coefficient of PQ. This means that the canonical image $\varphi(PQ)$ of PQ in $(\mathbf{Z}/n\mathbf{Z})\langle X\rangle$ vanishes. But $\mathbf{Z}/n\mathbf{Z}$ is a field, so $(\mathbf{Z}/n\mathbf{Z})\langle X\rangle$ is entire (Sect. 1); moreover, $0=\varphi(PQ)=\varphi(P)\varphi(Q)$, so $\varphi(P)=0$ or $\varphi(Q)=0$. This means that n divides all the coefficients of P or of Q, and contradicts the fact that P and Q are primitive.

(ii) By (i), $PQ/c(P)c(Q)=(P/c(P))(Q/c(Q))$ is primitive. So, by definition of the content of PQ, $c(PQ)=c(P)c(Q)$. Now, $\overline{PQ}=PQ/c(PQ)$ so that $\overline{PQ}=PQ/c(P)c(Q)=\bar{P}\bar{Q}$. □

Corollary 4.2. *Let $a_1, \ldots, a_n$ be polynomials. Then the continuant polynomials $p(a_1, \ldots, a_n)$ and $p(a_n, \ldots, a_1)$ are both zero or have the same content.*

Proof (Induction on n). The result is obvious for $n=0, 1$. Let $n \leqq 2$. By Lemma 2.5, we may suppose that both polynomials are $\neq 0$. Now we have, by Proposition 2.1

$$p(a_1, \ldots, a_n)p(a_{n-1}, \ldots, a_1)=p(a_1, \ldots, a_{n-1})p(a_n, \ldots, a_1)$$

By induction, either $p(a_1, \ldots, a_{n-1})=p(a_{n-1}, \ldots, a_1)=0$, in which case $p(a_1, \ldots, a_n)=p(a_1, \ldots, a_{n-2})$ by Eq. (2.1) and $p(a_n, \ldots, a_1)=p(a_{n-2}, \ldots, a_1)$, and we conclude by induction; or $c(p(a_{n-1}, \ldots, a_1))=c(p(a_1, \ldots, a_{n-1}))$, which implies by Eq. (2.4) and Theorem 4.1 that $c(p(a_1, \ldots, a_n))=c(p(a_n, \ldots, a_1))$. □

Corollary 4.3. *Let P_1, P_2, P_3, P_4 be nonzero polynomials in $\mathbf{Z}\langle X\rangle$ such that P_2 is invertible in $\mathbf{Q}\langle\langle X\rangle\rangle$ and such that $P_1P_2^{-1}P_3=P_4$. Then there exist polynomials R_1, R_2, R_3, R_4 in $\mathbf{Z}\langle X\rangle$ such that*

$$P_1=R_1R_2,\ P_2=R_3R_2,\ P_3=R_3R_4,\ P_4=R_1R_4$$

Proof. By Corollary 3.3 we have

$$P_1=Q_1Q_2,\ P_2=Q_3Q_2,\ P_3=Q_3Q_4,\ P_4=Q_1Q_4$$

for some polynomials Q_1, Q_2, Q_3, Q_4 in $\mathbf{Q}\langle X\rangle$.

Let $c_i=c(Q_i)$, $i=1, 2, 3, 4$. By Theorem 4.1. we have

$$c(P_1)=c_1c_2,\ c(P_2)=c_3c_2,\ c(P_3)=c_3c_4,\ c(P_4)=c_1c_4$$

Thus $c(P_4)=c(P_1)c(P_3)/c(P_2)$.

As by hypothesis and Eq. (4.2) $c(P_i)\in\mathbf{N}$, there exist positive integers d_1, d_2, d_3, d_4 such that

$$c(P_1)=d_1d_2,\ c(P_2)=d_3d_2,\ c(P_3)=d_3d_4,\ c(P_4)=d_1d_4$$

Moreover, by Theorem 4.1,

$$\bar{P}_1=\bar{Q}_1\bar{Q}_2,\ \bar{P}_2=\bar{Q}_3\bar{Q}_2,\ \bar{P}_3=\bar{Q}_3\bar{Q}_4,\ \bar{P}_4=\bar{Q}_1\bar{Q}_4$$

Put $R_i=d_i\bar{Q}_i$, $i=1, 2, 3, 4$. Then $R_i\in\mathbf{Z}\langle X\rangle$. Moreover,

$$P_1=c(P_1)\bar{P}_1=d_1d_2\bar{Q}_1\bar{Q}_2=R_1R_2$$

Similarly, $P_2=R_3R_2$, $P_3=R_3R_4$ and $P_4=R_1R_4$. □

Proposition 4.4. *Let Y be a primitive polynomial of degree 1 which vanishes for some integer values of the variables. Let $P, Q \in \mathbf{Z}\langle X\rangle$ and $\alpha \in \mathbf{Z}$, $\alpha \neq 0$ be such that $PQ \equiv \alpha$ mod. $Y\mathbf{Z}\langle X\rangle$. Then $P \equiv \beta$, $Q \equiv \gamma$ mod. $Y\mathbf{Z}\langle X\rangle$ for some $\beta, \gamma \in \mathbf{Z}$ such that $\alpha = \beta\gamma$.*

Proof. We have $PQ = YQ_2 + \alpha$ for some polynomial Q_2. As $\alpha \neq 0$, we have $Q \neq 0$ and we may apply Corollary 1.3. This shows that $P = \beta + YT$ for some β in $\mathbf{Q}$ and T in $\mathbf{Q}\langle X\rangle$. Hence $YQ_2 + \alpha = \beta Q + YTQ$. Since $\alpha \neq 0$ and $deg(Y) > 0$, we obtain $\beta \neq 0$. This shows that $Q \equiv \gamma + YS$ for some $\gamma \in \mathbf{Q}$ such that $\alpha = \beta\gamma$. Now, the assumption on Y and the fact that P, Q have integer coefficients imply that $\beta, \gamma \in \mathbf{Z}$. Since $YT = P - \beta \in \mathbf{Z}\langle X\rangle$, we obtain that $c(Y)c(T) \in \mathbf{N}$, by Eq. (4.2) and Theorem 4.1 (ii). But Y is primitive, so $c(Y) = 1$, which shows that $c(T) \in \mathbf{N}$ and $T \in \mathbf{Z}\langle X\rangle$ by (4.2). Similarly, $S \in \mathbf{Z}\langle X\rangle$. □

Exercises for Chapter VII

1.1. Let $P_1, \ldots, P_n, Q_1, \ldots, Q_n$ be polynomials. A relation $\sum_{i=1}^{n} P_i Q_i = 0$ is called *trivial* if for each i, either $P_i = 0$ or $Q_i = 0$. Note that $\sum P_i Q_i$ may be written

$$(P_1, \ldots, P_n)\begin{pmatrix} Q_1 \\ \vdots \\ Q_n \end{pmatrix}.$$

Show that if $\sum_{i=1}^{n} P_i Q_i = 0$, then there exists an invertible n by n matrix M with coefficients in $K\langle X\rangle$ such that the relation

$$[(P_1, \ldots, P_n)M]\left[M^{-1}\begin{pmatrix} Q_1 \\ \vdots \\ Q_n \end{pmatrix}\right] = 0$$

is trivial (cf. Cohn 1971).

1.2. a) Let A, B, A', B' be nonzero formal series such that $AB' = BA'$, with $\omega(A) \geqq \omega(B)$ (cf. Chap. I). Show that there exists a formal series U such that $A = BU$, $A' = UB'$.
b) Let S be a formal series and let C be its centralizer, i.e. $C = \{T \in K\langle\langle X\rangle\rangle \mid ST = TS\}$. Show that if T_1, $T_2 \in C$ and $\omega(T_2) \geqq \omega(T_1)$, then there exists $T \in C$ such that $T_2 = T_1 T$. (*Hint*: one may suppose $\omega(S) \geqq 1$; let n be such that $\omega(S^n) \geqq \omega(T_1)$, $\omega(T_2)$: use a) three times.) Let $T \in C$ such that $\omega(T) \geqq 1$ is minimum. Show that $C = K[[T]]$, i.e.

$$C = \left\{ \sum_{n \in \mathbf{N}} a_n T^n \mid a_n \in K \right\}$$

(see Cohn 1971).

2.1. Show that for $n \geqq k$ the continuant polynomials satisfy the identities

$$p(a_1, \ldots, a_n)p(a_{n-1}, \ldots, a_k) - p(a_1, \ldots, a_{n-1})p(a_n, \ldots, a_k)$$
$$= (-1)^{n+k} p(a_1, \ldots, a_{k-2})$$

with the conventions: $p(a_1, \ldots, a_{k-2}) = 0$ if $k=1$, $=1$ if $k=0$, and $p(a_{n-1}, \ldots, a_k) = 1$ if $k=n$. Show that the number of words in the support of $p(a_1, \ldots, a_n)$ is the n-th Fibonacci number $F_n(F_0 = F_1 = 1,\ F_{n+2} = F_{n+1} + F_n)$.

2.2. Show that if $a_1, \ldots, a_n$ are commutative polnomials, then

$$a_1 + \cfrac{1}{a_2 + \cfrac{1}{a_3 + \cfrac{1}{\cdots \cfrac{1}{a_n}}}} = \frac{p(a_1, \ldots, a_n)}{p(a_2, \ldots, a_n)}$$

2.3. Show that the entries of the matrix

$$\begin{pmatrix} a_1 & 1 \\ 1 & 0 \end{pmatrix} \begin{pmatrix} a_2 & 1 \\ 1 & 0 \end{pmatrix} \cdots \begin{pmatrix} a_n & 1 \\ 1 & 0 \end{pmatrix}$$

may be expressed by means of continuant polynomials.

3.1. Let M be an n by n polynomial matrix such that $M = M_1 M_2$ with $M_1 \in K\langle\langle X\rangle\rangle^{n \times p}$ and $M_2 \in K\langle\langle X\rangle\rangle^{p \times n}$. Show that then one may choose M_1, M_2 to be polynomial matrices (use the inertia theorem; see Cohn 1985).

Notes to Chapter VII

Most of the results of this chapter are due to P. M. Cohn. We have already seen a result concerning noncommutative polynomials in Chap. II (Corollary II.3.3): in P. M. Cohn's terminology, it means that $K\langle X\rangle$ is a *fir* ("free ideal ring"). The terminology "continuant" stems from its relation to continuous fractions (see Exercises 2.2 and 2.3). Corollary 3.2 is a special case of a more general result, stating that every polynomial matrix which is singular over the free field is not full (see Cohn 1971).

Chapter VIII

Codes and Formal Series

The aim of this final chapter is to present an application of formal series to the theory of (variable-length) codes. The main result (Theorem 4.1) states that every finite complete code admits a factorization into three polynomials which reflect its combinatorial structure.

The first section contains some basic facts on codes and prefix codes. These are easily expressed by means of formal power series.

Section 2 is devoted to complete codes and their relations to Bernoulli morphisms (Theorem 2.4). Concerning the degree of a code, we give, in Sect. 3, only the very basic results needed in Sect. 4.

This last section is devoted to the proof of the main result. It uses the material of the previous section and from Chapter VII.

1 Codes

Definition. A *code* is a subset C of X^* such that whenever $u_1, \ldots, u_n, v_1, \ldots, v_p$ in C satisfy

$$u_1 \ldots u_n = v_1 \ldots v_p \tag{1.1}$$

then $n=p$ and $u_i = v_i$ for $i=1, \ldots, n$. In this case, any word in C^* (= the submonoid generated by C) is called a *message*.

Note that if C is a code, then $C \subset X^+ \, (=X^* \backslash 1)$.

Example 1.1. The set $\{x, xy, yx\}$ is not a code, because the word xyx has two factorizations in it:

$$xyx = x(yx) = (xy)x$$

Example 1.2. The set $\{x, yx, yy\}$ is a code; indeed, no word in it is a left factor of another, so in each relation of the form (1.1), either u_1 is a left factor of v_1 or vice versa, so one has $u_1 = v_1$, and one concludes by induction on n.

Example 1.3. The set $\{y, xy, x^2y, x^3y, \ldots, x^ny, \ldots\} = x^*y$ is a code, for the same reason as in Example 1.2.

Example 1.4. The set $\{x^3, x^2yx, x^2y^2, xy, yx^2, yxyx, yxy^2, y^2x, y^3\}$ is a code for the same reason; note that in this case, moreover, no word is a right factor of another.

Example 1.5. The set $C=\{x^2, xy, x^2y, xy^2, y^2\}$ is a code. Indeed, let $\underline{C}$ denote its characteristic polynomial; then we have

$$\begin{aligned}
1-\underline{C} &= 1-x^2-xy-x^2y-xy^2-y^2 \\
&= (1-y-x^2-xy)+(y-y^2-x^2y-xy^2) \\
&= (1-y-x^2-xy)(1+y) \\
&= ((1-x-y)+(x-x^2-xy))(1+y) \\
&= (1+x)(1-x-y)(1+y)
\end{aligned}$$

Thus, in $\mathbf{Z}\langle\langle X\rangle\rangle$ we have

$$(1-\underline{C})^{-1}=(1+y)^{-1}(1-x-y)^{-1}(1+x)^{-1}$$

By the results of Sect. I.4, for any proper formal series S, $(1-S)^{-1}=\sum_{n\geq 0} S^n=S^*$ and $(1-x-y)^{-1}=X^*=\underline{X^*}$ is the sum of all the words on X (and hence, its nonzero coefficients are all equal to 1). Hence

$$\underline{X^*}=(1+y)\left(\sum_{n\geq 0}\underline{C}^n\right)(1+x)$$

This shows that the series $\sum_{n\geq 0}\underline{C}^n$ has no coefficient ≥ 2, since otherwise $\underline{X^*}$ would have such a coefficient. From $\underline{C}^n=\sum_{u_1,\ldots,u_n\in C} u_1\ldots u_n$, we obtain the fact that no word has two distinct factorizations of the form $u_1\ldots u_n(u_i\in C)$, so C is a code.

Recall that for any language L, $\underline{L}$ denotes its characteristic series (considered as an element of $\mathbf{Q}\langle\langle X\rangle\rangle$ in the present chapter). One of the arguments of the last example may be generalized as follows.

Proposition 1.1. *Let C be a subset of X^+ and let $\underline{C}$ be its characteristic series. Then C is a code if and only if one has in* $\mathbf{Z}\langle\langle X\rangle\rangle$:

$$(1-\underline{C})^{-1}=\underline{C}^*=\underline{C^*} \tag{1.2}$$

Proof. The first equality is always true, as shown in Sect. I.4. Let $C\subset X^+$. Then

$$\sum_{n\geq 0}\;\sum_{u_1,\ldots,u_n\in C} u_1\ldots u_n=\sum_{n\geq 0}\underline{C}^n=\underline{C}^*$$

If C is a code, then the words

$$u_1 \dots u_n \; (n \geqq 0, \; u_i \in C)$$

are all distinct, so the left-hand side is equal to $\underline{C}^*$. If C is not a code, then two of these words are equal, so the left-hand side is a series with at least one coefficient $\geqq 2$: it cannot be equal to $\underline{C}^*$, because the latter has only 0, 1 as coefficients. □

The previous result provides an effective algorithm for testing whether a given rational subset C of X^+ is a code. Indeed, one has merely to check if the rational power series $\underline{C}^* - \underline{C}^*$ is equal to 0; for this, apply Corollary II.3.4.

However, there are more direct algorithms. We give below, without proof, the algorithm of Sardinas and Patterson (see Lallement 1978; Berstel and Perrin 1985). Recall that for any language L and any word w, we denote by $w^{-1}L$ the language

$$w^{-1}L = \{u \in X^* \mid wu \in L\}$$

More generally, if E is a language, we denote by $E^{-1}L$ the language

$$E^{-1}L = \bigcup_{w \in E} w^{-1}L$$

Now let C be a subset of A^+. Define a sequence of languages C_0 by

$$C_0 = C^{-1}C \backslash 1$$

$$C_{n+1} = C_n^{-1}C \cup C^{-1}C_n \, (n \geqq 0)$$

Then C *is a code if and only if no* C_n *contains the empty word.* Note that if C is finite, then the sequence (C_n) is periodic (because each word in C_n is a factor of some word in C); hence we obtain an effective algorithm.

Another way to express the fact that a set of words is a code is by means of the so-called unambiguous operations. Let K, L be languages. We say that their *union* is *unambiguous* if they are disjoint languages. We say their *product* is *unambiguous* if u, $u' \in K$, $v, v' \in L$ and $uv = u'v'$ implies $u = u'$, $v = v'$. We say that the *star* K^* is *unambiguous* if K is a code.

Proposition 1.2. *Let* K, L *be languages.*
(i) *The union of* K *and* L *is unambiguous if and only if* $\underline{K \cup L} = \underline{K} + \underline{L}$.
(ii) *The product* KL *is unambiguous if and only if* $\underline{KL} = \underline{K}\underline{L}$.
(iii) *If* $1 \notin K$, *then the star* K^* *is unambiguous if and only if* $\underline{K}^* = \underline{K^*}$.

Proof. The first two assertions are a direct consequence of the definition. The last one is merely a reformulation of Proposition 1.1. □

We have already met a family of codes in Sect. II.3: the *prefix codes.* A code is a prefix code if no word in it is a left factor of another word in it (this condition is sufficient to ensure codicity). Symmetrically, one defines *suffix* codes. A code is called *biprefix* if it is both prefix and suffix.

Proposition 1.3. *Let C be a code such that for any word v in C^*, one has $v^{-1}C^* \subset C^*$. Then C is a prefix code.*

Note that for any set C of words and v in C^*, one has $C^* \subset v^{-1}C^*$.

Proof. Suppose $u=vw$, with u, v in C and $w \in X^*$. We have to show that $w=1$. Now, $w=v^{-1}u \in v^{-1}C \subset v^{-1}C^*$, hence $w \in C^*$. Therefore $w=c_1 \ldots c_n (c_i \in C)$ and $u= vc_1 \ldots c_n \in C$. The only possibility for C to be a code is $n=0$, i.e., $w=1$, and C is a prefix code.

Proposition 1.4. *Let C be a prefix code such that $CX^* \cap wX^*$ is nonempty for any word w. Let P be the set of proper left factors of the words in C. Then one has in $\mathbf{Z}\langle\langle X \rangle\rangle$*

$$\underline{C}-1=\underline{P}(\underline{x}-1)$$

Proof. Let $P'=X^* \backslash CX^*$. Then, by Proposition II.3.1, we have $X^*=C^*P'$. But, because C is a prefix code, the conditions $u_1 \ldots u_n q = v_1 \ldots v_p r$, u_i, $v_j \in C$, q, $r \in P'$ imply $n=p$, $u_i=v_i (i=1, \ldots, n)$, hence also $q=r$. This shows that the product C^*P' is unambiguous, hence by Proposition 1.2, we have $\underline{X}^*=\underline{C}^*\underline{P}'$. Now, by Proposition 1.1, $\underline{X}^*=(1-\underline{X})^{-1}$ and $\underline{C}^*=(1-\underline{C})^{-1}$. Moreover, the empty word is in P', so $\underline{P}'$ is invertible in $\mathbf{Z}\langle\langle X \rangle\rangle$. Hence $1-\underline{X}=\underline{P}'^{-1}(1-\underline{C})$, which implies $\underline{C}-1=\underline{P}'(\underline{X}-1)$.

It remains to show that $P=P'$. Let w be in P; then w is a proper left factor of some word in C and so has no left factor in C, C being a prefix code; hence $w \notin CX^* \Rightarrow w \in P'$.

Let w be in P'. By assumption, there are words $c \in C$, u, $v \in X^*$ such that $cu=wv$; as $w \notin CX^*$, w must be a proper left factor of c, so $w \in P$. □

Let C be a code. Define for any word u the series $S(u)$ inductively by:

$$S(1)=1$$

$$S(u)=x^{-1}[S(v)]+(S(v),1)x^{-1}\underline{C}, \qquad \text{for } u=vx(x \in X)$$

Note that, obviously, $S(u)$ has nonnegative coefficients. The reader may verify that the support of $S(u)$ consists of proper right factors of C (cf. Exercise 1.3).

Lemma 1.5. *Let C be a code. Then for any word u, $u^{-1}(\underline{C}^*)=S(u)\underline{C}^*$. In particular, $S(u)$ is a characteristic series. If C is finite, then $S(u)$ is a polynomial.*

Proof. We shall use the formulas of Lemma I.6.2.

We prove $u^{-1}(\underline{C}^*)=S(u)\underline{C}^*$ by induction on $|u|$. If $u=1$, it is clearly true. Let $u=vx(x \in X)$. Then by induction $v^{-1}(\underline{C}^*)=S(v)\underline{C}^*$. Thus, by Lemma I.6.2,

$$u^{-1}(\underline{C}^*)=x^{-1}v^{-1}(\underline{C}^*)=(x^{-1}S(v))\underline{C}^*+(S(v),1)(x^{-1}\underline{C}^*)$$

$$=(x^{-1}S(v))\underline{C}^*+(S(v),1)(x^{-1}\underline{C})\underline{C}^*=S(u)\underline{C}^*$$

Now, since $u^{-1}(\underline{C}^*)$ is obviously a characteristic series, the same holds for $S(u)$. If C is finite, the fact that $S(u)$ is a polynomial is easily verified by induction on the definition. □

One defines symmetrically the series $P(u) \in \mathbf{Z}\langle\langle X\rangle\rangle$ by:

$$P(1)=1$$

$$P(xv)=[P(v)]x^{-1}+(P(v),1)\underline{C}x^{-1} \qquad \text{for } x\in X \text{ and } v\in X^*$$

Now we define for any couple (u, v) of words another series, in the following way:

$$F(u,1)=0$$

$$F(u,xv)=(P(v),1)[S(u)]x^{-1}+F(u,v)x^{-1}$$

As above, the series $F(u, v)$ clearly has nonnegative coefficients.

Proposition 1.6. *Let C be a code. Then for any words u and v, $u^{-1}(\underline{C}^*)v^{-1}=S(u)\underline{C}^*P(v)+F(u,v)$. In particular, $F(u,v)$ is a characteristic series. If C is finite, then $F(u,v)$ is a polynomial.*

Proof. (Induction on $|v|$). The result is obvious if $v=1$, by Lemma 1.5. Let $x\in X$. Then $u^{-1}(\underline{C}^*)(vx)^{-1}=[u^{-1}(\underline{C}^*)v^{-1}]x^{-1}$ is equal, by induction, to

$$[S(u)\underline{C}^*P(v)]x^{-1}+F(u,v)x^{-1}$$

$$=S(u)\underline{C}^*[P(v)x^{-1}]+(P(v),1)S(u)[\underline{C}^*x^{-1}]$$

$$+(P(v),1)[S(u)x^{-1}]+F(u,v)x^{-1}$$

$$=S(u)\underline{C}^*[P(v)x^{-1}]+(P(v),1)S(u)\underline{C}^*[\underline{C}x^{-1}]+F(u,xv)$$

$$=S(u)\underline{C}^*P(xv)+F(u,xv)$$

This proves the formula.

Now, since $S(u)\underline{C}^*P(v)$ has nonnegative coefficients and since $u^{-1}(\underline{C}^*)v^{-1}$ is a characteristic series, the same holds for $F(u, v)$. If C is finite, it is easily seen by induction on the definition that $F(u, v)$ is a polynomial. □

2 Completeness

Definition. A language $C\subset X^*$ is *complete* if for any word w, the set $C^*\cap X^*wX^*$ is nonempty.

Lemma 2.1. *If C is complete, then any word w is either a factor of a word of C or may be written as*

$$w=smp$$

with $m\in C^*$ and where $s(p)$ is a right (left) factor of a word of C.

Proof. We have $awb \in C^*$ for some words a, b. Let us represent a word in C^* schematically by

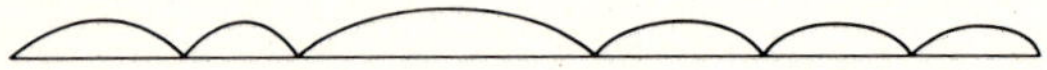

Then we have two cases:

1)

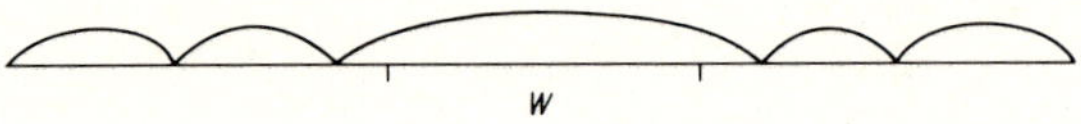

2)

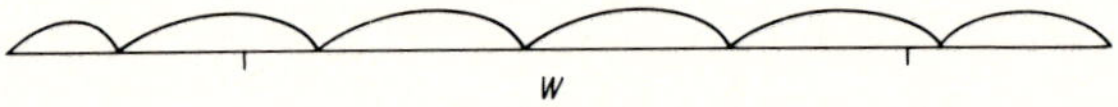

In the first case, w is a factor of a word in C. In the second case, $w = smp$, as in the lemma. □

Definition. A *Bernoulli morphism* is a mapping π: $X^* \to \mathbf{R}$ such that
(i) $\pi(w) > 0$ for any word w,
(ii) $\pi(1) = 1$,
(iii) $\pi(uv) = \pi(u)\pi(v)$ for any words u, v,
(iv) $\sum_{x \in X} \pi(x) = 1$.

It is called *uniform* if $\pi(x) = 1/|X|$ for any letter x. We define for any language L the *measure* of L by

$$\pi(L) = \sum_{w \in L} \pi(w)$$

(it may be infinite). We shall frequently use the following inequalities:

$$\pi(\cup L_i) \leqq \sum \pi(L_i)$$

$$\pi(KL) \leqq \pi(K)\pi(L)$$

Note that for any n, one has $\pi(X^n) = 1$.

Lemma 2.2. *Let C be a code. Then $\pi(C) \leqq 1$.*

Proof. Since C is the limit of its finite subsets, it is enough to show the lemma in the case where C is finite. Let p be the maximal length of words in C. Then

$$C^n \subset X \cup X^2 \cup \ldots \cup X^{pn}$$

Thus $\pi(C^n) \leqq pn$. Now, as C is a code, each word in C^n has only one factorization of the form $u_1 \ldots u_n (u_i \in C)$. As π is multiplicative, we obtain $\pi(C^n) = \pi(C)^n$. Hence

$$\pi(C)^n \leqq pn$$

This shows that $\pi(C) \leqq 1$. □

Lemma 2.3. *Let C be a finite complete language. Then $\pi(C) \geqq 1$.*

Proof. By Lemma 2.1, we may write

$$X^* = SC^*P \cup F$$

where S, P, F are finite languages. Thus

$$\infty = \pi(X^*) \leqq \pi(S)\pi(C^*)\pi(P) + \pi(F)$$

This shows that $\pi(C^*) = \infty$. Now

$$C^* = \bigcup_{n \geqq 0} C^n$$

so that $\pi(C^*) \leqq \sum_{n \geqq 0} \pi(C^n)$. Moreover, $\pi(C^n) \leqq \pi(C)^n$, π being multiplicative. So $\infty \leqq \sum_{n \geqq 0} \pi(C)^n$, which shows that $\pi(C) \geqq 1$. □

Theorem 2.4 (Schützenberger and Marcus 1959; Boë et al. 1980). *Let C be a finite subset of X^* and let π be a Bernoulli morphism. Then any two of the following assertions imply the third one*:

(i) *C is a code,*
(ii) *C is complete,*
(iii) $\pi(C) = 1$.

Note that this gives an algorithm for testing whether a given finite code is complete. We need another lemma.

Lemma 2.5. *Let L be a language and let w be a word such that $L \cap X^*wX^*$ is empty. Then $\pi(L) < \infty$.*

Proof. Let $l = |w|$ and for $i = 0, \ldots, l-1$

$$L_i = \{v \in L \mid |v| \equiv i \text{ mod. } l\}$$

Then $L_i \subset X^i(X^l \backslash w)^*$. Indeed, $v \in L_i$ implies $v = uv_1 \ldots v_n$ with $|u| = i$ and for any j, $|v_j| = l$; by assumption, w is not factor of v, hence w is none of the v_j's: thus $v_j \in X^l \backslash w$, which proves the claim.
Now

$$\pi(X^l \backslash w) = \pi(X^l) - \pi(w) = 1 - \pi(w) < 1$$

and

$$\pi[(X^l \backslash w)^*] = \pi\left[\bigcup_{n \geqq 0} (X^l \backslash w)^n\right] \leqq \sum_{n \geqq 0} \pi[(X^l \backslash w)^n] \leqq \sum_{n \geqq 0} [\pi(X^l \backslash w)]^n < \infty$$

Thus $\pi(L_i)=\pi[X^i(X^l\backslash w)^*]\leqq\pi(X^i)\pi[(X^l\backslash w)^*]<\infty$ and since $L=\bigcup_{0\leqq i\leqq l-1} L_i$, we obtain $\pi(L)<\infty$. □

Proof of Theorem 2.4. Lemmas 2.2 and 2.3 show that (i) and (ii) imply (iii).

Let C be a code with $\pi(C)=1$. Suppose C is not complete. Then for some word w, $C^*\cap X^*wX^*$ is empty. Hence, by Lemma 2.5, $\pi(C^*)<\infty$. As C is a code, $\pi(C^*)$ is equal to the sum $\sum_{n\geqq 0}\pi(C)^n$. The latter being finite, we deduce that $\pi(C)<1$, a contradiction.

Let C be complete and $\pi(C)=1$. Then C^n is complete for any n; indeed, for any word w, there are words u, v, $a_1, \ldots, a_p\,(a_i\in C)$ such that $uwv=a_1\ldots a_p$ (C being complete). Let r be such that $p+r$ is a multiple of n; then $uwva_1^r=a_1\ldots a_pa_1^r\in(C^n)^*$, which shows that $(C^n)^*\cap X^*wX^*$ is nonempty. Hence C^n is complete. Thus by Lemma 2.3, $\pi(C^n)\geqq 1$ for any n. But as, usually, $\pi(C^n)\leqq\pi(C)^n=1$, then $\pi(C^n)=\pi(C)^n$ for any n.

Suppose C is not a code. Then for some words $u_1, \ldots, u_n, v_1, \ldots, v_p$ in C we have $u_1\ldots u_n=v_1\ldots v_p$ and $u_1\neq v_1$. Hence $u_1\ldots u_nv_1\ldots v_p=v_1\ldots v_pu_1\ldots u_n$, and we have obtained a word in C^{n+p} which has two distinct factorizations. Hence

$$\pi(C^{n+p})=\pi(\{w_1\ldots w_{n+p}\mid w_i\in C\})<\sum_{w_1,\ldots,w_{n+p}\in C}\pi(w_1\ldots w_{n+p})$$
$$=\pi(C)^{n+p}$$

which is a contradiction. □

Let π be a Bernoulli morphism. Since π is multiplicative, it may be extended to an algebra homomorphism, still denoted by π,

$$\pi\colon \mathbf{Z}\langle X\rangle\to\mathbf{R}$$

by the formula

$$\pi\left(\sum_w (P,w)w\right)=\sum_w (P,w)\pi(w)$$

Note that, because the measure of X is 1, one has

$$\pi(\underline{X}-1)=0$$

Theorem 2.6. (Schützenberger 1965). *Let C be a finite code such that for any word w, the set $C^*\cap wX^*$ is nonempty. Then C is a prefix code.*

Proof. Let C' be the set of words in C having no proper left factor in C, i.e. $C'=C\backslash CX^+$. Clearly, C' is a prefix code. Moreover, if w is a word, then for some words $c_1, \ldots, c_n\in C$, $u\in X^*$, one has by assumption

$$c_1\ldots c_n=wu$$

Then either $c_1\in C'$, or c_1 has left factor in C'. Thus $C'X^*\cap wX^*$ is nonempty.

Let P be the set of proper left factors of the words in C'. Then by Proposition 1.4, $\underline{C}'-1=\underline{P}(\underline{X}-1)$. Apply the homomorphism $\pi:\mathbf{Z}\langle X\rangle\to\mathbf{R}$, obtaining $\pi(\underline{C}'-1)=0$, because $\pi(\underline{X}-1)=0$. Thus $\pi(C')=1$. As C is a code, we have by Lemma 2.2, $\pi(C)\leqq 1$. But $C'\subset C$ and π is positive. Hence $C=C'$ is prefix. □

Theorem 2.7 (Reutenauer 1985). *Let P in $\mathbf{N}\langle X\rangle$ be without a constant term such that $P-1=A(\underline{X}-1)B$ for some polynomials A, B in $\mathbf{R}\langle X\rangle$. Then $P=\underline{C}$ for some finite complete code C. Furthermore, if $B\in\mathbf{R}$ $(A\in\mathbf{R})$, then C is a prefix (a suffix) code.*

Proof. 1. Note that if S, T are formal power series, then

$$supp(ST)\subset supp(S)\,supp(T)$$

Moreover, if S is proper, then

$$supp(S^*)\subset supp(S)^*$$

2. We have $1-P=A(1-\underline{X})B$. By assumption, $1-P$ is invertible in $\mathbf{R}\langle\langle X\rangle\rangle$. The same holds for $1-\underline{X}$ since its inverse is $\underline{X}^*=\underline{X^*}$. This shows that A and B are also invertible. So we obtain

$$(1-P)^{-1}=B^{-1}(1-\underline{X})^{-1}A^{-1}$$

which implies

$$(1-\underline{X})^{-1}=B(1-P)^{-1}A$$

Thus

$$\underline{X^*}=BP^*A \tag{2.1}$$

By 1, this implies that each word w may be written $w=bma$ with $b\in supp(B)$, $m\in supp(P)^*$ and $a\in supp(A)$. Let $C=supp(P)$ and let u be a word such that $|u|>deg(A)$, $deg(B)$. Let v be any word. Then $w=uvu$ may be written $uvu=bma$ as above, which shows, by the choice of u, that $m=v_1vv_2$. Hence $C^*\cap X^*vX^*$ is nonempty: we have shown that C is complete. Thus, by Lemma 2.3, $\pi(C)\geqq 1$ (where π is some Bernoulli morphism). Now, as $P-1=A(\underline{X}-1)B$, we obtain $\pi(P)=1$. Hence

$$1\leqq\pi(C)\leqq\pi(P)=1$$

because P has nonnegative integer coefficients. This shows, π being positive, that $P=\underline{C}$ and that $\pi(C)=1$. Hence, by Theorem 2.4, C is a code, and thus a finite complete code.

Suppose now that $B\in\mathbf{R}$. Then, similarly to the above, Eq. (2.1) shows that for any word v, one has $vu=ma$ for some words $m\in C^*$, $a\in supp(A)$ (u being chosen as before). Then, as $|u|>|a|$, we obtain $m=vv_1$, which shows that $C^*\cap vX^*$ is nonempty. We conclude by Theorem 2.6. □

3 The Degree of a Code

Given a monoid M, recall that an *ideal* in M is a nonempty subset J which is closed for left and right multiplication by elements of M. Moreover, an *idempotent* is an element e which is equal to its square, i.e. $e^2=e$.

Theorem 3.1 (Suschkewitsch 1928). *Let M be a finite monoid. There exists in M an ideal J which is contained in any ideal of M. Let e be an idempotent in J. Then eMe is a finite group whose neutral element is e.*

This ideal will be called the *minimal ideal* of M.

Proof. 1. Let J be the intersection of all the ideals in M. Clearly J is closed for multiplication by elements of M. We have only to verify that it is nonempty. But let m be the product of all elements in M, in some order. Then m is in each ideal of M, and hence in J.

2. We use the following classical fact: if $a\in M$, then some positive power of a is idempotent. Indeed, choose $i,j\geqq 1$ such that $j\geqq i$ and that $a^i=a^{i+j}$ (this is possible since the set $\{a, a^2, \ldots, a^n, \ldots\}$ is finite). Let $k=j-i$. Then a^{i+k} is idempotent, because $a^{i+k}a^{i+k}=a^ka^{i+i+k}=a^ka^{i+j}=a^ka^i=a^{i+k}$.

3. Clearly, $eeme=eme=emee$ and $emeem'e=e(mem')e$, hence eMe is a (finite) monoid whose neutral element is e.

4. Let $a=eme$ be in eMe. We show the existence of $b\in eMe$ such that $ab=e$. We have $a=et$ for some $t\in M$. Now MaM is an ideal in M contained in J (because $MaM=MetM$, $e\in J$ and J is an ideal), hence $MaM=J$ (J being minimal). Thus $e=uav$ for some elements u, v of M. Next, $e=uetv=uuetvtv=u^ne(tv)^n$ for any $n\geqq 1$. Choose n such that $(tv)^n$ is idempotent. Then $e=u^ne(tv)^{2n}=u^ne(tv)^n(tv)^n=e(tv)^n=etv(tv)^{n-1}=aw$ (recall that $et=a$). But $a=eme$ implies $ae=eme^2=eme=a$, whence $e=aw=aew$ and $e=e^2=aewe$. Let $b=ewe\in eMe$. Then $e=ab$.

5. Symmetrically, we have $e=ca$ for some c in eMe. Then, classically, $c=ce=cab=eb=b$. This shows that each element of eMe has an inverse in eMe, that is, eMe is a group. □

Theorem 3.2. *Let C be a finite complete code. There exist a finite monoid M and a surjective homomorphism φ: $X^*\to M$ such that $C^*=\varphi^{-1}\varphi(C^*)$. Let J be the minimal ideal of M. There exists an idempotent e in $J\cap\varphi(C^*)$; further $\varphi(C^*)\cap eMe$ is a subgroup of the group eMe.*

It will not be shown here that the index of $\varphi(C^*)\cap eMe$ in eMe depends only on C; for this, we refer the reader to the book by Berstel and Perrin (1985). This being admitted, we introduce the following definition.

Definition. With the notation of Theorem 3.2, the index of $eMe\cap\varphi(C^*)$ in eMe is called the *degree* of C.

Proof of Theorem 3.2. Clearly, C^* is a rational subset of X^* (cf. Sect. III.1.) Hence, by Kleene's theorem (Theorem III.1.1), it is recognizable. This shows that there exists a finite monoid M, a monoid homomorphism $\varphi: X^* \to M$, and a subset N of M such that $C^* = \varphi^{-1}(N)$. Clearly, we may assume that φ is surjective; then $N = \varphi(C^*)$ and $C^* = \varphi^{-1}\varphi(C^*)$.

Let J be the minimal ideal of M and w a word in $\varphi^{-1}(J)$. Then $C^* \cap X^* w X^*$ is nonempty (because C is complete), hence there exist words u, v such that uwv is in C^*. Now $a = \varphi(uwv)$ is in $\varphi(C^*)$ and also in J (because $a = \varphi(u)\varphi(w)\varphi(v)$, $\varphi(w) \in J$, and J is an ideal). Some power $e = a^n (n \geqq 1)$ of a is idempotent and still lies in $\varphi(C^*) \cap J$.

Now, $\varphi(C^*)$ is clearly a submonoid of M. Hence, the product of any two elements of $eMe \cap \varphi(C^*)$ lies in $eMe \cap \varphi(C^*)$. Take $a \in eMe \cap \varphi(C^*)$. Then for some $n \geqq 2$, $a^n = e$ (eMe being a finite group). Then a^{n-1} is the inverse of a in eMe, and belongs to $eMe \cap \varphi(C^*)$. Thus, the latter is a subgroup of eMe. □

4 Factorization

Theorem 4.1 (Reutenauer 1985). *Let C be a finite complete code. Then there exist polynomials A, B, D in $\mathbf{Z}\langle X \rangle$ such that*

$$\underline{C} - 1 = A(d(\underline{X} - 1) + (\underline{X} - 1)D(\underline{X} - 1))B \tag{4.1}$$

and

(i) *d is the degree of C,*
(ii) *C is prefix (suffix) if and only if $B = 1$ ($A = 1$).*

Example 4.1. We have

$$x^2 + x^2y + xy + xy^2 + y^2 - 1 = (1 + x)(x + y - 1)(1 + y)$$

The corresponding code is neither prefix nor suffix, but *synchronizing* (i.e. of degre 1).

Example 4.2. Let C be the square of the code of Example 4.1. Then C is of degree 2 and

$$\underline{C} - 1 = (1 + x)(2(x + y - 1) + (x + y - 1)(1 + y)(1 + x)(x + y - 1))(1 + y)$$

Example 4.3. We have

$$x^3 + x^2yx + x^2y^2 + xy + yx^2 + yxyx + yxy^2 + y^2x + y^3 - 1$$

$$= 3(x + y - 1) + (x + y - 1)(2 + x + y + xy)(x + y - 1)$$

The corresponding code is a biprefix code and has degree 3.

The following corollary (which uses Theorem 2.7 also) characterizes completely finite complete codes.

Corollary 4.2 (Reutenauer 1985). *Let C be a language not containing the empty word. Then the following conditions are equivalent:*

(i) *C is a complete finite code.*
(ii) *There exist polynomials P, S in* $\mathbf{Z}\langle X\rangle$ *such that*

$$\underline{C}-1=P(\underline{X}-1)S \qquad \square$$

In order to prove Theorem 4.1, we need the following lemma.

Lemma 4.3. *Let C be a finite complete code of degree d. Then there exist words* $u_1, \ldots, u_d$, $v_1, \ldots, v_d$, *with* $u_1, v_1 \in C^*$, *such that for any i,* $1 \leqq i \leqq d$:

$$\underline{X}^* = \sum_{1\leqq j\leqq d} u_i^{-1}(\underline{C}^*)v_j^{-1} \text{ and for any } j,\ 1\leqq j\leqq d:$$

$$\underline{X}^* = \sum_{1\leqq i\leqq d} u_i^{-1}(\underline{C}^*)v_j^{-1}$$

Proof. By Theorem 3.2, there exist a finite monoid M, and a surjective homomorphism $\varphi: X^* \rightarrow M$ such that $C^*=\varphi^{-1}\varphi(C^*)$; moreover, there exists an idempotent e in $J\cap\varphi(C^*)$, where J is the minimal ideal of M, $G=eMe$ is a finite group and $H=eMe\cap\varphi(C^*)$ is a subgroup of G of index d.

Let $u_1, \ldots, u_d, v_1, \ldots, v_d$ be words in $\varphi^{-1}(G)$ such that

$$G = \bigcup_{1\leqq i\leqq d} \varphi(v_i)H \qquad (4.2)$$

and

$$G = \bigcup_{1\leqq j\leqq d} H\varphi(u_j)$$

(disjoint unions). By elementary group theory, we may assume that $\varphi(u_1)=\varphi(v_1)=e$ (hence $u_1, v_1 \in \varphi^{-1}(e) \subset \varphi^{-1}\varphi(C^*)=C^*$) and that $\varphi(u_i)$ is the inverse of $\varphi(v_i)$ in G.

Let $1\leqq j\leqq d$ and w be a word. Then there exists one and only one i, $1\leqq i\leqq d$, such that $w\in u_i^{-1}(C^*)v_j^{-1}$, that is, $u_iwv_j\in C^*$. Indeed, the element $e\varphi(wv_j)$ of G is in some $\varphi(v_i)H$, by Eq. (4.2). Hence, $\varphi(u_iwv_j)=\varphi(u_i)e\varphi(wv_j)\in\varphi(u_i)\varphi(v_i)H=eH=H$, which implies that $u_iwv_j\in\varphi^{-1}(H)\subset\varphi^{-1}\varphi(C^*)=C^*$. Conversely, $u_iwv_j\in C^*$ implies $\varphi(u_iwv_j)\in eMe\cap\varphi(C^*)=H$, because $\varphi(u_iwv_j)=e\varphi(u_iwv_j)e$ is already in eMe. Hence $e\varphi(wv_j)=\varphi(v_i)\varphi(u_iwv_j)\in\varphi(v_i)H$, and i is completely determined by j and w.

We have shown that one has the disjoint union, for any j, $1\leqq j\leqq d$:

$$X^* = \bigcup_{1\leqq i\leqq d} u_i^{-1}(C^*)v_j^{-1}$$

But this is equivalent to the last relation of the lemma. By symmetry, we have also the first. $\square$

We easily derive the following lemma.

Lemma 4.4. *Let C be a finite complete code of degree d. Then there exist polynomials P, P_1, S, S_1, Q, G_1, D_1 with coefficients* 0, 1 *such that*

(i) $d\underline{X}^* - Q = S\underline{C}^*P$.
(ii) $\underline{X}^* - G_1 = S\underline{C}^*P_1$.
(iii) $\underline{X}^* - D_1 = S_1\underline{C}^*P$.
(iv) P_1, S_1 *have constant term* 1.
(v) G_1, D_1 *have constant term* 0.
(vi) *If C is a prefix (suffix) code, then $S_1 = 1$ ($P_1 = 1$).*

Proof. We use Lemma 4.3 and the notation of Sect. 1. We have by Proposition 1.6, $u_i^{-1}(\underline{C}^*)v_j^{-1} = S(u_i)\underline{C}P(v_j) + F(u_i, v_j)$; moreover, by Lemma 1.5 and Proposition 1.6, $S(u_i)$, $P(v_j)$, and $F(u_i, v_j)$ are polynomials with nonnegative coefficients.

Now, by Lemma 4.3, for any i

$$\underline{X}^* = \sum_{1 \leq j \leq d} S(u_i)\underline{C}^*P(v_j) + \sum_{1 \leq j \leq d} F(u_i, v_j)$$

and for any j

$$\underline{X}^* = \sum_{1 \leq i \leq d} S(u_i)\underline{C}^*P(v_j) + \sum_{1 \leq i \leq d} F(u_i, v_j)$$

Let

$$P = \sum_{1 \leq j \leq d} P(v_j), \qquad S = \sum_{1 \leq i \leq d} S(u_i)$$

$$P_1 = P(v_1), \qquad S_1 = S(u_1)$$

$$G_1 = \sum_i F(u_i, v_1), \qquad D_1 = \sum_j F(u_1, v_j)$$

$$Q = \sum_{i,j} F(u_i, v_j)$$

Then we obtain

$$d\underline{X}^* = S\underline{C}^*P + Q$$

$$\underline{X}^* = S\underline{C}^*P_1 + G_1 \tag{4.3}$$

$$\underline{X}^* = S_1\underline{C}^*P + D_1$$

which proves (i), (ii), and (iii).

As $u_1 \in C^*$ by Lemma 4.3, $u_1^{-1}(C^*)$ contains 1, hence $u_1^{-1}(\underline{C}^*)$ has constant term 1. As $u_1^{-1}(\underline{C}^*) = S(u_1)\underline{C}^*$ by Lemma 1.5, $S_1 = S(u_1)$ must have constant term 1. The same holds for P_1, by symmetry, and proves (iv).

As $S = \sum_i S(u_i)$, the $S(u_i)$'s are nonnegative and as $S(u_1)$ has constant term 1, S has a nonnegative constant term. Moreover, P_1 has constant term 1. Hence, because $\underline{X}^*$

has constant term 1 and by Eq. (4.3), G_1 has constant term 0. Similarly, D_1 has constant term 0. This proves (v).

Suppose now that C is prefix. Then, by Proposition 1.3, $u_1^{-1}(C^*)=C^*$ (because $u_1 \in C^*$). Hence $u_1^{-1}(\underline{C}^*)=\underline{C}^*$. As by Lemma 1.5, $u_1^{-1}(\underline{C}^*)=S(u_1)\underline{C}^*$, we obtain $S_1=S(u_1)=1$. Similarly, if C is suffix, then $P_1=1$. This proves (vi). □

Given a Bernoulli morphism π, define a mapping λ for each word w by

$$\lambda(w)=\pi(w)|w|$$

For each language L, define $\lambda(L)$ by

$$\lambda(L)=\sum_{w\in L}\lambda(w)\in \mathbf{R}_+\cup\infty$$

This is called the *average length of* L. On the other hand λ extends to a linear mapping $\mathbf{Z}\langle X\rangle \to \mathbf{R}$ by

$$\lambda(P)=\sum_{w}(P,w)\lambda(w)$$

Lemma 4.5. *Let $P_1, \ldots, P_n$ be polynomials. Then*

$$\lambda(P_1\ldots P_n)=\sum_{1\leqq i\leqq n}\pi(P_1)\ldots\pi(P_{i-1})\lambda(P_i)\pi(P_{i+1})\ldots\pi(P_n)$$

Proof. For $n=2$, it is enough, by linearity, to prove the lemma when $P_1=u$, $P_2=v$ are words. But in this case

$$\lambda(uv)=\pi(uv)|uv|=\pi(u)\pi(v)(|u|+|v|)$$

$$=\pi(u)|u|\pi(v)+\pi(u)\pi(v)|v|$$

$$=\lambda(u)\pi(v)+\pi(u)\lambda(v)$$

Now the general case is easily proved by induction. □

Proof of Theorem 4.1. 1. First, note that the "if" part of (ii) is a consequence of Theorem 2.7. We use the notation of Lemma 4.4. We have $\underline{X}^*-G_1=(1-\underline{X})^{-1}-G_1=(1-\underline{X})^{-1}(1-(1-\underline{X})G_1)$. As $\underline{X}^*-G_1=S\underline{C}^*P_1$ and P_1 has constant term 1 (Lemma 4.4), P_1 is invertible in $\mathbf{Z}\langle\langle X\rangle\rangle$ and we obtain from

$$S\underline{C}^*P_1=(1-\underline{X})^{-1}(1-(1-\underline{X})G_1)$$

by multiplying by $1-\underline{X}$ on the left and by P_1^{-1} on the right,

$$(1-\underline{X})S\underline{C}^*=(1-(1-\underline{X})G_1)P_1^{-1} \tag{4.4}$$

Multiply the relation (i) of Lemma 4.4 by $1-\underline{X}$ on the left. This yields

$$d-(1-\underline{X})Q=(1-\underline{X})S\underline{C}^*P$$

Hence, by Eq. (4.4),

$$d-(1-\underline{X})Q=(1-(1-\underline{X})G_1)P_1^{-1}P$$

Note that, because G_1 has no constant term, $1-(1-\underline{X})G_1$ is invertible in $\mathbf{Z}\langle\langle X\rangle\rangle$, so that we obtain, by multiplying the previous relation by $P_1(1-(1-\underline{X})G_1)^{-1}$ on the left

$$P=P_1(1-(1-\underline{X})G_1)^{-1}(d-(1-\underline{X})Q)$$

2. We apply Corollary VII.4.3 to the last equality: there exist E, F, G, H in $\mathbf{Z}\langle X\rangle$ such that

$$P_1=EF, \qquad 1-(1-\underline{X})G_1=GF \tag{4.5}$$
$$d-(1-\underline{X})Q=GH, \qquad P=EH$$

By Proposition VII.4.4 (with $1-\underline{X}$ instead of Y), we obtain

$$G\equiv \pm 1 \; mod.(1-\underline{X})\mathbf{Z}\langle X\rangle$$

Replacing if necessary E, F, G, H by their opposites, we may suppose that $G\equiv +1$, and hence we obtain, again by Proposition VII.4.4, and by Eq. (4.5), that $H\equiv d\, mod.(1-\underline{X})\mathbf{Z}\langle X\rangle$, which implies

$$P=E(d+(\underline{X}-1)R), \; R\in\mathbf{Z}\langle X\rangle \tag{4.6}$$

3. We have $\underline{X}^*-D_1=(1-\underline{X})^{-1}(1-(1-\underline{X})D_1)$ so that, by Lemma 4.4 (iii),

$$S_1\underline{C}^*P=(1-\underline{X})^{-1}(1-(1-\underline{X})D_1)$$

As D_1 has constant term 0, $1-(1-\underline{X})D_1$ is invertible in $\mathbf{Z}\langle\langle X\rangle\rangle$; moreover, S_1 is also invertible, because it has constant term 1. So we obtain, by multiplying by $(1-\underline{C})S_1^{-1}$ on the left and by $(1-(1-\underline{X})D_1)^{-1}(1-\underline{X})$ on the right,

$$(1-\underline{C})S_1^{-1}=P(1-(1-\underline{X})D_1)^{-1}(1-\underline{X})$$

Now we use Eq. (4.6) and multiply by $-S_1^{-1}$ on the right, thus obtaining

$$\underline{C}-1=E(d+(\underline{X}-1)R)(1-(1-\underline{X})D_1)^{-1}(\underline{X}-1)S_1$$

4. By Corollary VII.4.3, there exist E', F', G', H' in $\mathbf{Z}\langle X\rangle$ such that

$$E(d+(\underline{X}-1)R)=E'F', \; 1-(1-\underline{X})D_1=G'F' \tag{4.7}$$
$$(\underline{X}-1)S_1=G'H', \; \underline{C}-1=E'H'$$

Let π be any Bernoulli morphism. Replacing if necessary E', F', G', H' by their opposites, we may assume that

$$\pi(F') \geqq 0$$

So, by Eq. (4.7) and Proposition VII.4.4, we obtain

$$G' = 1 + (\underline{X} - 1)G'', \; F' = 1 + (\underline{X} - 1)F'' \tag{4.8}$$

for some $G'', F'' \in \mathbf{Z}\langle X\rangle$. This and Eq. (4.7) imply that

$$(\underline{X} - 1)S_1 = (1 + (\underline{X} - 1)G'')H' = H' + (\underline{X} - 1)G''H'$$

Thus, we have

$$H' = (\underline{X} - 1)H'', \; H'' \in \mathbf{Z}\langle X\rangle \tag{4.9}$$

Now, Eqs. (4.7) and (4.8) imply also

$$E(d + (\underline{X} - 1)R) = E'(1 + (\underline{X} - 1)F'')$$

5. We now apply Theorem VII.2.2 to this equality and denote by p_i the continuant polynomial $p(a_1, \ldots, a_i)$ and $\tilde{p}_i = p(a_i, \ldots, a_1)$. Thus, we obtain the result that there exist polynomials U, V in $\mathbf{Z}\langle X\rangle$ such that

$$\begin{aligned} E &= Up_n, \; d + (\underline{X} - 1)R = \tilde{p}_{n-1}V \\ E' &= Up_{n-1}, \; 1 + (\underline{X} - 1)F'' = \tilde{p}_n V \end{aligned} \tag{4.10}$$

Applying Corollary VII.1.3 to the second and last equalities (with $A \to \tilde{p}_{n-1}$ or $\tilde{p}_n$, $B \to \underline{X} - 1$, $Q_1 \to 0$, $P \to V$, $R_1 \to d$ or 1), we obtain the result that the left Euclidean division of $\tilde{p}_{n-1}$ and $\tilde{p}_n$ by $\underline{X} - 1$ is possible, i.e. $\tilde{p}_{n-1}$ and $\tilde{p}_n$ are both congruent to a scalar *mod.* $(\underline{X} - 1)\mathbf{Q}\langle X\rangle$. This implies by Proposition VII.2.3 that

$$p_{n-1} \text{ and } \tilde{p}_{n-1} \text{ (and } p_n \text{ and } \tilde{p}_n\text{)} \tag{4.11}$$

are congruent to the same scalar *mod.* $(\underline{X} - 1)\mathbf{Q}\langle X\rangle$. Moreover, by Corollary VII.4.2, they have the same content

$$c(p_{n-1}) = c(\tilde{p}_{n-1}), \; c(p_n) = c(\tilde{p}_n) \tag{4.12}$$

6. As D_1 has coefficients 0, 1, the polynomial $1 - (\underline{X} - 1)D_1$ is primitive. Hence, by Eq. (4.7) and by Gauss's Lemma, G' and F' are primitive. As by Eqs. (4.10) and (4.8)

$$\tilde{p}_n V = 1 + (\underline{X} - 1)F'' = F'$$

we obtain by Gauss's Lemma

$$c(\tilde{p}_n)c(V) = 1$$

and

$$\bar{\bar{p}}_n \bar{V} = F'$$

Hence, by Proposition VII.4.4,

$$\bar{V} = \varepsilon + (\underline{X} - 1) V', \ \varepsilon = \pm 1, \ V' \in \mathbf{Z}\langle X \rangle \tag{4.13}$$

Furthermore, $\underline{C} - 1$ is primitive, hence so is E' by Eq. (4.7). As $E'F' = E(d + (\underline{X} - 1)R)$ by Eq. (4.7) and E', F' are primitive, we obtain by Gauss's Lemma that $d + (\underline{X} - 1)R$ is primitive. Thus, by Eq. (4.10) and Gauss's Lemma again

$$d + (\underline{X} - 1)R = \bar{\bar{p}}_{n-1} \bar{V}$$

This implies, by Proposition VII.4.4 and Eq. (4.13),

$$\bar{\bar{p}}_{n-1} = \varepsilon d + (\underline{X} - 1)L, \ L \in \mathbf{Z}\langle X \rangle$$

By Eqs. (4.11) and (4.12), we obtain the result that $\bar{p}_{n-1}$ and $\bar{\bar{p}}_{n-1}$ are congruent to the same scalar modulo $(\underline{X} - 1)\mathbf{Q}\langle X \rangle$. Hence

$$\bar{p}_{n-1} = \varepsilon d + (\underline{X} - 1)M$$

with $M \in \mathbf{Q}\langle X \rangle$. But $\bar{p}_{n-1} - \varepsilon d = (\underline{X} = 1)M$ and $\underline{X} - 1$ is primitive, so that $c(M) = c(\bar{p}_{n-1} - \varepsilon d) \in \mathbf{N}$, and $M \in \mathbf{Z}\langle X \rangle$, by Eq. (4.2) in Chap. VII.

We have seen that E' is primitive, so that by Gauss's Lemma and Eq. (4.10), we have

$$E' = \bar{U} \bar{p}_{n-1}$$

which implies

$$E' = \bar{U}(\varepsilon d + (\underline{X} - 1)M)$$

Hence, by Eqs. (4.7) and (4.9),

$$\bar{C} - 1 = \bar{U}(\varepsilon d + (\underline{X} - 1)M)(\underline{X} - 1)H''$$

where all the polynomials are in $\mathbf{Z}\langle X \rangle$ and where $\varepsilon = \pm 1$. This shows that we have a relation of the form

$$\underline{C} - 1 = A(\varepsilon' d + (\underline{X} - 1)D)(\underline{X} - 1)B$$

where

$$A = \pm \bar{U}, \ B = \pm H'', \ \varepsilon' d + (\underline{X} - 1)D = \pm(\varepsilon d + (\underline{X} - 1)M)$$

are chosen in such a way that, for some Bernoulli morphism π, one has

$$\pi(A) \geq 0, \ \pi(B) \geq 0$$

7. Apply Lemma 4.5 to this relation, using the fact that $\pi(\underline{X}-1)=0$; we obtain

$$\lambda(\underline{C}-1)=\pi(A)\varepsilon' d\lambda(\bar{X}-1)\pi(B)$$

Now $\lambda(1)=0$, $\lambda(\underline{C})>0$, $\lambda(\underline{X})>0$, and we obtain

$$\varepsilon' d\pi(A)\pi(B)>0$$

This shows that $\varepsilon'=1$ and proves Eq. (4.1) and (i).

8. Now, if C is a prefix code, we have by Lemma 4.4 (vi) that $S_1=1$. Hence, by Eq. (4.7), $\underline{X}-1=G'H'$, which implies by Eq. (4.9), $\underline{X}-1=G'(\underline{X}-1)H''$. Hence $H''=\pm 1$, and we obtain $B=\pm 1$. But $\pi(B)\geqq 0$, so $B=1$.

On the other hand, if C is a suffix, then $P_1=1$ by Lemma 4.4 (vi). Then, by Eq. (4.5), $E=\pm 1$, which implies by Eq. (4.10) and Gauss's Lemma, $\bar{U}=\pm 1$. Thus $A=\pm 1$. As $\pi(A)\geqq 0$, we obtain $A=1$. This proves the theorem. □

Exercises for Chapter VIII

1.1. Show that a submonoid of X^* is of the form C^*, C a code, if and only if it is free (i.e. isomorphic to some free monoid). Show that a submonoid M of X^* is free if and only if for any words u, v, w

$$u,\ uv,\ vw,\ w\in M \Rightarrow v\in M$$

1.2. Show that, given rational languages K, L, it is decidable whether their union (their product, the star of K) is unambiguous.

1.3. Show that $S(u)$ $(P(u), F(u, v))$ as defined in Sect. 1 is a sum of proper right factors (left factors, factors) of words of C.

2.1. Show that for a finite code C the three following conditions are equivalent:
(i) C is a complete and prefix code.
(ii) For any word w, $wX^*\cap CX^*$ is nonempty.
(iii) For any word w, $wX^*\cap C^*$ is nonempty.

2.2. Let C be a finite complete language. Show that for any word w, there exists some power of a conjugate of w which is in C^* (two words w, w' are *conjugate* if $w=uv$, $w'=vu$ for some words u, v).

3.1. Show that if e, e' are idempotents in the minimal ideal J of a finite monoid M, then there exists an idempotent e_1 in J which is a right multiple of e and a left multiple of e'. Show that the mapping

$$a \mapsto ae_1$$

defines a group isomorphism $eMe\to e_1Me_1$. Deduce that all the maximal groups in J are isomorphic.

3.2. Let C be a finite complete code. Show that C is synchronizing (i.e. of degree 1) if and only if for some word w, one has $wX^*w \subset C^*$.

4.1. Let C be a finite complete code which is biprefix. Let n be such that $x^n \in C$ for some letter x.

a) Show that for any i, $1 \leqq i \leqq n$, $C_i = x^{-i}C$ is a prefix set such that $C_iX^* \cap wX^*$ is nonempty for any word w.
b) Show that the set of proper right factors of C is the disjoint union of the C_i's.
c) Deduce that $\underline{C}_i - 1 = P_i(\underline{X} - 1)$ and that

$$\underline{C} - 1 = n(\underline{X} - 1) + (\underline{X} - 1)\left(\sum_{i=1}^{n} P_i\right)(\underline{X} - 1)$$

Show that n is the degree of C. Show that it is also equal to the average length of C (cf. Perrin 1977).

Notes to Chapter VIII

Theorem 4.1 is a noncommutative generalization of a theorem due to M. P. Schützenberger (1965). Corollary 4.2 is a partial answer to the main conjecture in the theory of finite codes, the *factorization conjecture*, which states that P and S may be chosen to have nonnegative coefficients (or equivalently coefficients 0 and 1).

Finite complete codes are maximal codes, and conversely, every maximal code is complete. Most of the general results on codes are stated here in the finite case. However, they hold for rational and even for "thin" codes. For a general exposition of the theory of codes, see the book by Berstel and Perrin (1985).

Another illustration of the close relation between codes and formal series is the following result (roughly): a thin code is biprefix if and only if its syntactic algebra is semisimple (Reutenauer 1981).

References

Amice, Y. (1975) Les nombres p-adiques. Presses universitaires de France, Paris

Bergmann, G. M. (1967) Commuting elements in free algebras and related topics in ring theory. Thesis, Harvard University

Benzaghou, B. (1970) Algèbres de Hadamard. Bull Soc Math France 98, 209–252

Berstel, J. (1971) Sur les pôles et le quotient de Hadamard de séries N-rationnelles. C R Acad Sci Paris, Série A 272, 1079–1081

Berstel, J., Mignotte, M. (1976) Deux propriétés décidables des suites récurrentes linéaires. Bull Soc Math France 104, 175–184

Berstel, J., Perrin, D. (1985) Theory of Codes. Academic Press, London New York

Berstel, J., Reutenauer, C. (1982) Recognizable formal power series on trees. Theor Comput Sci 18, 115–148

Bezivin, J. P. (1984) Factorisation de suites récurrentes linéaires et applications, Bull Soc Math France 112, 365–376

Boë, J. M., De Luca, A., Restivo, A. (1980) Minimal complete set of words. Theor Comput Sci 12, 325–332

Cahen, P. M., Chabert, J.-L. (1975) Eléments quasi-entiers et extensions de Fatou. J Algebra 36, 185–192

Carlyle, J. W., Paz, A. (1971) Realizations by stochastic finite automaton. J Comput System Sci 5, 26–40

Chabert, J. L. (1972) Anneaux de Fatou. Enseignement Math 18, 141–144

Cohn, P. M. (1961) On a generalization of the Euclidean algorithm. Proc Cambridge Philos Soc 57, 18–30

Cohn, P. M. (1969) Free associative algebras. Bull London Math Soc 1, 1–39

Cohn, P. M. (1982) The universal field of fractions of a semifir I: numerators and denominators. Proc London Math Soc (3)44, 1–32

Cohn, P. M. (1985) Free Rings and Their Relations. Academic Press, London New York (2nd ed.)

Conway, J. H. (1971) Regular algebra and finite machines. Chapman and Hall, London

Cori, R. (1975) Un code pour les graphes planaires et ses applications. Astérisque 27, Société Mathématique de France, Paris

Duboué, M. (1983) Une suite récurrente remarquable. Europ J Combinatorics 4, 205–214

Ehrenfeucht, E., Parikh, R., Rozenberg, G. (1981) Pumping lemmas for regular set. Siam J Computing 10, 536–541

Eilenberg, S. (1974) Automata, Languages and Machines, Vol. A. Academic Press, London New York

Eilenberg, S., Schützenberger, M. P. (1969) Rational sets in commutative monoids. J Algebra 13, 173–191

Fatou, (1904) Sur les séries entières à coefficients entiers. C R Acad Sci Paris. Série A 138, 342–344

Fliess, M. (1971) Formal languages and formal power series. Séminaire IRIA Logique et Automates, Le Chesnay, 77–85

Fliess, M. (1974a) Matrices de Hankel. J Maths Pures Appl 53, 197–222, + erratum 54 (1975)

Fliess, M. (1974b) Sur divers produits de séries formelles. Bull. Soc. Math. France 102, 181–191

Fliess, M. (1975) Séries rationnelles positives et processus stochastiques. Ann Inst H Poincaré, Sect B 11(2), 1–21

Fliess, M. (1981) Fonctionnelles causales non linéaires et indéterminées non commutatives. Bull Soc Math France 109, 3–40

Hansel, G. (1986) Une démonstration simple du théorème de Skolem-Mahler-Lech. Theor Comput Sci 43, 1–10

Harrison, M. A. (1978) Introduction to Formal Language Theory. Addison-Wesley, Reading, Mass

Isidori, A. (1985) Nonlinear control systems: an introduction. Lect Notes in Control Inform Sci 72, Springer, Berlin Heidelberg New York

Jacob, G. (1975) Représentations et substitutions matricielles dans la théorie algébriques des transductions. Thesis, University of Paris

Jacob, G. (1978) La finitude des représentations linéaires des semi-groupes est décidable. J Algebra 52, 437–459

Jacob, G. (1980) Un théorème de factorisation des produits d'endomorphismes de K^n. J Algebra 63, 389–412

Karhumäki, J. (1977) Remarks on commutative N-rational series. Theor Comput Sci 5, 211–217

Katayama, T., Okamoto, M., Enomoto, H. (1978) Characterization of the structure-generating functions of regular sets and DOL growth functions. Information and Control 36, 85–101

Kleene, S. C. (1956) Representation of events in nerve nets and finite automata. In: Shannon, C. E., McCarthy, J. (eds.) Automata Studies. Princeton University Press, Princeton, 3–42

Koblitz, N. (1974) p-adic numbers, p-adic analysis, and zeta functions. Springer, Berlin Heidelberg New York

Kuich, W.; Salomaa, A. (1986) Semirings, Automata, Languages. EATCS Monographs in Theoret. Comput. Science, Vol. 6. Springer, Berlin Heidelberg New York

Lallement, G. (1978) Semigroups and Combinatorial Applications. Wiley, New York Chichester

Lang, S. (1965) Algebra. Addison-Wesley, Reading, Mass

Lascoux, A. (1986) Suites récurrentes linéaires. Advances in Appl Math 7, 228–235

Lascoux, A., Schützenberger, M. P. (1985) Formulaire raisonné de fonctions symétriques. LITP, Université Paris VII

Lech, C. (1953) A note on recurring series. Ark Mat 2, 417–421

Lewin, J. (1969) Free modules over free algebras and free goup algebras: the Schreier technique. Trans Amer Math Soc 145, 455–465

Lyndon, R., Schupp, P. (1977) Combinatorial Group Theory. Springer, Berlin Heidelberg New York

Mahler, K. (1935) Eine arithmetische Eigenschaft der Taylor-Koeffizienten rationaler Funktionen. Akad Wetensh Amsterdam, Proc 38, 50–60

Mandel, A., Simon, J. (1977) On finite semi-groups of matrices. Theor Comput Sci 5, 101–111

Manin, Y. I. (1977) A Course in Mathematical Logic. Springer, Berlin Heidelberg New York

McNaughton, R., Zalcstein, I. (1975) The Burnside problem for semi-groups. J Algebra 34, 292–299

Perrin, D. (1977) Codes asynchrones. Bull Soc Math France 105, 385–404

Pólya, G. (1921) Arithmetische Eigenschaften der Reihenentwicklungen rationaler Funktionen. J reine angew Math 151, 1–31

Pólya, G., Szegö, G. (1964) Aufgaben und Lehrsätze aus der Analysis, Band 2, 8. Abschn. Springer, Berlin Heidelberg New York

Restivo, A., Reutenauer, C. (1984) On cancellation properties of languages which are support of rational power series. J Comput System Sci 29, 153–159

Reutenauer, C. (1977a) On a question of S. Eilenberg. Theor Comput Sci 5, 219

Reutenauer, C. (1977b) Une caractérisation de la finitude de l'ensemble des coefficients d'une série rationnelle en variable non commutatives. C R Acad Sci Paris, Série A 284, 1159–1162

Reutenauer, C. (1978a) Variétés d'algèbres et de séries rationnelles. Actes du ler Congrès Maths Appl AFCET-SMF 2, 93–102

Reutenauer, C. (1978b) sur les séries rationnelles en variables non commutatives, Lectures Notes in Comput Sci 62. Springer, Berlin Heidelberg New York 372–381

Reutenauer, C. (1980a) Séries formelles et algèbres syntactiques. J Algebra 66, 448–483

Reutenauer, C. (1980b) Séries rationnelles et algèbres syntactiques. Thesis, University of Paris

Reutenauer, C. (1980c) An Ogden-like iteration lemma for rational power series. Acta Informatica 13, 189–197
Reutenauer, C. (1981) Semisimplicity of the algebra associated to a biprefix code. Semigroup Forum 23, 324–342
Reutenauer, C. (1982) Sur les éléments inversibles de l'algèbre de Hadamard des séries rationnelles. Bull Soc Math France 110, 225–232
Reutenauer, C. (1985) Noncommutative factorization of variable-length codes. J Pure applied Algebra 36, 167–186
Ryser, H. J. (1963) Combinatorial Mathematics. Wiley, New York Chichester (Carus math monographs)
Salomaa, A., Soittola, M. (1978) Automata-Theoretic Aspects of Formal Power Series. Springer, Berlin Heidelberg New York
Schützenberger, M. P. (1961a) On the definition of a family of automata. Information and Control 4, 245–270
Schützenberger, M. P. (1961b) On a special class of recurrents events. Annals Math Stat 32, 1201–1213
Schützenberger, M. P. (1962a) On a theorem of R. Jungen. Proc Amer Math Soc. 13, 885–889
Schützenberger, M. P. (1962b) Certain elementary families of automata. Proceedings of symposium on mathematical theory of automata, Polytechnic Institute Brooklyn, 139–153
Schützenberger, M. P. (1962c) finite counting automata. Information and Control 5, 91–107
Schützenberger, M. P. (1965) Sur certains sous-monoïdes libres. Bull Soc Math France 93, 209–223
Schützenberger, M. P. (1970) Parties rationnelles d'un monoïdes libre. Proceedings of international mathematics conference 3, 281–282
Schützenberger, M. P., Marcus, R. S. (1959) Full decodable code-word sets. IRE Trans Information Theory 5, 12–15
Skolem, T. (1934) Ein Verfahren zur Behandlung gewisser exponentialer Gleichungen und diophantischer Gleichungen. C R 8 Congr Scand Stockholm, 163–188
Soittola, M. (1976) Positive rational sequences. Theor Comput Sci 2, 317–322
Sontag, E. D. (1975) On some questions of rationality and decidability. J Comput System Sci 11, 375–385
Sontag, E. D., Rouchaleau, Y. (1977) Sur ls anneaux de Fatou forts. C R Acad Sci Paris, Série A 284, 331–333
Steyaert, J. M., Flajolet, P. (1983) Patterns and pattern-matching in trees: an analysis. Information and Control 58, 19–58
Suschkewitsch, A. K. (1928) Über die endlichen Gruppen ohne das Gesetz der eindeutigen Umkehrbarkeit. Math Ann 99, 30–50
Turakainen, P. (1985) A note on test sets for N-rational languages. Bull Europ Assoc Theor Comput Sci 25, 40–42
Wedderburn, . H. M. (1932) Noncommutative domains of integrity. J reine angew Math 167, 129–141

Subject Index